BEYOND THE BASICS

Excelling at
SQUASH

By the same author

SQUASH — THE SKILLS OF THE GAME
TEACH YOURSELF — SQUASH
IMPROVE YOUR SQUASH
FIT FOR THE GAME — SQUASH
THE SQUASH WORKSHOP

BEYOND THE BASICS

EXCELLING AT
SQUASH

A Practical Reference Manual for Players and Coaches

IAN McKENZIE

Hodder & Stoughton
LONDON SYDNEY AUCKLAND

ISBN 0-340-57663-4
Copyright © Ian McKenzie 1994
The right of Ian McKenzie to be identified as the Author of the Work
has been asserted by him in accordance with the Copyright, Designs
and Patents Act 1988.

Photographs © Stephen Lines

First published in Great Britain in 1994 by Hodder and Stoughton
A division of Hodder Headline PLC
10 9 8 7 6 5 4 3 2 1

British Library Cataloguing in Publication Data
CIP data is available from the British Library

Set and designed by John Youé
with drawings by Ethan Danielson

Printed and bound in Great Britain by
BPCC Hazell Books Ltd
Member of BPCC Ltd

Hodder and Stoughton Ltd
A division of Hodder Headline PLC
338 Euston Road
London NW1 3BH

Contents

Contents

Foreword

My friend Ian McKenzie has arguably written more about our sport than any other squash scribbler. He has earned a reputation for thoughtful, concise and authoritative analysis and such a book as this has been long overdue.

There is a myriad of coaching manuals, but the player who really does wish to excel has rarely been satisfactorily provided for. In *Beyond the Basics* Ian has more than filled the gap. We have here the most formidable combination of simple, basic and sound coaching fundamentals, forged in a most skilful way with the core of a keen player's ambition: how to improve in the short term and, above all, how to achieve excellence with long-term planning. The McKenzie experience – working with Ross Norman, the Men's World Champion in 1986, and our own shining star, Lucy Soutter, so successful during the 1980's – has placed him in pole position as a player support and back-up service.

He is very much a squash guru, has served a priceless apprenticeship as a good player, fine coach and enquiring squash journalist. Yet again he has done well for our sport with this splendid book, a valuable addition to any squash library.

Jonah Barrington

Jonah Barrington
SRA DIRECTOR OF EXCELLENCE

ACKNOWLEDGEMENTS

I am grateful to the SRA for giving me the opportunity to write this book. My thanks go to Professor Frank Sanderson of Liverpool's John Moore University, Dr Craig Sharp now of Limerick University, to the National coaching foundation and to Jonah Barrington MBE for advice and support. Thanks to all the players and pupils, great and small, who have provided ideas on excelling at squash for this book and for the *Squash Player* magazine. I am also grateful to James E Loehr for permission to use material from his book *Mental Toughness Training for Sports*. Special thanks to squash's number one photographer Stephen Line for showing us exactly what the top players do, so that perhaps we can be a little more like them.

Ian McKenzie

Introduction

A PLAYER'S APPROACH

Squash involves and rewards effort, but to excel at squash, effort is not enough. It is the approach you take to your game that is important. This book takes a player's approach. It gets you to think about squash and particularly your game, your needs, strengths and weaknesses, about the things that can be improved and it tells you how you can go about improving them. Little can be achieved without effort but with this book your efforts will be directed to where they will be most productive.

Perhaps you would like to excel at squash without training and practising. For you there is plenty of useful information you can use immediately, but the player's approach will encourage you to incorporate some practice and training into your overall programme and to adopt a longer-term approach to your game. This is one of the problems of trying to excel at squash. We like playing and often judge our game by short-term results. In this book there is much short-term advice, particularly in the Problem Solving and Match Play chapters, but there is also the theme of taking a longer-term approach to your game.

The first two chapters, Watching Squash and Playing Squash, help to clarify exactly what we are trying to do when we play. If you don't know exactly what you are trying to do, you can't get better at it can you? We use these exact ideas and analyses to look at Your Game, to see how you can play better and at what can be improved.

Some of these things you will know already and perhaps Problem Solving on page 36 will have the immediate answers to some of your problems but others will require a longer-term effort. Improving Your Game shows you the things to do. Perhaps it

is your concentration that is letting you down, or that your speed or tactics aren't the best. Perhaps your shots aren't up to scratch. All these can be improved.

A longer-term approach doesn't mean that you need to stop enjoying playing squash, it just means that as well as your short-term activity, you will have some long-term aims and there will be some parts of your game you will be trying to improve in the long term. If you only take a short-term approach you may never achieve the longer-term improvement you are capable of and you may never excel at squash.

Two chapters are particularly concerned with this longer-term approach, one is Practising, the other Planning. The Planning chapter could have been called Goal Setting, Programming and Training. That is not meant to sound ominous. Probably you already have some goals and you certainly have a programme, even if it is just playing squash three times a week – you may just not recognise it as such. You will be able to do many of the practices in practice games, although I will also recommend solo and pairs practice. Why? Because they are the best ways to improve your shots.

It is quite possible that the ideas you have on goals, planning, training and practice are vague, half thought out and only half implemented, if at all. This section clarifies all that for you. It helps you sort out where you are going and how to plan getting there.

One of the attitudes that players who excel at squash have is that they are always looking at improving their games. Advanced Shots and Techniques give you further ideas on this, but it does give a warning – 'the top players do the basic things better'.

Plate 1 –
The two great players of the modern era:
Jahangir Khan, the ten-times British Open
Champion, is all power and concentration as he
strikes the ball, while his Pakistani compatriot,
World Champion Jansher Khan, is watching
intently and is already moving

Squash is a fairly continuous sport. There is so little time to think in matches that our play can get stuck in a rut, we don't do the things we are capable of doing, we can play it all wrong and often wish we had another chance. The chapters on Match Preparation and Match Play are a bit like another chance. They give the opportunity to learn from your mistakes, rather than repeating them over and over. They show you how to prepare and plan your matches so that much of your thinking is done before you are rushed and pressurised by the battle.

There is much in this book that you can use immediately. Seize on it and use it but also try to take a longer-term approach. That is really what the players who excel at squash do.

YOU AND SQUASH

FITNESS AND HEALTH

Squash, one of the most vigorous of sports, strongly taxes both the aerobic and anaerobic energy systems. It will make you fitter but you also want to ensure that it makes you healthier. For the very unfit or the good player getting back into the sport after a lay-off, it will be useful and safer to get fit for the sport. Start easily and progressively build up aerobic fitness.

Heart

The vigorous aerobic exercise that squash players above beginner level get, helps to reduce the risk of coronary heart attack although there are risks for anyone who has a heart malformation from birth; a viral condition such as influenza or glandular fever; or coronary heart disease. Some of the factors that affect this third category are being overweight, smoking, stress, high blood pressure, too much dietary fat and salt and too little or too mild exercise. Men over 45 and those with known coronary disease or coronary risk should approach squash with caution and are advised to seek medical advice before playing.

Dr Craig Sharp, the former director of the British Olympic Medical Centre, provides this advice.

'If you are really unfit, carry out a four-to-eight -week conditioning period before taking up or going back to the game. Especially if you are a more extrovert personality, and particularly if you have a good eye for the ball.'

- Never play when feeling ill, or within forty-eight hours of getting up from an illness which has given you a temperature and caused you to stay in bed. This applies to players of all ages.
- Always warm up for two or three minutes and always warm down afterwards; never come straight off court and stand still. Jog gently for two or three minutes.
- Go easy on very hot days, and drink a little water between games.
- Don't have a hot bath or shower immediately after playing. Either have a luke-warm shower, or cool down first.
- Do not smoke within thirty minutes of playing, and if you feel you may be at risk, don't drink alcohol within the same period.

Never ignore the possible early signs of an underlying heart condition while playing. These include: unexpectedly severe breathlessness, chest pain, faintness, nausea and a feeling of 'indigestion' a hand's-width above your navel.

If you have a family history of heart disease, heart or blood pressure problems or of diabetes, then pay special attention to all the above.

The role of preparticipation medical screening has simply not been adequately assessed, although a simple interview and medical examination would reveal those who have overt cardiovascular disease.

Eyes

One of the most serious dangers implicit in squash is eye injury. *Squash Player* magazine says that 'there are few objects better designed to cause eye injury than a squash ball'.

The eye sockets are reasonably well protected against the swing of a racket but the obvious and sensible advice is that if there is the slightest risk of hitting anyone with racket and ball, stop. It's very simple, the rules encourage the playing of lets. Proper eye protectors with strong frames are an option players can consider. They are compulsory for competition in the United States. For those who wear spectacles, plastic lens are a must and soft, not hard, contact lens must be worn.

Back

Moving quickly from a sedentary job to violent activity on a squash court can be a shock for the spine, so it is vital that the back and pelvis are kept as supple as possible. This is done by lying on the floor and raising your head and trunk, using your arms as support, while keeping the legs and hips in constant contact with the floor. (*see* page 85.) It is also important to stretch the hamstrings. *See* the Fitness section and Match Preparation chapter on pages 84 and 160.

Sweat

Squash players sweat and need to replace this liquid. In extreme cases liquid loss could result in dehydration, leading to high heart rates, fatigue and increased body temperature.

Before playing make sure you have consumed sufficient liquid and that this is replaced as needed. *See* Match Preparation on page 157.

Injury

The management of bruises, muscle, tendon and ligament injuries should be carried out with the 'RICE' treatment. This is designed to stop continuing bleeding in the damaged tissue and aid early recovery. This is: R – rest the inured part
I – apply ice
C – compression bandaging
E – elevation

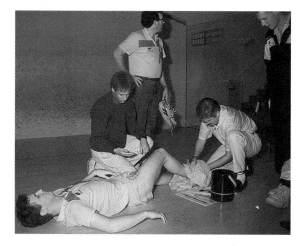

Plate 2 –
In the event of muscle pulls or tears apply ice immediately and follow the RICE treatment

Treat these soft tissue injuries with ice packs or ice wrapped in a damp flannel. Protect the skin from burning by applying a layer of grease or a bandage. The ice should stay on for five to fifteen minutes until the skin turns red. Compression bandaging can then be applied with tubular or crepe bandages. Elevation limits swelling. For example, when in a lying position an injured foot could be elevated on cushions for up to twenty-four hours.

Rest an injury for twenty-four to seventy-two hours after which movement within the limits of pain may be started. Gradually increase the exercise over a seven-day programme by which time most minor injuries will have recovered. It's best not to play squash until you have fully recovered.

In general, if it hurts don't play on it.

THE SRA SAFETY CODE

1 Don't play if you are not fit enough. Start with a less strenuous training activity, such as jogging, swimming, calisthenics or a moderate keep-fit class.

2 Don't play competitively until you really know how to play. Don't be unreasonably ambitious in choosing opponents when new to the game.

3 Always limber up before you begin to play competitively.

4 Don't play if you are unwell in any way before or during a game.

5 Don't play for at least two hours after a heavy meal.

6 Don't play after drinking alcohol; avoid smoking before the game if you can. If you do smoke, wait for at least thirty minutes after the end of a game before smoking a cigarette.

7 Never have a very hot or very cold shower after a game, the water should be tepid.

8 Wear suitable shoes. Make sure your clothes, shoes and equipment are properly maintained and are in a safe condition.

9 If you wear glasses, they must be unbreakable, (lenses as well as frame should be plastic); contact lenses should be soft.

10 Eye guards must be strong enough not to break with the impact of the ball or racket, they must keep the ball out of contact with the eyeball and they must not restrict peripheral vision.

11 Never look directly round if your opponent is hitting a ball from behind you.

12 The safety of your opponent is in your hands. If you cannot hit the ball without hitting your opponent, ASK FOR A LET.

Watching Squash

I magine that you have just arrived in the middle of a match and you are looking over the balcony. The first questions you would ask are: 'Who is winning?' and 'What is the score?' Then you would start to watch the game yourself and begin to note the winning shots and the mistakes. Perhaps mentally you would keep the score, especially if it was close when squash is at its most interesting, and calculate how far a player has to go to win a game or draw level with his opponent. In the contest you would be focusing on the outcome of the rallies, any major events like a confrontation with the referee, a very long rally or spectacular shot.

Besides observing the contest you may start to work out why one player is dominating the other. Initially you would look at who plays the best finishing shots and at who makes the mistakes, but then you might consider where the shots are being played from, how the opportunities and difficulties occurred – you will have begun to consider the quality of shots and the sequence of events. This is what we do when we analyse matches. All that really happens is that we note these down and add them up, so that we have a systematic analysis rather than just relying on some overall impression.

There are often so many events going on in squash that it is hard to select the really important items that affect the outcome of a contest. But this is what we try to do in match analysis which we will consider shortly.

WATCHING AND LEARNING

You can learn a lot by watching squash. The ideas in this book that can help you to raise your standard of play can mostly be observed in good squash players. How top players hit the ball, where they hit it to and how they try to play the right shots at the right time.

Top players have individual styles of hitting the ball but watch and you will see good footwork, positioning and balance, early preparation for the

Plate 3 –
Intense concentration from the
New Zealand's number one Ross Norman
and team coach Dardir Ali El-Barkary as
they analyse the matches at the Royal Albert
Hall during the 1987 World Team
championships final

shot, a pause and a full and unrestricted swing. Beginners marvel at this but are often a little disappointed that it is not more spectacular. They are surprised at how much time the top players have to play their shots.

Watch top squash players and you will see how they nearly always seem to get the ball back and recover position ready for the next shot before their opponent hits.

When we watch squash and see exactly where the ball is going, we can work out the target areas where it is really difficult for an opponent to recover the ball, where it gives time for recovery and where it can be played to die quickly to win points. Often this precision in shot-making is lost in our play. Working out exactly where to place the ball is discussed in Chapter 2: Playing Squash and learning to do this consistently is discussed in Chapter 5: Improving Your Game.

When we watch squash it is easy to see where things go wrong, where a player hits back to his opponent instead of away, where players play the wrong shot at the wrong time. It will help your play if you watch for these situations when you next watch squash. Watch for the times when a player: takes the decision of playing a risky shot off a difficult ball; hits short when his opponent is ready in the middle and easily able to seize on the opportunity; hits back to his opponent; leaves himself out of position; aims too low; tries to do too much; plays lots of loose crosscourts and boasts; fails to attack when there is a good opportunity; and lets balls go that he could have volleyed and so applied pressure on his opponent. We could call these tactical errors and list them below.

It is all easy from outside the court, of course, but you can learn a lot about squash by trying to analyse the game and by applying this type of thinking to Your Game.

TACTICAL ERRORS

1 Attacking difficult balls.
2 Attacking when your opponent is on the T.
3 Hitting back to your opponent.
4 Leaving yourself out of position. Not Covering your shots.
5 Aiming too low. Not using a margin for error above the tin.
6 Hitting hard when under pressure. Not lobbing or varying the pace in your game.
7 Trying to do too much when you are making errors, playing loose shots or making tactical errors. Not returning to defence when required and not setting up rallies.
8 Playing too many crosscourts and boasts.
9 Playing defensively when you have opportunities to attack, to move an opponent and to apply pressure.
10 Leaving the ball when you can volley it.

MATCH ANALYSIS

SCORES, EVALUATION AND DIARY

The simplest record we can keep of a match is the score. This may seem so glaringly obvious that it is not worth writing down but imagine that you had the scores of your matches for the last season. Perhaps there would be some patterns that would be useful to you. Which games did you tend to win and which did you lose? A diary of your results with a short evaluation could be very useful in working out how to improve your game. Perhaps you have noted that you have been nervous for a number of matches and had very poor starts; lost longer matches when you got tired; lost to opponents the second time round when they were used to your game.

Written evaluations of your own matches, or someone else's, can help you to form impressions on such things as whether you got the ball past your opponent or attacked enough.

SCORE SHEETS

It is amazing how players who have not performed up to expectation avoid asking for the score sheets, as if they want to obliterate the match from their memories. Learn from your mistakes or you will keep making them over and over again.

The score sheets will tell how the run of points went. Was there a time when you lapsed, or let your opponent dominate, rush you or catch up when you could have pressed home your advantage?

WINNERS AND ERRORS

One of the most basic tactical ideas in squash is to know where the points come from. A simple method of recording this is to write the score and record whether the rally ended on a winner or an error and what the final shot was. Codes that can be used for the final shots are listed below:

Codes

These simple codes can easily be adapted into individual forms of shorthand.

F	– forehand
B	– backhand
s	– short
c	– crosscourt
d	– drop
b	– boast
ra	– reverse angle
v	– volley
db	– drop boast or trickle boast
w	– winner
m	– mistake

(mistake assumed a tin unless marked otherwise.)

mh	– mishit
o	– out
fe	– forced error

Shots are assumed to be straight length unless otherwise noted.

Example 1

	C		D
0.			
		0.	Cm Fb (fe)
		1.	Dw Bd
0.			
.1			Cw Fvs
2.			Cw Fd
.3			Cw Bd
4.			Cw Bd
.5			Dm Fb
			Cw Bvs

So far we see that

	Winners	Errors
C	5	1
D	1	1

C's winners are the significant factor. They were a short forehand volley, a forehand straight drop, two backhand straight drops and a backhand volley.

Example 2

Let's look at a real match, the first game of the 1992 British Open final between Susan Devoy and Martine le Moignan . (Le Moignan is a left-hander.)

Le Moignan v Devoy

	0		
		0.	w Bd
		.1	w Bd
		2.	w Bc
w Bc	0.		
		.2	w Bd
		3.	w Bd
	0.		m Fb
		3.	w Bd
w Fb	0.		
w Bd	.1		
	2.		m Bk
	.3		m stroke
		3.	w Bvd
		.4	w Bk
m Bb	5.		
m stroke	.6		
m B	7.		
		.8	w Fd
	3.		m Fv out
		8.	w Bd
		.9	w Bd
	3	**9**	

	Winners	Errors
Le Moignan	3	3
Devoy	11	4

In winning her eighth British Open title Susan Devoy hit eleven winners in the first game, seven from her backhand drop. Having played Devoy many times before, Le Moignan should have known that this was a threatening shot. She should have been prepared to rally deep, play on Devoy's forehand more and avoid the backhand boast, (being a left-hander). *See* Game Plan page 167.

Although Martine minimised her mistakes she was unable to deprive Devoy of opportunities to play her backhand drop. It was an error of judgement that she was unable to recover from as Devoy collected the Open title 9-3, 9-5, 9-3.

SEQUENCE ANALYSIS

It is not easy to note the whole sequence of shots used in a rally (although this can be done with computer techniques and also by Sanderson's shorthand notation method), but it can still be very

Plate 4 –
Susan Devoy uses her backhand drop shot to
attack an opening prised from Martine Le
Moignan in the British Open final

useful to record the events preceding the final point.

The penultimate shot (the one preceding the final shot) may have given the opportunity for playing a winner or forcing an error. This can be recorded in a score-related analysis such as in example 1, simply by recording the penultimate shots as well as the final one.

Example 3

	C		D	
	0.			
			0.	Cm Fb (fe), Bc
			.1	Dw Bd, Bs
	0.			Cw Fvs, Bc
	.1			Cw Fd, Bb
	2.			Cw Bd, Fb
	.3			Cw Bd, Fb
	4.			Dm Fb, F
	.5			Cw Bvs, Fc

C's winners (two short volleys and three drops) we saw in Example 1 are in fact two short volleys off crosscourts and three drops off the boast. Even from this short analysis it seems that D is commit-ting two basic faults – playing loose boasts and crosscourts.

SHOT ANALYSIS

In looking at a player's game and trying to analyse it, one of the key areas we require information on is the quality of shots. How good are the shots, what are the relative strengths and weaknesses and what are the problem areas?

There can be a number of ways of doing this. One, as shown below, is to select the very good (/) and bad (x) shots and just note these. Another is just to note the weak shots.

	Forehand	Backhand
Straight	/xx/xx	//x/x
Crosscourt	x//x///	x//xxx
Boast	x/xx/xx	x///x/

From the above analysis we can see that the backhand crosscourt, forehand boast and forehand straight drive are relatively weak. The latter two may be a problem relating to the forehand back-corner. This is a problem we could analyse in the same way.

A more in-depth analysis of selected shots could be performed by rating them on a scale of say 1 to 5 where 1 is poor, 2 is below average, 3 average, 4 above average and 5 very good.

In rating shots we have to have some criteria – this can be subjective, or we can specify special areas or targets. Very simply we could work out overall where the ball lands.

Front quarter
Middle half
Back quarter

Criteria other than / and x could be used. We may want to know whether a shot is short or loose. For short we could use an s and x (or L) for loose.

TACTICAL ANALYSIS

A large part of squash is playing the right shots at the right time. We can analyse the effectiveness of shot selection by analysing tactics and tactical errors. We may want to know, for example, whether a player is varying the pace (lobbing at the right time), taking opportunities to attack (using the drop, boast and kill), applying pressure (volleying and hitting hard), moving his opponent (hitting away) and using combinations.

Analysis of tactical decisions can note the correct and incorrect decisions but it is probably easier to note where there has been a tactical error with an x as in the example below or if using a scoring method with a ?.

Example:
Not lobbing **xxxxxx**
Not volleying **xxxxx**
Not attacking **xx**
Not moving an opponent **xx**

Further analysis could be more specific by analysing selected areas in depth. For example with a player who is attacking but losing points we would want to know if he is:

Attacking when his opponent is on the T
Attacking difficult balls
Attacking when out of position
Not using a margin for error

For a player who is not attacking, we could look at which basic opportunities, (*see* Combinations page 116), are being lost and analyse these. We would then be in a position to make specific criticisms and suggestions on exactly what a player was doing in his game.

VIDEO

It is difficult to analyse all these different aspects of matches during play – that is errors, shots and tactics together – but it is possible to do this by analysing videos of matches. Here you can slow down and rewind the tape as you need. It is a powerful technique where players can see exactly what they are doing.

ADAPTING METHODS

The most important point about developing analysis methods is that they are found to be useful. Try to pinpoint exactly what you want to know. Adapt the methods above and develop your own. With a little practice, you will develop abbreviations and your own shorthand. The score and tallying methods can be combined where you just select and note important weak shots and tactical errors.

YOUR ANALYSIS

Watch squash in an enquiring way. Analyse why one player is winning and the other losing. Ask who is making the mistakes, where are they making them and why? Where are the winners played from and why? Are there weaknesses the players are homing in on or loose shoots they are taking advantage of? Are there tactical errors?

Use some of the methods above to practise analysing games.

Apply this type of analysis to your game. If you wish to improve your game, having some analysis of it rather than just pressured impressions is very useful. It could tell you, for example, that half your drives are landing in front of the back of the service box, that your crosscourts are weak and being volleyed and that you are boasting at the wrong time.

Have advisers or a coach watch and analyse your game. File these analyses away. Use them to make a list of things to improve on. Have a video made of your game and analyse it yourself. Take this list and go into action. *See* Chapter 5: Improving Your Game.

Plate 5 –
Former World Champion Ross Norman plays a
full-length straight drive that rebounds to cling
and present his opponent with a problem in the
back corner

Playing Squash

This is a book for players and as a player it will be so easy for you to skip over this section, for you already know how to play, don't you?

You know that you want to: hit the ball away from your opponents; play shots they can't get back; manoeuvre them into positions where recovering your shots is going to be difficult. You know you have to run, that it will be tiring and that you will have to show persistence and determination, and as a competitive person this is what you will do. You know you will have to concentrate because it is easy to lose your concentration on court.

Shortly we will look at how you can do these things but firstly let us consider exactly what you are trying to do when you are playing squash. If you know exactly what you are trying to do you are in a position to improve. If you don't know exactly what you are trying to do, it is going to be difficult to improve. This chapter will help you clarify exactly what you are trying to do in a game of squash.

In squash we win points by playing shots our opponents can't get to and by forcing errors. We attempt to minimise the chances of our opponents winning points by avoiding mistakes and by depriving them of the opportunity to play winning shots.

The further we can make an opponent run to the ball the more chance we have of playing a winner or of forcing a mistake. We make opponents run by hitting to the extremities, that is, to the corners, and by hitting away from them. We play safe by putting the ball where it is difficult for an opponent, that is, close to the side and back walls, where there is little risk of our making a mistake or of providing opponents with opportunities. These

are the key concepts of *placement* and *tactics*.

You can skip this section if you have a perfect understanding of where you want your shots to go and when you want them to go there.

CORNERS

Beginners hit the ball into the middle, average players get it in the corner sometimes, good players get it into the corners often, very good players hit it in the corners more often and hardly ever in the middle.

This is squash: low and often soft shots to the front corners (we will call these attacking shots) and high shots to the back corners (we call these defensive shots). Remember better players are better at getting the ball in the corners.

TARGETS

Where are the most difficult balls to play?

Close to the side wall, close to the back where your swing is restricted, low in the front, and out of the nicks where the bounce can be low and awkward. And those that pass out of reach and don't give us a second chance to return.

LENGTH

Shots aimed into the back corners are called length shots. Playing length means that we are taking our opponent out of the dominant middle position and placing him in the back corners where we want to give him a problem, by restricting his shot to a defensive one, or even better, forcing a mistake or a weak ball we can attack. As well as taking your opponent out of the middle, a length shot will give you time to recover. Playing a ball short of a length

Plate 6 –
The striker struggles to recover a pressure drive
from the front court played for dying length to
the back of the service box

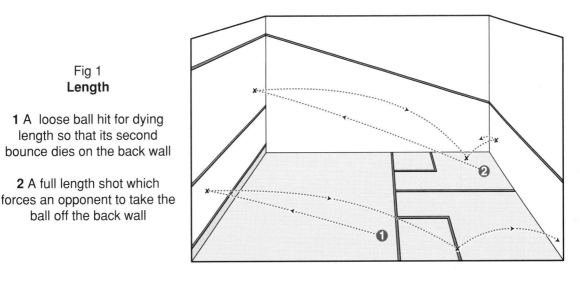

Fig 1
Length

1 A loose ball hit for dying length so that its second bounce dies on the back wall

2 A full length shot which forces an opponent to take the ball off the back wall

means an opponent won't have a restricted position from which to play and won't have to move as much from the centre.

There are two types of length – full length and dying length. Full length forces an opponent to take the ball off the back wall and a dying length forces him to play it before the back.

A full length is the basic defensive shot and will force an opponent deeper into the corner as well as giving you more time to recover.

Dying length is a special pressure shot. It has the advantage that it doesn't rebound and give your opponent a second chance to recover it. However, there is the disadvantage that it can allow an opponent to keep the middle by playing the ball well before the back and hence recover the T more quickly. This would give you less time to recover. We use these pressure drives when an opponent is out of position.

TIGHTNESS
We have all experienced the difficulty of trying to scrape the ball off the wall and the frustration of playing opponents who invariably angle their shots

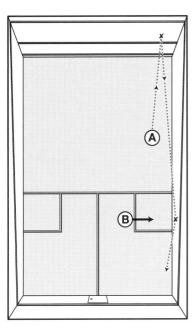

Fig 2 *(left)*
Tightness

Player **A** plays a tight drive into the side to pass an opponent who threatens to volley

Fig 3 *(right)*

1 A tight drive targeted at the side wall behind the service box

2 A tight drive targeted for length to rebound and cling

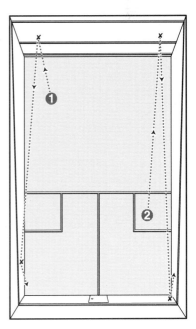

so that they seem to be almost magnetically drawn into the wall.

Tight shots, that is, those close to the side are not easily intercepted. They move us out of the middle and provide difficult and restricted returns. Clingers, those that roll along and cling to the wall, can force weak returns or errors.

Shots can rarely be tight to the side for their whole path, so ideally we would choose to put the ball on the wall at the point where an opponent would want to play it. If an opponent is hanging into the side looking to volley this is where we angle the ball to touch.

On length drives we try to hit the side wall behind the service box, at the point an opponent would want to drive it from. When an opponent is going to take the ball after it has rebounded off the back, we ideally aim the ball to rebound and then cling.

Dying length drives should be designed to angle continually into the wall and not rebound out from it to provide an easier shot. Straight drops, the most frequent and important type, should be played to bounce and cling so that an opponent running to retrieve has the problem of scraping them off the side.

WIDTH

Crosscourt shots spend most of their time out from the side wall. They involve the danger of being intercepted, allowing an opponent to keep the middle and catch us out of position. Perhaps we should call crosscourts passing shots, as they are designed to get past an opponent. To do this they need to be played at the right angle (and the right time), or to put this another way, at the right width across the court. Too narrow an angle and the ball can be intercepted. Too wide an angle and it will rebound back into the middle providing an easy opportunity for an opponent.

Aim wide enough to beat an opponent. If a volley intercept threatens we should try to play wide enough to beat it and put the ball into the side. At times when an opponent is up the court and threatens an intercept, this can necessitate extra width, that is, putting a very sharp angle on the shot so that it reaches the side before an opponent reaches it – even if later it bounces out into the court behind an opponent. If an opponent is well up the court this is less of a problem. When an opponent is close to the side we should put the ball on the side at the point he would wish to play it, as we do with straight drives and lobs. This idea gives us one of the target areas for the serve.

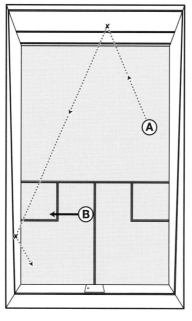

Fig 4
Angle crosscourts wide enough
to beat an opponent's volley

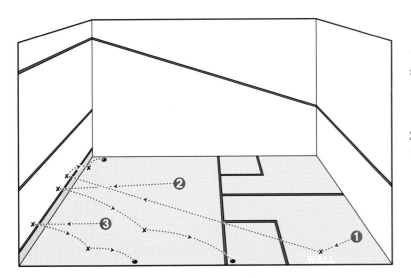

Fig 5

1 A boast played to die on the side or the nick on the second bounce

2 A crosscourt kill played for a width that will die just on or in the nick before the side and not rebound

3 A straight drop played to cling and die on the side

DYING

Part of the essence of squash is to play shots an opponent can't get to before they have bounced twice. The walls, however, often rebound the ball back into the court and this gives opponents a second chance to recover them. Part of the time when we are directing shots we are trying to get the ball to die and not rebound.

Dying is a term used to refer to the fall of shots near the second bounce. *Dying length* is a shot that bounces twice just before the back or falls for its second bounce off the back making recovery impossible or very difficult. *Dying width* is a shot that bounces twice just before the side or which doesn't rebound enough off the side to allow a second attempt. *Dying short* are kills, drops and cut drops which we hope will bounce twice as soon as possible.

You could ask: if these dying shots are more likely to be winners why do we bother with length and width shots that rebound back into the court?

The answer to this is crucial in understanding exactly what you are trying to do with the ball. Dying shots must of necessity be bounced nearer the centre of the court than full length and width shots, giving an opponent the opportunity of playing them early before the side and back. This can allow him to keep the middle more easily. Playing them does not give us the time a full length or width shot would.

The decision to play dying length and width shots, then, depends on the position you are hitting from (can you recover the T easily to cover your opponent's counter shots?), your opponent's position, and the difficulty of the ball you have (you don't want to play a loose shot). Select openings to play dying length shots when your opponent is out of position, so that he will not have an easy shot before the side or back and so that he may be forced to scramble in his attempt to retrieve the ball.

The dying shot is one of the ways of winning points but there is another – the nicks.

NICKS

Walls mean joins and these joins between the wall and floor provide ideal targets for winners. A ball played into the nick can sit low, roll along the floor or bounce unpredictably.

Play drops, attacking crosscourt volleys and kills for the nicks when there is enough angle. They are best played from the middle crosscourt or straight from outside the service box width. In the front court there is also the nick boast (or three-wall boast).

In the back court, hard crosscourts are often aimed for the nick behind the service box and we also have the back wall nick used frequently by Jahangir on the hard bodyline serve.

SHORT

Short has two main meanings in squash. Firstly it refers to the front court or short shots; also called the short game. Secondly it refers to drives that

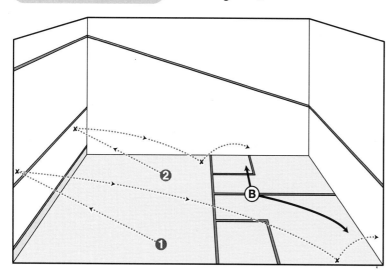

Fig 6

1 A full-length shot pulls player **B** out of the middle and places him in the back corner

2 A short shot allows Player **B** to get to the ball early and keep the middle

allow an opponent to take the ball easily before the back and that don't move him out of the middle. It is the second meaning we will be generally referring to.

LOOSE

Loose shots are those that are not tight or of good width. On a straight drive a loose shot will be moving out from the side wall rather than in towards it; crosscourts may be too narrow and not pass an opponent.

A loose game is one that has too many 'loose' shots out from the side wall providing opportunities for opponents. We also use the term to refer to those games characterised by an abundance of crosscourts and boasts and the looser shots that spend much of their time out from the side walls. One of the first tactical things we learn to do in squash is to play straight frequently so that we play 'tight'.

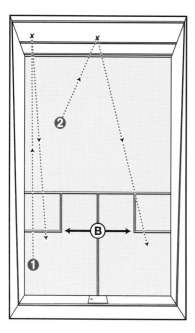

Fig 7 *(Left)*

1 A loose straight drive out from the side gives Player **B** an easy opportunity to intercept the volley

2 A loose crosscourt of poor width can be easily intercepted on the volley

Plate 7 – *(Right)*
Former World Junior Champion Simon Parke seizes the opportunity to attack a loose ball

Plate 8 –
Placing Simon Parke in the back corner has given his opponent time to take the T. Note how he is on his toes, in a ready position and watching intently

T AND TIME

Getting to the ball is everything in squash. If you can get to every ball and return it without making a mistake it is impossible to be beaten.

To recover the ball, you will want to be in the best position from which to run and cover all your opponents options and to run as soon as your opponent hits. Be ready, watching, anticipating the starting gun. If you are still recovering from a previous shot when your opponent strikes, standing out of position or are not ready to run, you have left an opening. Here is an opportunity for your opponent to play a shot that is going to take you longer to get to, provide less chance of a successful recovery and which will be more difficult to recover. The best position from which to cover all your opponent's options is the T.

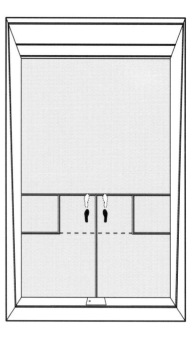

Fig 8
On the T

Ready position on the T,
astride the half-court line, and
between the short line and the
back of the service boxes.
Move forward to the short line
when expecting a short shot

This position 'on the T' is astride the half-court line and between the short line (the line short of halfway) and the imaginary line joining the back of the service boxes. There is some flexibility in this. If expecting a short shot you will move forward, if a drive back a little, but always forward of the imaginary line joining the back of the boxes. Being too far forward or too far back will leave a gap.

Squash is a continual pattern of movement to and from the T. Quick bursts of movement to recover the ball and then equally important, a quick recovery movement to the T, so as to be ready to run again before an opponent hits. Poor recovery leaves gaps an opponent can exploit, forcing you to move further and giving you less time for your next attempted return.

Likewise you seek delays in your opponent's recovery pattern which leave gaps you can exploit. As your opponent is recovering you will be looking to intercept and take the ball early before he has recovered the T.

In many ways this is the essence of the game. Attempting to get your opponent off the T by rallying and then exploiting the gaps.

PACE AND PRESSURE

Pace is the speed at which we propel the ball. Pressure is the time we deprive an opponent of by taking the ball early and by using pace. Jahangir was the great pressure player. He not only got there faster, but being superbly fit he sustained this throughout a match. When he arrived at the ball he cracked it at a relentless pace other players couldn't live with.

Pace can create pressure if it deprives an opponent of time he needs; it can help pass or beat an opponent, make timing more difficult and can force mistakes or weak balls; but it does have its dangers. Play can easily become rushed, 'loose' or 'short', the ball can rebound back further into the court and hard hitting can be more tiring and make recovery more difficult.

Hard hitting can pressurise an opponent by depriving him of time but it will also deprive you of recovery time. In match play we vary the pace of shots to apply pressure on opponents and to relieve pressure on ourselves.

SHOTS

In playing squash we place shots around the court in an endeavour to outmanoeuvre opponents and by adding pace to pressurise them. Now let's look at exactly where we would like to place these.

STRAIGHT DRIVE

The straight drive for full length is designed to pass

opponents, take them from the T to the back corner and force them to take the ball off the back wall. If a volley is threatening it should be angled into the side to be tight at this point, if not, the straight drive should be targeted to cling on rebound from the back at the point an opponent would wish to hit it.

Dying length, hit from the centre area, or when there is an opening, forces an opponent to get the ball before the back and, unless an intercept is threatening, should be faded in to die on the side and not rebound.

CROSSCOURT

The full-length crosscourt should pass a player with width and be played into the side, floor and back just dropping off the back wall to be unplayable or force a restricted reply – a boast or recovery straight drive.

A dying length crosscourt, hit from the central area or when there is an opening, is targeted on the nick behind the service box, or the floor just before the side, to give a spiralling dying length bounce which an opponent must intercept before it dies on the back.

LOB

The high crosscourt lob should drop down into the side wall behind the service box, bounce on the floor and die on the back to force a boast or a recovery backwall lob.

SERVICE

The serve should be played for width to beat the volley and for length to force an opponent into the back – that is for the side, floor and back. A whole range of paces and variations is available.

RETURN OF SERVICE

The standard return of service is as for the full-length straight drive. The crosscourt return is again for width and full length giving time to recover the T. Attack weak serves with dying length drives and volleys and the occasional short shot.

VOLLEYS

The volley is a pressure shot played for dying length or an attacking shot played for the nick or to cling short.

DROP

Whether they are cut or touch drops, these should be played high enough above the tin so as not to make mistakes – that is, a margin for error which varies depending on the difficulty of the shot. Straight drops inside the service-box width should be played to cling. Straight drops played from the middle and crosscourt drops should be played for the nick.

TACTICS

These are the shots we use in our endeavour to earn points and not to lose them. As we have said, we earn points by playing winners and forcing our opponent to make mistakes; and try to avoid losing points by minimising our mistakes and our oppo-

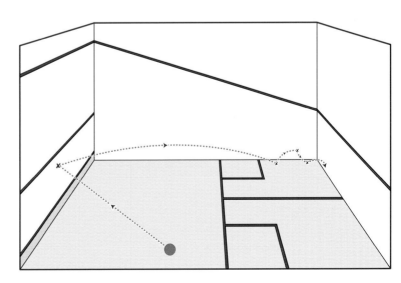

Fig 9
Dying length crosscourt targeted for the nick or floor behind the service box to give a spiralling, dying bounce

Fig 10
Target areas for: **1** dying length drives both
straight and crosscourt; **2** full-length drives;
3 full-length crosscourts, serves and lobs to
rebound into **4**; **5** straight and crosscourt drops;
6 fading boasts which land in this area and die
in **5**; **7** straight kills; this is also the area where
crosscourt kills should die

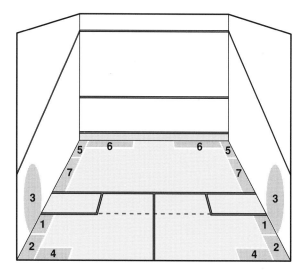

nent's opportunities to play winners.

The first endeavour here is in general termed the attacking part of our game, the second the defensive. Overall it is useful to look at our shot play as fitting into four types of play: defence, attack, positional and pressure, each of which revolves around the T and Time.

Before we look at tactics, let us look a little further at winning and losing points. (Here I use points in a very general sense, when in traditional scoring I really mean winning rallies which can result in either a point or the service won.)

We win points on our winners and through our opponent's errors.

Our winners, often off an opponent's weak shots, (loose, short and middle balls) win points. We try to force these weak shots by providing difficult tight, restricted and dying shots. For example, a dying length, forcing a weak boast which we can drop, or an attacking boast forcing a weak lob which we can volley.

Opponents' mistakes will give us points. To earn these we play the ball into areas where unforced errors occur and set up situations where we can force errors.

We lose points on our mistakes and our opponent's winners.

Our mistakes, those we are forced to make and those which are unforced, give an opponent points. What we will look at is where and why they are made. Where is an opponent forcing us into errors and how?

Our opponent's winning shots are played off our weak balls and tactical errors. The key question to ask of our opponent's winners is where are they played from.

Knowing how to win points and how not to lose them is important, but it is really the setting up of these point-winning and point-losing opportunities that is vital. This we do in rallies and throughout the match. Your thinking on court and your match play is something you can improve and we will come to this, but first you must master the ten basics of squash tactics.

1 DEFENCE

We use defensive play to: avoid mistakes; deprive opponents of the opportunity to attack, apply pressure and make us move; put opponents out of position; win the T. We are in the best place to recover all of our opponent's shots and to take advantage if openings occur from the T.

Defence gives us the time to recover the T before an opponent has played his shots. Other shots don't always give us this time and as a result we can be caught off the T, that is, out of position.

The defensive game uses shots that go right into the back corners – full-length, straight drives, length crosscourts that pass an opponent with width, and lobs. It puts an opponent in the back, gives you possession of the T and gives you time.

Tight shots pull an opponent out of position off the T to the side and may force an opening or even a mistake. Length shots pull an opponent out of position into the back from where his returns may give us the chance to play the ball before he has recovered position, hence allowing us to make him run further.

Good defensive play will give your opponent few opportunities to attack and tight defensive play may force him to make mistakes or provide openings you can exploit.

Defence is the first part of your game. You build on this foundation.

2 VARY THE PACE

Slower shots take longer and therefore create time which can be used to recover the T when needed. It is especially important to play slower shots when under pressure, that is, when you are deprived of time. Use crosscourt and straight lobs to create recovery time.

Also use these slower shots if you need recovery time after a hard rally or if you are tiring. Use more high, wide crosscourts and medium drives.

When you don't need time, but your opponent does, hit hard to provide him with even less time than he has.

Keep an opponent guessing, break up his rhythm, create and restrict time by varying the pace of your shots throughout a match.

3 PRESSURE

Apply pressure, that is, deprive an opponent of time, by hitting hard, playing the ball early on the bounce and volleying, before an opponent has fully recovered the T.

Move into pressure play when you don't need time to get to the T, and when you can catch your opponent off it. This often happens when you hit from the centre area. Apply pressure with bursts of hard hitting.

4 VOLLEY

Take opportunities to volley. This applies pressure and will let you dominate the middle. The player who is in front and who dominates the middle wins. Volley both short and long.

Plate 9 –
Jahangir Khan turns on the pressure. Exploding into action, he seizes the opportunity to take the ball early and crack it away with pace

5 POSITIONAL PLAY

Take opportunities to hit the ball away from your opponent. This is the essence of the game. The further you can make your opponent run, the more chance there is of his not getting to the ball and of not returning it, the more difficult stopping and recovering will be and the more tired he will get.

If your opponent is off to one side, hit to the other. If your opponent is back off the T, hit to the front and if your opponent is in the front, hit to the back. If an opponent is off the T, that is, out of the T box, or has not recovered to a ready position, there is an opening to play the ball away from him.

6 ATTACK

Attacking has the reward of winning points – and the risks of making mistakes, of setting an opponent up with an easy shot in the front court and of being caught out of position.

Attack when you have the following two conditions – a) an opponent out of position, and b) an easy ball. Generally we use the defensive game to get opponents back and then attack short when an easy ball comes along and they are behind. Minimise mistakes by using a margin of error. We will come to this.

7 T

The player who controls the T wins. Recover the T and use this as the position from which to cover your opponent's shots. Give yourself time for recovery. Use length and width and vary the pace to give yourself recovery time. Deprive your opponent of recovery time and move him away from the T. Practise movements that will allow you to pull out of your shots and recover the T quickly and smoothly.

Don't play shots that will leave you out of position and unable to cover all of your opponent's options if he recovers the ball.

8 RETURN TO DEFENCE

Return to defensive play in your rallies and your games. If play becomes loose, short or scrappy, create time and establish control of the T again by returning to defence and varying the pace. If one attack fails to win a rally, or a burst of pressure or positional play fails to force a mistake or opening, return to defence and wait for or create another opening.

Squash is the continual moving in and out of defence, of forays into attacking, pressure and positional plays and back to defence again.

9 RALLY

Squash is not a shot-making sport but a rallying sport. Set up rallies.

Good players don't play a random selection of shots but play to a pattern with standard moves and combinations plus lots of variations. Set up rallies. We will learn to do this better in the match play section.

10 MATCH PLAY

Vary your tactics to counter an opponent's strengths and probe his weaknesses. Develop plans prepare for matches and set up rallies but adapt these to the match situation to seize opportunities and adapt to new threats.

SUMMARY
The ten Basic Tactics

1 **Defence**, first, wins the T with length and width.

2 **Vary the Pace** to create time and recover the T.

3 **Pressurise** your opponent by taking opportunities to take the ball early and hit hard.

4 **Volley** to dominate the middle and apply pressure.

5 **Positional Play** is used to hit the ball away from an opponent when openings occur.

6 **Attack** when an opponent is out of position and you have an easy ball.

7 **T** recovery and domination control the game.

8 **Return to Defence** to tighten your game and move in and out of defence to make attacking, pressure and positional plays.

9 **Rally** to set up opportunities for winners and to force errors.

10 **Match Play** is where you adapt your tactics to an opponent's strengths and weaknesses.

Your Game

To improve your game, play better squash, lift your standard to a new level or become a champion, it's important to know where you are in Your Game. If you know where you are, you will find it a lot easier to get to where you want to go. Your destination is something we look at in Goal Setting (*See* Chapter 7, p, 140).

So before you rush out and enthusiastically play lots of matches, get even fitter or practise your favourite shots, it is important to assess Your Game. What are you good at? What are you not so good at? What are the important areas to work on if you are really going to improve your game? Strangely, so much of the effort players put into improving their game goes into working at what they are good at and familiar with, rather than what they do not do so well.

Firstly, look for areas of weakness that you can improve on and then look at where you are limited in your play. Of course you will want to improve everything overall but try to focus on the key areas for you. Self-criticism is not usually much fun so we tend to avoid it, but there will be much satisfaction in improving your performance so it's worth putting your efforts into where you will get the best results.

Below, we discuss five methods which will help you to assess your game – observation, advice, analysis, experience and player assessment. At the end of this section you will be asked to list ten things you need to work on to improve your overall game, focusing particularly on areas of relative weakness. (An experienced coach who knows your game may be able to tell you these areas straight off.) You will also be asked to complete a skills profile, on which you will note any points you need to work on to improve your game.

This list, The Things I Need To Improve On, can be added to or subtracted from as you read this book. Perhaps when you have finished the book you can come back and look at the profile once again and make another assessment.

OBSERVATION

Arrange for a coach or adviser to watch you play, and ask him to make notes and give an assessment of how you play, including comments on your overall game. The first thing he focuses on may be your weaknesses and the types of problems we shall be discussing in Problem Solving – mistakes, loose shots and tactical errors. However, in an appropriate match, an experienced observer will be able to assess your overall game.

Arrange for someone to video one of your matches. Observe yourself on video and use this technique to analyse your game.

These are useful observations that have been made about my game:

ADVICE

The young player who is excited about playing one of his heroes and keen to tell everyone about the experience always misses a valuable opportunity. What did he say about your game I ask? What did you ask him? 'Well, I didn't ask,' comes the reply.

Ask for advice from better players, senior players and coaches you play or who see you play and write the advice down. It's simple to ask for. Try: 'What do you think of my game?' 'What do you think I have to do to improve my game?' And then perhaps slip in, 'Would you like to play another game or do some practice sometime – I'll fit in with you?'

This is useful advice I have received about my game:

....
....
....
....

ANALYSIS

Arrange for someone to use the methods we discussed in Chapter 1: Watching Squash to analyse your game. Adapt these results and devise forms of assessment that are particularly relevant to your game. A simple dash or cross on a bit of paper will tell you whether or not you achieved success in some aspect of your play. For example, your straight shots from the back of the court may tend to land short. A dash could show that it landed behind the back of the service box, a cross that it was short. Perhaps fold the paper in half keeping the left side for the backhand the right for the forehand.

The analysis criteria are limitless. What proportion of your serves hit the side wall? What proportion of your crosscourts get past an opponent?

How many volleys do you hit and how many does your opponent hit? How many winners do you play on the drop, as opposed to mistakes and the times your opponent takes advantage combined? Develop analysis criteria that are relevant to your game. You can't do everything at once.

Analyse videos of your matches.

Analysis of my matches shows:

....
....
....
....

YOUR EXPERIENCE

Observation, advice and analysis will be useful in helping you to understand your strengths and weaknesses but they are also something you will experience in your game.

What are the problems and successes you are having with your opponents? Your mistakes are obvious, although players often don't appreciate the overall effect of these. The tightness of your game, that is, your ability to get opponents out of the middle to the side and back, is its defensive base. Every time an opponent has an opportunity to play a shot out from the walls or back, you have given him this opportunity. Consider where you tend to play loose shots in your game. What is the cause of these? Have you mastered the basics and

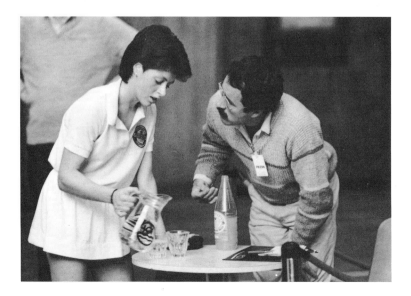

Plate 10 –
The author advises former
National Champion Lucy
Soutter between games

is your technique giving you good control?

Think about your game and the players you play. What problems do you experience? Where do opponents give you trouble, catch you out and take advantage? Do you have a tendency to give away 'cheap points' with mistakes and rash shots. What type of players do you have trouble with? What shots don't you get to?

The shot-making part of your game comes into play when you have the opportunity to attack, apply pressure and move an opponent. Your success in this area is measured by the ease with which you can make these plays and how they affect your opponent. The overall control you manage to establish in your play is reflected by the time you have on the T. A tight game will give you time to recover your position. If you are covering the court in furious bursts of speed to retrieve your opponent's shots after you have left gaps, this will not aid your control over the ball or the rallies.

Try to pinpoint the problems you experience on court and work out the areas that you should improve. This will give you the potential to improve your game. For example, in rallies establish what shots you are trying to play and if you make a tactical error pick up on it immediately. Analyse what you experience before matches and whether anxiety, lack of confidence and concentration are problems during play. How does your fitness affects your results?

Use practice sessions to help you to analyse your game. If you can't do it in practice you won't be able to do it in a game. Here is what former World Champion Ross Norman has to say about it.

Practice is a good way of analysing your game and of finding mistakes. If you know what you are trying to do – you're halfway there. Basic practices will show up where your weaknesses are. For example, if your straight drives are only going three-quarters of the way down the court, rather than right into the back, you can recognise the problem and practise correcting it.

If you don't practise, you'll find that you just have not got time to work out what to do in a game when you are in trouble. If you are used to correcting problems in practice, then it's a lot easier to do it in a game. If you have not worked them out in practice, you won't have time to think about it in a match.

When considering my experience on court I think I should work on:

....

....

....

....

YOUR PLAYER PROFILE

Your standard as a player is set by your skill level. (Here we use skill in a loose sense to categorise the different parts of your game and the different attributes you have.) Squash is a game of many ingredients. Improve these and you improve your standard.

Below is a list of ten important ingredients in your game. Consider carefully how important each is to your game and what impact improving each ingredient would have on your play. Rate yourself in each area on the 1 to 10 scale and total the score for your skills profile total.

1 TECHNIQUE

Your technique helps to give you control over the ball and to place it accurately, consistently and sometimes powerfully into the target area.

Improving technique is discussed under the basics of racket control – grip, wrist, racket face, preparation and swing – and movement control – position, balance, distance, stance and shoulder turn. (*See* Basic Control pages 52–66.)

Rate your technique out of 10:
Do you need to improve it?

I need to improve:

....

....

....

2 TARGETS

Do you have a clear idea of your target before hitting? Do you regularly have that feeling of being early and in the right place for the ball, of having the ball 'lined up', and of knowing where it is going?

Adjusting your position with your feet and knees, early racket preparation, adapting swing size and pausing while waiting for the ball to fall to just the right impact point will help to give you this accuracy. Use these to place the ball accurately into the target area. Read the section on targets and shots in Chapter 2: Playing Squash on pages 19 and 26 and the section on lining up the ball in Improving Your Game on page 65.

Rate your target ability out of ten: ☐

I need to improve:

....
....
....
....

3 SHOTS

Assess the accuracy and consistency of your shots Consider all of the ten basic shots (*see* Chapter 5: Improving Your Game pages 87–111). What are you really doing with each and how effective are they? Are any weak and in need of work? ☐

Rate your shots out of ten:

The shots I need to work on are:

....
....
....
....

4 TACTICS

Read the section on Tactics in Chapter 2: Playing Squash (page 127) and then consider the ten tactical errors discussed in Chapter 1: Watching Squash (page 14). How often do these infringements occur in your game? ☐

Rate your tactical ability out of ten:

I need to eliminate these tactical errors from my game and to improve these tactics:

....
....
....
....

5 THINKING

Consider how well you think on court. How does your mental performance in the areas of concentration, determination, anxiety, frustration, tolerance, confidence and decision-making affect your game? (*See* Chapter 5: Improving Your Game, pages 120–127.) ☐

Rate your thinking out of ten:

I need to improve my thinking on court in these areas:

....
....
....
....

6 MOVEMENT

How would you rate your court movement? Consider your take-off, whether it is early or late and include how well you read your opponents' shots. Is your movement fast and efficient? Can you stop and change direction quickly and how well do you push back to the T from your shots? Are you usually ready on the T before your opponent hits? ☐

Rate your movement out of ten:

I can improve my movement by:

....
....
....

7 FITNESS

For your standard of play does your fitness level get you through hard matches without flagging? Does it give you an edge over your opponents? If you want to go up a level is your fitness level going to be good enough to let you survive there against better players? ☐

Rate your fitness out of ten:

I need to improve my fitness in these areas:

....
....
....

8 PREPARATION

Match preparation includes: how you organise the day of a match so that you arrive unhassled, nourished, hydrated and early; having thought about who you are going to play and how you want to play, and having worked out a game plan; having warmed up physically, warmed up mentally using mental rehearsal; and using a check list in your knock-up. In general consider when you play well, not so well and how your preparation has affected this. ☐

Rate your preparation out of 10:

I can improve my match preparation by:

....
....
....
....

9 MATCH PLAY

For your level of ability and skill what are you really like at playing matches? Do you construct a good game tactically and mentally and try to impose your game on your opponents? Do you adapt your game as you go along to concentrate on your opponent's weaknesses and your strengths? Do you make the same mistakes over and over again and get caught out regularly by the same shots, or are you quick to sort out these problems? Do you vary your shots and change your game when necessary? Do you show determination and can you win or is something always going wrong?

Rate your match play out of ten:

These are the really important things I can improve in my match play:

....
....
....
....

10 PLANNING

Under planning we include programming and goal setting. By planning we really mean, do you think much beyond your next match and take steps to play better in the future or do you just play from match to match? Goals can be both long- and short-term and provide logical steps towards your long-term aims. Do you divide your season into cycles? Do you organise a programme to include fitness, practice, whether it is solo or pairs, and do you play different types of games and players?

Rate your planning ability out of ten:

I can improve my planning by:

....
....
....
....
....

Profile Aggregate: *Total:*

Total your individual scores in each of the ten categories. This is a self-assessment and the categories cannot be assumed to have equal value, so profile aggregates of different players cannot be compared. This is a useful process to help you to assess your own game. If you scored 100, you need not read any more of this book. If you scored less than 100, it is good news, you have room to improve your game.

TEN THINGS I NEED TO IMPROVE ON

From the notes and reflections you have made in Observations, Advice, Analysis, and your consideration of Your Experience and Your Player Profile, make a list of the things you need to do to improve your game. List them in order of priority.

1 ....
....

2 ....
....

3 ....
....

4 ....
....

5 ....
....

6 ....
....

7 ....
....

8 ....
....

9 ....
....

10 ....
....

Problem Solving

Jonah Barrington often tells the story about a pupil of Azam Khan who sought advice from his coach on the inordinate number of times he tinned the ball. The advice of the four-times British Open Champion was simple, direct and given with a clarity that needed no further discussion: 'Aim vee bit higher,' said Azam in his characteristic Pakistani accent.

Now, solutions to all squash problems may not be so simply explained, but at least this pupil recognised the problem and asked the right question. And of course Azam gave the right answer.

In this chapter we provide answers to the most common squash problems: enforced errors, loose shots, a loose game and tactical errors. Are these problems in your game? Ask yourself the right questions and look for the answers here.

ERRORS

The matches you lose are often lost because of your errors. Remember, there are four ways that points and rallies are won and lost – on your winners and mistakes, and on your opponents' winners and mistakes.

What is an acceptable number of errors?

There is no figure or range we can give you except to say that your winners minus your errors must total more than your opponent's in at least three out of five games.

Let us take an example. Chris Dittmar, after years of trying, won his first ever victory over Jahangir Khan in the World Open semifinal in Kuala Lumpur in 1989 with a 15-9, 12-15, 15-9, 9-15, 15-13 victory, in one hour fifty-one minutes. Dittmar only hit forty winners to Jahangir's forty-six, but he made only fifteen errors to Jahangir's twenty-six.

Aim to minimise errors in your game as Dittmar did against Jahangir.

Errors can be divided into two types – forced and unforced. The greater number are usually unforced. These are the ones you have control over. With forced errors we must look at the opportunities you have given an opponent to force you into error. This is something we will cover in Loose Shots and Tactical Errors,

How many errors are you making in your game? Where are they? Can you decrease this number while still playing a similar number of winners? This is the vital information that you should know about your game. Use the analysis method we discussed in Chapter 1: Watching Squash (page 19) and Chapter 3: Your Game (page 31).

Be aware of mistakes. Plan your game to avoid the danger areas where you make them. Recognise mistakes while you are playing – not an easy task when you are under pressure and rushing about. Unforced errors should hurt. Be hard on yourself. Say 'Stop it'. Sort out where mistakes happen and resolve not to make them again.

When I asked the father of the modern game, the seven-times British Open Champion, Hashim Khan, what players should concentrate on to improve their games, he responded with a succinct answer I have often quoted. In clear, if truncated English, he dispensed his wisdom.

Any time you make an error, don't forget – think the reason, what's the reason, what's the reason you make errors – you rush, you not watch, you not in time, ball going away from you. There must be reason. Think for reason. Find reason. Don't do it.

Plate 11 –
In an epic World Open semifinal in
Kuala Lumpur in 1989, Jahangir Khan goes
on the attack against Chris Dittmar.
Is it a winner or an error?

Work to minimise errors, but I must add a word of caution. Squash is both a defensive (minimising errors and loose shots) and an attacking (winning points) game. Don't become obsessed with eliminating errors to the extent of playing negatively. Learn to minimise risk and calculate percentages. We will come to this in Match Play. For now, work out where unforced errors are being made in your game, what is causing them – whether the reasons are technical, tactical, mental or physical – and work to minimise them. The troubleshooting guide lists the ten top causes of unforced errors and suggests action you can take to stop them.

TROUBLESHOOTING: ERRORS

PROBLEM	SOLUTION
1 Aiming too low	Allow a small margin for error above the tin (perhaps four inches, eight centimetres, but if you are hitting the tin this is still too low). Vary this margin for error. Aim a little higher when playing a more difficult ball or a shot from deeper in the court.
2 Choosing the wrong ball to attack	Don't pick difficult balls to attack – the chances of a mistake are high. Wait for the easy ball and for your opponent to be out of position so you have a greater margin for error. Don't attack when you are under pressure and in general don't attack from the back court or when you have a clinger.
3 Losing concentration	Focus your thoughts on the next rally. Start with length and be aware of the danger areas where you could lose concentration. *See* Chapter 10: Match Play.
4 Rushing	Stop for your shots. Vary the pace of your game and create time when you need it. Walk. Try not to get overexcited when opportunities occur.
5 Faults	Mistakes can occur because you are poorly positioned, too close to the ball, or lose control of your swing. A faulty grip or wrist action can mean that the ball is pulled down into the tin. Overcome faults with the technique practices. *See* Chapter 5: Improving Your Game.
6 Weaknesses	Errors will tend to occur when you play your weaker shots. Practise to overcome these weaknesses. Take care of these areas in a game.
7 Mishits and eye off-the-ball	Try to be prepared for your shots so that you don't misjudge them and mistime at the last minute. Stop on balance, keep your head still and your eye on the ball throughout the shots. Use a shorter swing when under pressure or when playing a difficult ball.
8 Impatience	Impatient players make mistakes. Wait for the easy ball and for an opponent to be out of position. Pick the time when it is best to take a risk.
9 Anxiety	Anxious players make mistakes because they make wrong calculations and because tension spoils their timing. Try to overcome anxiety (*see* Chapter 5: Improving Your Game), take more care on shots, concentrate on good preparations, and when anxiety strikes in matches, play more defensively until it passes.
10 Fatigue	When tired, slow down the game using more lobs and high drives. Still try to recover the T, walk as much as possible but play positively without going for rash shots that could easily end up as a string of errors.

ACTION
Unforced errors cost matches. Try to minimise them.

1 Work out where you are making unforced errors in your game.
2 Work out why you are making these errors. Use the Troubleshooting Chart.
3 Practise and plan to overcome errors.
4 Recognise errors when playing and resolve to eliminate them. Stop them.
5 Discipline yourself to follow the rules of attacking play.
6 Look out for danger areas that could lead to mistakes and lapses in concentration.

PRACTICE
Practise your shots in solo and pairs practice using good margins and aim for consistency. In solo practice give yourself regular tests. How many shots out ten can you get into your target area? And how many can you play without a mistake?

Practise pressure exercises with a partner or coach with random feeding from the front where you are practising either drops or boasts. How many shots can you play without a mistake? Play practice games where you are playing lots of shots but concentrate on not making errors.

LOOSE SHOTS

We say 'good shot' to our opponents too easily after they slot in another winner, but this is a poor attitude. Don't think in terms of your opponents' good shots but of the opportunities you have provided them with.

Again Hashim Khan puts it succinctly: 'Any time your opponent plays a good shot there must be reason. You give him chance to play good shot. Don't do same thing. Don't do again.'

If your opponent plays a winner or a good shot ask yourself, where did he play that from? How did my opponent dominate the rally or pressurise me?

To deprive your opponents of the opportunity of playing good shots you should aim to play a tight game emphasising length and width, playing the ball into difficult positions where it is relatively safe for you. An opponent scraping the ball off the side and digging it out of the back is less likely to be hitting winners and playing good shots than an opponent who has the luxury of loose shots. 'Free shots' Ross Norman calls these, shots that can be hit anywhere.

RECOGNISING LOOSE SHOTS
In Chapter 2: Playing Squash we defined target areas for where we would like the ball to go and identified 'short' shots – those that didn't get an opponent in the back when we wanted to – and 'loose shots' – those that came out from the side walls. It's easy to talk about these shots here but recognising them in a game is not so easy. There are two things to help you do this:

First, have a clear idea of exactly where the ball should be going. Establish length, width and tight-

Plate 12 –
Former World Champion Rodney Martin takes the opportunity to go on the attack after Simon Parke plays a loose ball

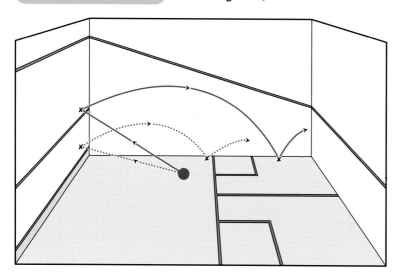

Fig 11
Higher for Length

If a shot lands short, immediately hit higher for length

Fig 12 *(below)*
Tight and Straight

1 striking the ball at a right angle to the side wall will send it parallel to the wall
2 let the ball come past the right angle, to angle it into the side

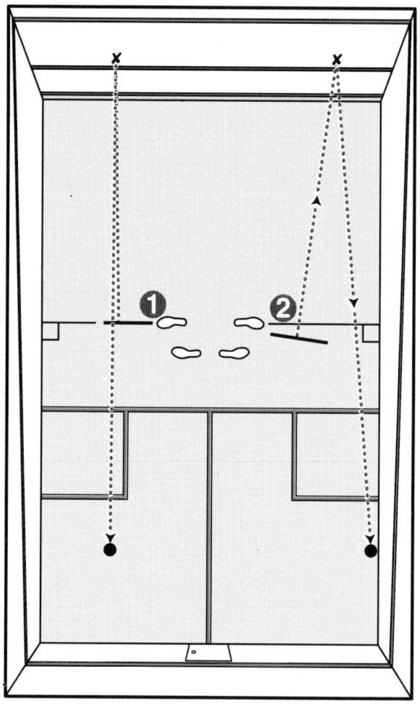

ness in the knock-up, concentrate on it from the first rally and don't let it go. One slip, one short ball and you should pick up on it immediately. As Ross Norman says 'You are monitoring your game the whole time'. One of the things you are looking for is loose shots.

Second, see where your opponent is taking advantage. This takes us back to where we started. If your opponent plays a winner or grabs the advantage, ask yourself: 'Where did he play that shot from?'

HIGHER FOR LENGTH

Recognise the short balls that creep into your game, that is, where opponents play your straight drives and crosscourts easily before the back. Immediately this happens hit higher for length.

Remember height is more important than pace in making the ball go deep. Use an open racket face and get under the ball. Aim above the cut line.

BEHIND THE RIGHT ANGLE

Angle straight drives into the side so that they are tight. Position yourself to the side of the ball so that it is between you and the side at impact. To angle or fade the ball into the side you must always let it come behind the right angle your racket makes to the side wall.

BEAT THE VOLLEY

The crosscourt is a dangerous shot because it spends most of its time out in the middle away from the protecting walls. Position yourself behind crosscourts in a more open stance and angle your shots wide to reach the side wall before an opponent can volley.

Plate 13 –
A supreme effort to get under the ball and lift it
higher for length. Note the open racket face and
how low the player is

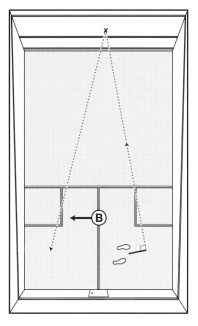 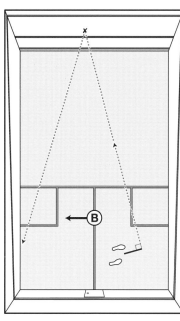

Figs 13 and 14 *(left)*
Beat the Volley

Position more behind the ball
in a more open stance to get
more width on a crosscourt to
beat an opponent's volley

TROUBLESHOOTING: LOOSE SHOTS

TO CORRECT IN A GAME	TO CORRECT IN PRACTICE

Short Shots

Aim higher: use the cut line as a reference point. Play all shots above the cut line (unless attacking) until length is established. Use an open racket face and get under the ball.

Solo practice: drive continuously from the back corners so the ball bounces and rebounds off the back.
Pairs practice: boast and drive, making sure that the ball forces your partner to take it off the back. If one shot is short, over correct on the next.
Condition games: play the High Game, Back Game and Middle Game. *See* Chapter 5: Improving Your Game, Tactics (page 112).

Loose Shots

Angle the ball into the side: don't run at the ball, position to the side of it. Try to stop for your shots and not to rush. Don't try to do too much. Keep it simple. Tighten up your game before moving on.

Solo practice: straight drive from the back targeting the side wall behind the service box. Vary the pace.
Pairs practice: use the boast and drive practice and the circling practice. See if you can roll the ball along the side wall. Slow down.
Condition game: Side Game.

Narrow Shots

Cut down on crosscourts. When you do play a crosscourt make sure that you are in position behind the ball and can get it across the court into the side.

Solo Practice: straight drive for length from the back and pick appropriate balls to crosscourt. Repeat from the other side.
Pairs Practice: boast and crosscourt targeting the side and use the drop and crosscourt; volley and boast practice seeing if you can beat your partner's volley.
Condition Game: play a Back Game where crosscourts must hit the side on the full.

LOOSE GAME

In match play things can go wrong. For example, imagine that your opponent is in front dominating and you have no time to play your shots well. You're rushed. Recovering the T is difficult. Your opponent always seems to be in front, recovers the T easily and although you try harder nothing seems to work.

Now imagine what you would do in a game where your shots ricochet around the court and an opponent easily reads and intercepts them, playing shots seemingly at will. What would you do if your crosscourts came through the middle and straight drives drifted out from the side?

Looking at the first situation above from outside the court, the problem is simple: you have 'lost your length'. With it you have lost the time full-length shots give you to recover the T and the ability to move an opponent out of the middle with your drives. Inside the court you may not see the situation so clearly but you experience the symptoms of 'losing your length' – rushing; feeling pressured; an opponent in front with time who is reading your shots; and an opponent who is taking opportunities to make you run.

The second problem above exists because your 'game is loose' and you are giving your opponent opportunities. In this situation it is easy to become a little depressed (with resulting tactical errors), anxious (resulting in more nervous, less precise shots) and you will almost certainly rush (resulting in mistimed shots).

CORRECT IMMEDIATELY

Try to recognise these problems – 'losing length' and 'loose play'; which often occur together – and correct them immediately. If length is lost, hit higher. Hit high enough on the front wall to achieve good length even if this means a slower pace. It is better to make a definite, even exaggerated, change in height on the front wall rather than a minor adjustment that can result in another short ball. Perhaps play all your drives above the cut line until length is restored.

If your game in general is loose try to eliminate the opportunities you are giving to your opponent. Pick up on your loose shots and correct them immediately as in the troubleshooting guide above.

Picking up on short and loose shots immediately as we discussed in the previous section is the best way to avoid your game becoming even looser.

CREATE TIME FOR CONTROL

When you do lose length or your game becomes loose there is a tendency to rush and run directly to the ball to play straight drives, rather than positioning to the side. This pulls the ball out from the wall when hitting from the front court and deflects it off the side when hitting from the back. Rushing can lead to hard hitting in an effort to get out of trouble, which often results in shots being even less controlled. What can you do?

When you rush, or are anxious, you tend to mistime slightly and your shots aren't as accurate as ones that are well lined up. This gives your opponent the opportunity of putting you under more pressure, and hence the problem is compounded. The only way to break out of this vicious circle is to slow down; take more time on your shots; prepare your racket as you move; make a definite stop before hitting and hit higher and softer to give yourself more time.

BACK TO BASICS

The standard advice when a game becomes loose is to go back to basics. Concentrate on the basic game – get your length right, play mainly straight shots and when you cross make sure it's wide

enough to beat an opponent's volley. Vary the pace and concentrate on tight, accurate shots. Once this tight base has been established and you are playing on automatic pilot you can begin to concentrate on other things, but be careful not to lose it. 'Keep monitoring your game.'

Thinking in a squash match is not easy – there is little time. Think about how you want to play before you go on court, prepare a game plan and practise it. Use the knock-up to groove shots for the game and then set up and control rallies. If things go wrong it is back to basics and building again. This is one of the top ten tactical ideas in the game – Return to Defence.

STRAIGHTEN UP

The crosscourt and the boast are the two loosest shots in the game. If your game is loose, cut down the number of crosscourts and straighten up your game.

A boast fed to the front when an opponent is on the T provides an easy ball that can be cut short, killed or driven to the back again. Try not to be

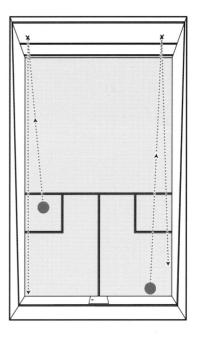

Fig 15
Straighten Up

The first thing you should try to do when you realise that your game has become loose is to hit straight for length

forced to boast from the back corners. Practise so you don't have to do it and certainly don't choose to do so unless you have special reasons. These include an opponent who watches the front wall, who has his feet to the side, a tired opponent or one who is back off the T.

The general rule is simple: don't boast when you're behind your opponent unless you're forced to.

ACTION
If you lose your length:

1 Aim higher. Try to pick up on short shots immediately. Play your game above the cut line until length is established again. Play some practice games in this area.

If your game is loose, providing opportunities for your opponent:

2 Slow down. Concentrate on three things – prepare for your shot, make a definite stop on balance, play more high shots, both straight and high wide shots to give yourself time.

3 If your crosscourts and boasts are loose, stop playing them.

4 Go back to basics in your game and establish length and width before making other plays.

5 Play mainly straight, especially from the back.

TACTICAL ERRORS

It is difficult to recognise your own tactical errors – as discussed in Chapter 1: Watching Squash it is much easier to see them in others than ourselves. Learn the tactical vocabulary, watch squash, see when others make tactical errors and then apply this thinking to your own game. Arrange for a coach or experienced player to watch you play and make notes of your performance. Arrange to have a video made of your game and analyse your play for tactical errors.

Your tactics can be improved. Read Chapters 9 and 10 on Match Preparation and Match Play and establish a structure to your game. Try to recognise tactical errors as you play – such as mistakes and loose shots which we have discussed.

When in trouble ask yourself why your opponent has taken the advantage? Was it because you gave him the opportunity with loose play or a tactical error? Or was it just all his good play? Recognise the opportunities you give your opponents and work to eliminate them.

In Chapter 5: Improving Your Game (page 112) we will look at how to improve tactics with practice, and practice games. For now give yourself tactical rules to play by and if you break them occasionally stop as soon as you are caught out. Recognise any tendency in your game to lapse into tactical errors.

Below are the ten tactical errors outlined in Chapter 1 and some ideas on how to go about eliminating them from your game.

Plate 14 –
Jansher Khan still perfectly balanced improvises a straight drive from a difficult position

Plate 15 – *(above)*
Many of the classic squash battles of the 1970's were between eight-times British Open Champion Geoff Hunt and Pakistan's Qamar Zaman. The superbly fit Hunt was the great mover, Zaman the attacking wizard. Here Zaman has played short when Hunt has been in position on the T giving Hunt a good chance of retrieving the ball

Plate 16 – *(right)*
The player to the left has failed to lob when under pressure and has provided a volleying opportunity for his opponent who has followed up on his original shot looking for a volleying opportunity

TROUBLESHOOTING: TACTICAL ERRORS

TACTICAL ERROR	SOLUTION
Attacking difficult balls	**'Attack the easy ball.'** Don't be overeager to attack. Set up rallies and wait for an easy ball. Attack when you have a sense of time so that everything is ready, focused and lined up before you hit. Prepare for a shot so that you have the option of attack or defence. If there is too much risk in attacking, select the defensive option or try to put pressure on your opponent. Play practice games where you keep the rallies going and wait for the right opportunities.
Attacking when an opponent is on the T	**'Get your opponent back.'** Think of your driving game as the first part of your game which is designed to get your opponent back. Only attack when your opponent is back off the T. Get your opponent behind you, then attack.
Hitting back to an opponent	**'Hit to the gaps.'** Hit away from your opponent. If your opponent is on one side, hit to the other. If your opponent is in the front or in the middle, hit to the back. If your opponent is in the back and you have the right ball, hit to the front. Don't confuse deception with poor positional play. Practise combinations, (*See* Chapter 5: Improving Your Game page 116), in pairs practice and in your practice games.
Leaving yourself out of position	**'Cover your opponent's options.'** Ideally you want to be back on the T before your opponent plays his shot and be able to cover all of his options. It is risky to play shots that leave an opening for your opponent and if you take this risk you need to feel that you have a reasonable chance of success. If you are caught out, don't do it again. Use crosscourt lobs, straight lobs and length shots to give yourself time to recover the T.
Hitting the tin	**'Aim a wee bit higher.'** Leave a margin for error above the tin and vary this depending on the difficulty of the ball and the distance from the front wall. Play attacking and working shots when an opponent is out of position and you can afford to aim a little bit higher. Play condition games. Use the front/back game and practise games playing all shots short. When you practise count the number of shots you can play without a mistake.

continued overleaf

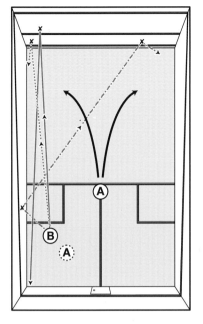

Fig 16 *(left)*
'Get your opponent back'

Player **A** is in the best position to move quickly into the front court and seize on a loose ball. To boast or drop here is a tactical error. In this situation **B** should drive and attack only when **A** is back, out of position

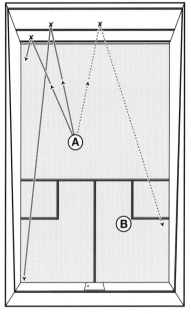

Fig 17 *(right)*
'Hit to the gaps'

Player **A** hits back to **B** rather than seizing the opportunity to hit away using a straight drop, or straight drive or perhaps playing a dying length and fading the ball into the side

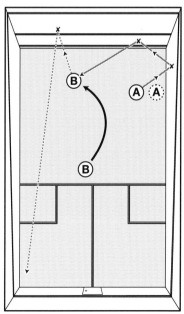

Fig 18 *(right)*
'Cover your opponent's options'

A under pressure plays an angle and finding it difficult to recover ends up out of position near the side wall. His problems are compounded by **B** who is front court. **B** is quickly on to the ball and plays it into the gap

TROUBLESHOOTING: TACTICAL ERRORS

TACTICAL ERROR	SOLUTION
Not lobbing when under pressure	**'Lob to create time.'** Being under pressure either temporarily or regularly means you are deprived of time. Create this time by lobbing and vary the pace throughout your match. Pressure or hard-hitting players will play fewer slow shots but it is still a part of their game and it is a tactical error not to lob at the right time. (Many players will try to hit their way out of trouble but before this extreme course is attempted it is tactically astute to explore variations of pace.) Try lobbing or playing slow in your practice games.
Not playing defensively	**'Back to defence.'** There are times in a match when to take the risk of losing points is dangerous and moments in a rally when the percentages are against you. Recognise these times and play defensively even if in the case of a rally it is for a shot or two. Play more defensively when you are a match or game ball down, when receiving and when in a neutral or disadvantaged situation on court. Practise rallying. Use the back game. Practise attacking when you serve and defending when you receive.
Overplaying crosscourts and boasts	**'Straighten up.'** Overplaying these shots gives your game a loose structure. Have a plan for your rallies, (*See* Chapter 10: Match Play page 167) and set them up. Use a game plan and a check list in your knock-up. Recognise loose shots and try to eliminate them in your game. Play mainly straight from the back. Play the condition game where crosscourts must hit the side on the full.
Failing to take attacking opportunities	**'Attack the easy balls when an opponent is back.'** It is just as much a tactical error to fail to attack when the opportunity presents itself as failing to defend when the conditions dictate. Practise attacking shots so that you are familiar with them and can play them easily. Practise combinations and conditioned games like the front/back game, (*see* Chapter 5: Improving Your Game), and play some easier practice games where you play defensively and concentrate on just picking a small selection of attacking shots at a time.
Failing to volley	**'Volley to keep the middle.'** Volleying is the opportunity to keep the middle, pressurise an opponent and, at times, to play winning shots. Practise volleys in solo and pairs routines and play conditioned games on the volley. Play some easier practice games where you are volleying as much as possible and a few where you are trying to volley everything. In your matches set up rallies, look for volleying opportunities and try to anticipate these. If in doubt, volley.

PROBLEM SOLVING

Q & A: Answers to questions on common squash problems.

Opponents read my play
Q *Opponents seem to read my game easily. Perhaps I lack variety. What should I do?*

A There are two things you can do – one technical, the other tactical. Technically develop some disguise and perhaps some deception in your play. Tactically use variations, that is, the ability to play a variety of shots from the same position on court. Don't use up all these variations at once. Set up patterns, then change them to add a little surprise to your game. *See* Advanced Shots and Tactics, page 150.

Always stuck behind Opponent
Q *I always seem to be stuck behind my opponent and often I just can't get to the ball. What is going wrong?*

A This is your own fault. You are behind your opponent either because your shots are short or because you are providing volleying opportunities. Get your opponent back with length shots. Hit higher, perhaps playing your drives above the cut line. Try the High Game. *See* page 117.

How to improve length
Q *My length is poor. How do I improve it?*

A Practise full length in solo and pairs practice then play some easier practice games where you are mainly concentrating on this part of your game.

Opponent volleys crosscourts
Q *My opponents frequently volley my crosscourts. What should I do?*

A Stop playing crosscourts, or play fewer of them, and when you do crosscourt, pick a time when your opponent is slightly out of position to the side you are hitting from. Play straight until your opponent moves in a little to look for the straight shot and then crosscourt. Crosscourt wide enough to beat an opponent's volley.

Opponent dominates with the volley
Q *My opponent dominates the middle on the volley and whatever I do I find it very difficult to get the ball past him. What should I do?*

A This is one of the classic confrontations in squash, that between the good-length hitter and the volleyer.

Play mainly straight, varying this with wide crosscourts when your opponent hangs in to the side. (Hold, disguise and snap these crosscourts a bit harder if your opponent still reads and volleys them.)

Play your straight drives lower and harder, targeting the medium-paced ones into the side at the point where your opponent would wish to volley them. Try not to be rushed when you move to lower, harder drives but keep a tight game.

Try some very high shots. Your opponent may not be as good very high, as he is at shoulder height.

Anticipate your opponent's volleys. Start moving early to the areas where you are caught out. Still play short shots if you can cover your opponent's options.

Caught by opponent's angles
Q *My opponent invariably catches me out with little, front-court angles. What should I do?*

A Be careful about giving your opponent these opportunities. When you do play short, move him from the back to the front corners. Learn from your match experience and anticipate his likely reply. Look for the angle. Expect it. Move up on the T, move early.

Whenever caught out by an opponent's shot ask yourself where did he play it from.

Losing concentration
Q *Often when winning I lose concentration and never seem to get it back. What should I do?*

A This is a problem we can look at in more depth in Improving Your Game, pages 124–125 but briefly you should try to keep your concentration narrowed and focused on the immediate task throughout. Think in simple terms. Use checks, a game plan and set up rallies.

Be aware of the danger areas such as lapsing after a lead is won. If it is lost, learn to refocus on the next rally.

Not fit enough

Q *I often seem to run out of steam near the end of a match. What should I do?*

A Quite possibly you are not fit enough and might consider a fitness programme, (*See* Improving Your Game, pages 78–86), at the right time – ideally using a pre-season build-up programme and then a maintenance programme throughout the season.

Several hard matches a week will also help to build and maintain fitness.

It may, however, be that lack of fitness is not your whole problem. Learn to pace yourself throughout a match, vary the pace in rallies to allow recovery time, try not to rush, develop smooth economical movement and don't play loose shots your opponent can seize on to make you run, or play tactical errors that mean you are often having to do extra work.

Poor start

Q *It really takes me quite a time to get into my game. When I look back at my results I see that I invariably seem to lose the first game. Often I'm a bit nervous. What should I do?*

A If you really want to perform properly, good preparation is vital, so that when the match starts you are physically, mentally and tactically prepared and have your main shots grooved in.

Think of other sports and consider, say, a high or long jumper preparing and focusing. If you are casual about your preparation, you will get casual results. *See* Match Preparation, page 156.

Slow recovery

Q *My length is not too bad but I seldom seem to win the T. What should I do?*

A The best players push back as they are pulling out of their shots and are already on their way to the

T. They recover it before their opponent hits the ball. Some players are still moving forward when they hit, making recovery difficult.

Try to stop for your shot and push back while completing it. *See* Improving Your Game, page 73. Use some speed drills, not just for taking off but also for recovery.

Poor at reading play

Q *I'm on the T but it's always a struggle getting to the ball. Sometimes it's gone before I've moved. I just don't know where it's going. What should I do?*

A There are two extremes in this problem. One, the front wall-watcher who always picks up the ball late and the other, the player who reads it well and always seem to know where it is going.

If your opponent is playing both straight and crosscourt shots in the knock-up, study him. Try to pick the crosscourt before it has been hit, say 'crosscourt' to yourself just before he hits it. Study his footwork, body and ball position (usually a little further forward for the crosscourt than the straight drive) and stroke. Study all your opponent's shots like this and start anticipating without over committing yourself.

Problems with a hard hitter

Q *I have problems with hard hitters and never really seem to settle down. I'm always rushed. What should I do?*

A Don't play a hard hitter at his strengths. Create time, slow the pace with high drives and lobs and wait for openings to attack. Hit hard in bursts. Countering with hard hitting overall can easily lead to loose play and can become tiring.

In Chapter 10: Match Play we consider different game types which could give you problems and consider how you should counter these.

YOUR PROBLEMS

Quite probably you have further questions on different problems. Hopefully you have, because if you do everything perfectly it's going to be very hard to improve your game.

Ask the question, define the problem, be it big or small, and you are part of the way to solving it. In this chapter we have looked at mistakes, loose shots, a loose game, tactical errors, and answered some common problems. Now it is your turn. Do this process yourself and list your squash problems below. Focus on these problems and look for solutions either in this chapter or the whole book. Later you can come back and note what action you will be taking and which pages will help. You are then on the way to improving your game.

Problem		Action
1	....	....
2	....	....
3	....	....
4	....	....
5	....	....
6	....	....
7	....	....
8	....	....
9	....	....
10	....	....

Improving Your Game

Having discussed Your Game and Your Problems and having selected the areas you wish to improve we must now consider how you can go about improving them.

Squash is a game of habits. There is little time in matches to work out how to improve things as we rush around while trying to win. As Jonah Barrington says: 'Everything seems to happen so quickly in squash that even the minutest amount of method can alleviate the madness of conflict.'

This chapter provides the methods for improving your play. Many of these methods include practice and training and setting time aside for these is something every player who is ambitious to improve should do. In the end though, any improvement must be demonstrated in your game. Having worked out the areas of your game you would like to improve and selected what you need to do from this chapter and the following one on practice, use the programming chapter (*see* page 144) to help you organise your personal improvement programme.

BASIC CONTROL

The best players in squash do the basic things better. Their level has not been achieved by their expertise in accomplishing fancy shots but is largely due to accuracy and consistency in the basic things. Good control of the placement and pace of the ball comes from control over the things that affect this basic control – that is, the technique. Improving these 'basics' is not just a matter for the beginner but for players at all levels – the more accurate and consistent you are from difficult positions the harder you will be to beat.

Even when ball control is satisfactory, ambi-

tious players will work to groove technique and shots further and build up the pace of these while keeping rhythm. They will practise preparing early for strokes so that the ball can be taken earlier. Like the top professionals they will 'line up the ball', so that while hitting they will seem to have time to choose exactly where they want to impact with the ball.

Remember that you build your game on basics. This is not something just for beginners. Technique can be broken down into two parts, movement control and racket control. In this section we will cover: the basics of technique; how to line up the ball; developing the basics even at an advanced level; and also the faults that can spoil control.

POSITION

A golfer has it easy. There is plenty of time to position carefully to the side of the ball, comfortably measure the distance and shuffle in minute adjustment. The squash player in comparison has a second or so to do all of this to be in the best place for his stroke. Imagine a golfer a couple of feet too far away from the ball, or behind or right on top of it. We would reasonably expect him to make a fearful hash of the shot, but this is what squash players often do.

Plate 17 –
The classic closed forehand stance from Rodney Martin. Note the strong stance ready to push back in recovery, the comfortable balance, easy positioning of the upper body, and the excellent control of the racket on a follow-through that has come right across the body

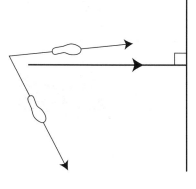

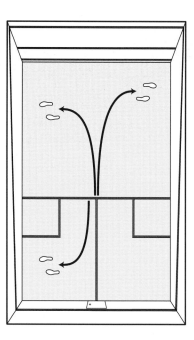

Fig 19 *(left)*
Positioning

The line of the shot is at right
angles to the direction of
the body

Fig 20 *(right)*
For straight shots we move up
and down the middle to
position ourselves to the side
of the ball

When you watch top squash note how the players invariably seem to be in position and prepared for these shots while beginners and club players are smashing themselves in the kneecaps, over-reaching and stumbling or twisting awkwardly from poor positions.

The secret of squash positioning is not to run to the ball but to move to the place you want to hit it from and to do this early. The position we use is the same side-on position as in golf but the action we use is a sidearm throwing action – that is, we stand side on to the direction we want to hit, our shoulders giving the line of the shot.

Many of the shots we hit are straight and this means facing the side, that is, at right angles to the direction we want to hit the ball. The path to these straight shot positions is more up and down the middle than directly to the ball.

Good positioning will allow a grooved stroke (the most accurate) without compensation with the wrist or body, as well as fast recovery, and will often give a position from which, with a minimum of adjustment, a variety of shots can be played.

STANCE

Squash court movement is a there and back run – you run, stop and run back. In that stop you must brake, adjust position, distance and level; brace and prepare to push back at the end of the stroke. If you don't brake well you will have less control as you are moving through the shot on impact and wasting time pushing off walls; if you don't adjust by bending your back and knee, and turning on your hips, you will not 'line up the ball' well; if you don't brace you will spin like a top with the swing losing control and power; and if you don't push back from your shot, you will be slow to recover and get to the next ball – a problem that will compound and restrict your performance.

A squash stroke is not just a flick of the arm. It incorporates an unwinding of power throughout the body, including a transfer of weight which gives the shot power. A good stance will allow all these things. It is the undercarriage for the shot, providing balance (through the suspension system of the knees), and putting the upper body in the best place. We can use different stances but the correctness of a stance is something you can feel – it will allow a smooth movement into and out of the shot and a rhythmic stroke. Try staying on balance after your shot – this is the balance check for a good stance. Briefly let us look at some basic stances.

Closed Stance

Stand facing the side wall (if off court imagine you are facing the side), step forward on the front foot, (the one nearest the front wall) bend the knee so that it covers the toe, have some space between the feet, let your weight go on to the front foot, bend the back knee slightly and let the heel come up. Rock back and forwards to check your balance –

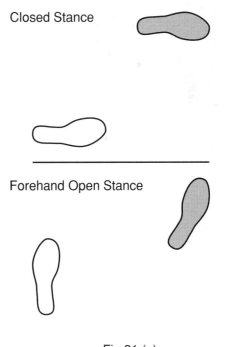

Closed Stance

Forehand Open Stance

Fig 21 (a)
Closed Stance
Forehand Open Stance
(weight is on shaded foot)

Plate 18 – *(left)*
This backhand closed stance from Jansher Khan is a brilliant study in control and balance that shows just how hard it is to beat him with the ball. At full stretch he has excellent control of the racket head and is concentrating on the ball

can you adjust for different impact points?

This is the orthodox or traditional stance. It puts the body in the right place for the shot. Generally we teach this stance first for this reason, although most players use an open stance on the forehand, especially when going forward.

Forehand Open Stance

Lunge forward towards the front right corner on the right foot and take up a strong stance. In this position your body faces the corner and is in position for a crosscourt shot. Moving into and out of this stance is quicker than the closed stance and allows more reach, but there is a tendency to hit across frequently. To hit straight a player must twist to the side from the hips.

Backfoot Stance

When taking the ball behind the T area but before the back wall, we often use a backfoot stance where we step back on the back foot and turn the body to the side on the hips.

Backcorner Stance

Here we use a squat type of stance with knees bent and weight evenly balanced on both feet. Come to the side of the ball, let the toes face the corner and the trunk faces the back. Using both feet and bent knees allows reach to different impact points over a wide area.

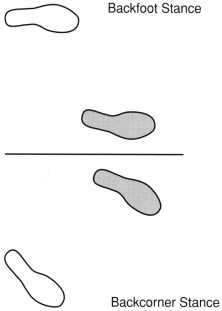

Backfoot Stance

Backcorner Stance

Fig 21 (b)
Backfoot Stance
Backcorner Stance
(weight is on shaded foot)

Plate 19 – *(left)*
Jahangir Khan using a backfoot stance. Note how he has prepared the racket in a low and compact backswing ready to lift the ball

Plate 20 – *(right)*
English National Champion Phil Whitlock using an open stance on this forehand. He has turned his body and is holding it braced as he swings. The photograph catches the slingshot-like pronating action of the forehand that the human eye does not see

SHOULDER TURN

Although you have the best control over your stroke when you are stopped and balanced there is a limited body movement that unwinds like a spring with the shot. Crucial in this is the shoulder turn which transfers weight into the shot and generates power in a fuller swing.

Jahangir Khan was the master at this, arriving in position for his shot with his trunk and shoulder turned and unwinding power no other player could live with.

Part of this turning action is from the hips, especially in open and backfoot stances, but concentrating on the turning of the shoulder early as part of your preparation will allow you to unwind the power smoothly.

Plate 21 – *(above)*
Jahangir Khan already prepared as he moves into a backcorner stance. Note how he is perfectly balanced on one leg but is moving into a stance using both feet which will give him more stability when hitting

Plate 22 – *(right)*
Susan Devoy turns her shoulder and winds up for a backhand crosscourt drive. Note how the toe is angled forward for the crosscourt, the racket in a perfect backswing position, and the concentration intense

GRIP AND WRIST

There is an old saying in squash that 'the racket is an extension of your arm'. The link with this additional appendage is through the grip and wrist which provides control of the racket head and of the angle of the racket face. If the racket flaps around loosely on the end of your arm you are unlikely to develop precise control of your swing and hence your shots. If the angle of the racket face is not easily adjusted to the most appropriate for the shot, you will be limited in your shot-making and may need to make wristy and inconsistent last-minute adjustments.

Bounce the ball up and down on your racket. Here you are lifting it straight up in the air with a completely open racket face. Look at the front wall. In your game you want to take advantage of the full height of this wall. To hit upwards at a trajectory of 30 degrees you would want your racket to be 30 degrees open. The wrist makes this adjustment easy.

Hold the racket face vertically and when you take it back, take the racket edge in a direct line to the backswing position (the quickest preparation). This is easily achieved by cocking the wrist back towards the right shoulder for the forehand and the left shoulder for the backhand.

Imagine your racket is a long hammer ten feet long or so and that you are going to put a tack in for a picture frame with it. Try it. Can you feel the control in your racket head.

Your racket head is the thing that hits the ball and your control over it is the most important part of your game. You can get this control with the V grip. To master this there are three important things to remember:

1 The V

Hold your hand out level with the ground, palm down and make a clear V between thumb and forefinger.

This V sits on top of the handle, on the inside edge – on a square-shafted racket it will be in line with the top inside edge (the edge towards the body) of the shaft.

2 Knuckle Up

Spread the fingers so that they fit diagonally around the head in line with the grip. Leave a finger gap between the index and middle finger. (Try pointing the index finger along the outside edge of the shaft and then slipping it around the handle like pulling the trigger on a gun.) Sit the knuckle up on the outside edge.

3 Diagonal Thumb

Run the thumb diagonally down the inside of the handle. The butt of the handle should be below the heel of the hand. Traditionally this has been just below the heel but today with lighter rackets a number of top players are holding the racket higher up on the handle.

Keep your wrist up and use the V grip. A little shake of the racket head will let you feel if you have control. If you drop the racket head well below wrist level the gripping action will be weaker and hence if you hit like this you will have less control.

Develop good racket head control then with the V grip, keep the wrist up and take the racket edge back at the most appropriate angle for the shot.

Fig 22
The V grip with the V along the inside edge of the handle, the knuckle sitting up on the outside edge and the thumb diagonally along the inside face

SWING

The path of the swing and angle of the racket face control the flight and placement of the ball. The better the swing, the better the control. Too many players have a very limited attitude to developing their swing and rush around the court whacking at the ball in a crude and uncontrolled way. Try to develop the best swing you can. It will help you improve your control and your game.

Golfers are excellent examples of sportsmen interested in technique and aware of how it affects their control of the ball. In squash there is much more going on but try to develop an awareness of your swing and an attitude that will allow you to improve it. Develop your swing by practising with and without the ball.

Develop an easy, economical, rhythmic action that gives power and control. The best control comes from a grooved swing. Imagine a swing that makes a smooth curve, almost mechanically grooved. Although in reality all swings will really be a little different, the more grooved this action, the more accurate and consistent it will be.

Early preparation for the backswing position by the most direct path saves time and aids timing of the ball especially in pressurised situations. When you watch top squash, this early preparation is one of the very strong impressions you are left with and one worth emulating.

The squash swing goes from a V to a V and hinges on the elbow. The forehand action is the sidearm throwing action we use to skip a stone on a lake or in cricket to throw in quickly a low pick-up of the ball. The backhand is like a slapping action or the throwing of a frisbee.

Plate 23 –
National Champion and former World Junior Champion Cassie Jackman demonstrates the forehand swing. Note the excellent preparation, the steady backswing position, the V in the arm and the balancing symmetry of the left arm

Forehand Swing

Initially to find the backswing position stand facing the side wall, lift your wrist, open the racket face and take it to a position in line with your shoulders and the back wall, just above your head. Let the elbow bend to make a V and sit over the hip – for a more powerful swing lift the elbow taking the racket further overhead. Swing down, back and then through, stopping at the impact point where your racket has made a right angle with the side wall. At impact, the wrist should be up, the racket roughly parallel with the floor and the racket face open.

Let the elbow come through and the swing move across the body and up into a V, with the wrist up.

Once you have explored these three points – backswing, impact and follow-through, practise your swings by taking the racket directly to the backswing position.

The swing will move from a V to a V. A slight pause on the backswing adds control providing a precise point from which to swing. Swing through to a definite stop point on the follow-through. Try to prepare early and develop a smooth and grooved swing between these two points. Swing precisely from A to B.

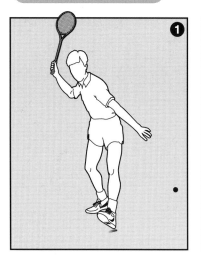

1 Take the racket back and up overhead, bending the arm into a V shape. Let the weight come forward as you are about to swing.

2 The racket goes back and down, and the elbow and butt of the racket handle are pulled through.

3 In the horizontal part of the swing, the forearm turns through the impact point. This turning action is called pronation.

THE FOREHAND SWING SEQUENCE

THE BACKHAND SWING SEQUENCE

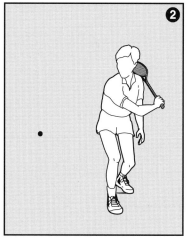

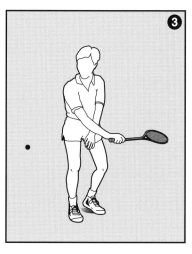

1 For the backhand swing, turn the shoulders and take the racket edge around behind the head. Bend the arm to make a V and again keep the wrist up.

2 Let your weight move forward as the racket moves down and around the body into line for the horizontal part of the swing.

3 The elbow and butt of the racket are pulled through and the forearm is about to turn and accelerate the racket head through the impact point. This action is called supination.

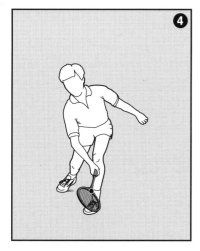

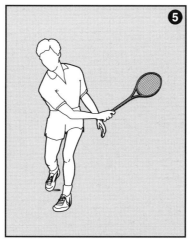

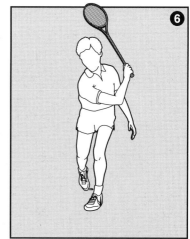

4 At impact keep your wrist up for good control over the racket head. The swing should be roughly parallel with the floor without the racket head dropped. Brace yourself on balance as the racket moves through the impact point.

5 Let the swing come across the body in a relaxed action while you stay balanced. Let it hinge on the elbow and keep the wrist up to keep control of the racket head.

6 Let the racket swing through to a full follow-through position. A full swing will have swung from a V behind the body to a V across the body.

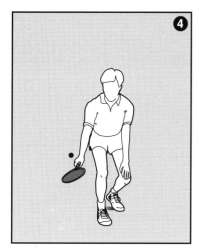

4 The impact point on the backhand should be forward of the leading foot as on this stroke the shoulder is in front of the body. The arm straightens and the body is held on balance as the racket moves through the impact point.

5 The swing flows through across the body, the arm turning at the elbow and shoulder. Keep the wrist up for good control over the racket head and a grooved swing.

6 Let the racket swing right through in line with the shoulders while maintaining balance. Keep control of the racket head and stop it at a precise point. Try to develop a smooth curve and a grooved action

Backhand Swing

To find the backswing position on the backhand, turn your shoulder, point the racket at the back, bend your elbow and then take the racket up behind your head. Push your elbow across your stomach. Don't come down too tightly on the ball but come down and around behind it, then accelerate the racket through the impact zone into a follow-through in line with the shoulders, with your elbow bent and wrist up.

Adapting the Swing

We use a whole range of swings in squash – little pushes and occasional flicks, half volleys that go over the ball, punches on volleys, and short, compact and full swings. It is a mistake to try to use the same swing and swing size for every shot, so don't be afraid to adapt them but don't let this flexibility distract you from the task of developing a smooth, flowing and if possible grooved swing. Use a short swing for touch, that is, to hit softly, a full swing for power, and a compact swing for control.

FAULTS

Faults are bad habits that can spoil your technique, making it limited and inconsistent, and they can lead to difficulties in timing the shot. Try not to rush your shots as they will tend to be less accurate. Practise lining up the ball. Try not to move excessively or swing your body with the shot. Use stances that will give you balance and allow you to stay steady. Don't get too close to the ball and cramp your stroke. Use an appropriately sized swing. A loose or dropped wrist leads to less control of the racket head and hence less accuracy. Taking your eye off the ball leads to missed and mistimed shots.

Try to eliminate any faults in your game with practice.

CONTROL UNDER PRESSURE

Technique breaks down under pressure – that is, in situations where you are forced to play the ball from poor positions, awkward stances and with little time.

Even when under pressure try to stop for your shot, force yourself to prepare your racket early, reduce the size of your swing and concentrate on watching the ball. When pressurised and scrambling it is not the time for full or flamboyant swings.

Tactically the answer is to relieve the pressure, but this is something we will come to in Match Play (*see* pages 163-174).

LINING UP THE BALL

Being in the best position, having a stable stance, good racket control and a grooved swing won't necessarily give precision to your shot if you have not lined up the ball. Lining up the ball refers to when you have positioned and prepared for the shot before you want to swing and can take the ball at exactly the impact point you want. Watch the top players, they always seem to have time to play their shots – everything is ready, the racket waits, the shot is lined up, the ball falls to the desired impact point and – whack!

We can guide the ball a little with the wrist and swing but the most important part of aiming the ball is to take it at the right point in relation to the body. (Usually we don't look at the target area.)

GROOVING THE SWING

The more your swing is grooved the more consistent and accurate your shots will be. One of the easiest ways to develop this is to have a clear idea of exactly where your racket is. Take it directly to the backswing position and pause, holding it steady. Develop a smooth swing from here to the follow-through position – from point A to B.

Practise your racket preparation and pause in solo driving to the service box; develop rhythm off the back wall. Practise grooving your swing by having a coach or partner feed for drives and work on it in the knock-up and in pairs practice.

Plate 24 –
Two-times former British National Champion Del Harris demonstrates the backhand swing. Note the steady and precise backswing position and the V in his arm. See how he has turned his shoulder and pushed that arm right across his body

PRACTISING TECHNIQUE

1 Without the Ball

Practise your swing without the ball, concentrating on quick racket preparation and a pause at the start of the backswing and end of the follow-through. Develop a smooth, flowing action.

Also practise the complete stroke from the ready position, co-ordinating your position, stance, shoulder turn, racket preparation, pause, swing and recovery. Move in and out of a ready position. This may be practised off and on court. Refer to the Movement sections on pages 67–77, for ideas on court movement and incorporate these with those on technique in your ghosting sessions.

2 Service-Box Drives

Lift the ball above the cut line and into the service box. Initially give yourself time to step back from and into each shot so that you are practising positioning, footwork, stance and recovery. Stop the racket on the backswing and follow-through. Gradually build up the pace from:

1) all above the cut line; 2) one above, one below; 3) all below.

3 Volley

Volleying straight halfway between the short line and front wall is excellent technique practice as it necessitates a firm wrist action, good racket head control in the short, punching action and quick preparation.

4 Backcorner Drives

Start out from the side wall and develop a rhythm in your continuous solo drives from the back corners. This is where you can develop a full, flowing, grooved swing and build up power. Again step in and out of the shot and pause on the backswing and follow-through positions as this will help your awareness of technique. Use a faster ball if this helps.

5 Feeding

From behind feed high and soft for your partner to move from the T and practise straight driving. Allow time between feeds. This practice in an unpressurised situation allows the player to become more aware of technique.

6 Knock-Up

The knock-up, especially an extended knock-up before practice, is an excellent time to concentrate on aspects of technique.

Practise first stepping in and out of each shot, concentrating on particular aspects of the shot in turn, such as the stance with a pause on balance, racket preparation when the ball hits the front wall and on a grooved swing pausing to check the racket head control at the end.

SUMMARY

Improving your Game: Basic Control

The best players play better shots more of the time. They seem always to be in the right place and

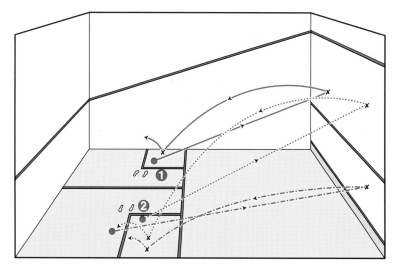

Fig 23

1 Service-box drives all above the cut line

2 Service-box drives one above the cut one, one below

to be prepared. What you are doing with the ball in your game goes back to your basic control – don't ignore it. You will know whether you need to work on it systematically, but even if it is satisfactory, develop an attitude of trying to line up the ball all the time. Be aware of your technique and take time to concentrate on it in knocking-up and in practice. These basics are the foundation of your game.

MOVEMENT

If a player can get to every ball and hit it without making a mistake it is impossible to be beaten. The nearer you are to this ideal and the longer you can sustain it, the harder you will be to beat. This is the raw guts of squash. You cannot talk your way round it.

Three things are vitally important if you want to achieve this: your movement to the ball; speed to get there in time; and your endurance to sustain this. In this section we look at your court movement and how you can improve it. In the Fitness section we consider your speed in recovering the ball and your ability to sustain this.

In moving, if we use a broad definition, a player must read the play, anticipate, react, take off, move efficiently to position, brake, balance, brace, push back and recover a position ready to run through

Plate 25 –
Chris Walker, anticipating well, is already under way as the Finn Sami Elopuro goes short

this pattern again and again.

The average time between squash shots is approximately one and a half seconds, so you will repeat this pattern every three seconds. In a thousand-shot match (very roughly one hundred rallies at an average of ten shots), you would repeat this five hundred times. Each movement would be different but similar.

Perhaps you have never really thought about your squash movement. If you have watched the top players you will invariably see they are back on the T before their opponent hits the ball. From the time their opponents hit the ball they go through the movement pattern described above and are back at the start ready to dart off again before an opponent's next shot. Some people are naturally better than others at this, but your movement is something you can improve by being aware of it and working at it.

ANTICIPATION

Study your opponent and his position in relation to the ball. If you go to see the top players, watch the nippy, little Australian Chris Robertson, his eyes big as saucers transfixed on his opponent. When the ball is hit his feet leave the ground in a fast little astride jump and he is already airborne, his head snapping to the front as he seeks to pick up the ball again.

Watch Chris Dittmar, marginally slower, stronger, steadier, close down his opponent's options of shot and be already moving before an opponent has hit, smoothly cruising to intercept and ruthlessly working the ball away.

Study your opponent. Limit his opportunities and anticipate. For example, if a ball passes an opponent and will not come off the back enough to allow a crosscourt, his options are a straight shot or boast – the crosscourt has been eliminated so you don't have to cover this. Move in a little looking to volley the straight shot and keep studying him for signs of a boast.

If your opponent has stretched for a ball that is well in front and is reaching forward for it, a crosscourt is most likely. What will you do? Move up to the short line, of course, and volley. Where? Straight for dying length.

Observe your opponent's position in relation to the ball and be ready for limitations in the variety of shots he can play. Is your good crosscourt going to force a boast? Yes. Then you are already on your way forward to straight drop. Study your opponent – his position, footwork and swing. Ask yourself which shot is next? Is he shaping to hit straight, crosscourt or boast? Is it a full swing for power or a short swing for touch?

Work out your opponent's patterns. Does he mainly crosscourt from the back right-hand cor-

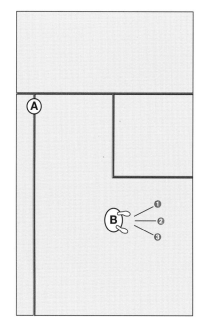

Fig 24
Anticipation

A studies **B** and notes
where he hits the ball
in relation to his body:
1 is likely to be a
crosscourt, **2** a
straight drive and **3** a
boast

Plate 26 –
Jansher Khan hangs into the side when he
sees that Ross Norman doesn't have the
crosscourt option

ner? Are you ready for this and preparing for a straight backhand volley drop?

Does your opponent always crosscourt from the front right? Are you ready to intercept on the volley.

When you boast him short, does he invariably try a tricky angle? Are you already moving forward anticipating?

Practise your anticipation. Watch squash. Study players from outside the court and just before they hit, ask yourself: what shot is this? How have they prepared to play it?

Study your opponents. Work out their patterns of play and likely shots in each situation. Use the knock-up. Study your opponents and practise reading straight and crosscourt shots. Try to make a decision before the ball has been hit but don't rush off before this has been confirmed. Play some easier practice games where you concentrate on anticipating and intercepting.

Be careful, however, because there is a difference between anticipating and guessing. If you don't have real cues on your opponent's shot and he has a range of variations available you must be ready to move to cover all these. In play, look at your opponent enquiringly, trying to work out what the next shot will be rather than giving a vague glance that may miss the shot altogether. Ask yourself: 'What shot is coming up?'

READY POSITION

It is unfortunate that the one and a half seconds you have to get to the ball in squash is only a rough average. Often you only have a split second and when it is your turn to run you must be ready.

In the ready position you should be like a sprinter crouched and ready to go, but there is an important difference – you must be ready to move in any direction.

'On your toes' really sums it up. You can't push off from your heels. Crouch forward on the balls of your feet like a boxer. When Dittmar, the biggest of the top players, is crouched ready to pounce he lifts his heels right up off the ground.

The best place from which to cover all of your opponent's shots is from a ready position on the T. That is, toes forward crouched astride the half court line between the short line and the imaginary line joining the back of the service box. Generally you will be around the middle of this area, a racket length or so behind the short line or, in deep rallies, a little further back. You must, however, always get both feet over the line joining the back of the service box, otherwise you will be out of position.

With more all-court rallies you will move forward and if expecting a short shot move right up to the short line. When an opponent is restricted to a straight shot you will move over to that side.

Generally you should have your toes forward so that you can move to either side without needing a time-consuming turn, and if the ball is behind, you should twist your trunk so that you have a good view of your opponent.

TAKE-OFF

Most top players use a fast, little astride jump as their opponents hit, so that their weight is forward, down and wide in a position from which they can push off in any direction. Practise this in your skipping or in the warming exercises of your warm-up.

MOVING

Squash players have individual styles of moving. Jahangir Khan, cat-like, accelerates fastest springing to the ball, twisting his trunk ready to unleash the power; the tall Jansher cruises smoothly, then darts in blurred steps, faster than the eye can see, his racket extended like a rapier to make recoveries we find difficult to believe; Robertson bounces, scurrying around opponents, changing direction easily in midair and possesses the uncanny ability to push off in all directions. Rodney Martin hovers elegantly on the T, seeking intercepts and Ross Norman's telescopic stride doesn't waste a step.

We move differently and use all sorts of steps – running and walking steps, lunges, jumps, astrides, side steps, crossovers, turning and little adjusting steps. Use all these steps but try to keep them to a minimum and eliminate all unnecessary steps.

Plate 27 – *(left)*
Australian Chris Dittmar astride the T and on his toes in a ready position

Plate 28 – *(right)*
Australia's speedy Chris Robertson demonstrating the stride jump that the top players use when they take off

Plate 29 –
Jansher Khan diving for the ball, racket open
and outstretched. If you look closely you can
see that he has just got his racket under the ball

Try to move smoothly and efficiently. Don't rush. Use long strides to get into position, but don't overstride as this is tiring. Use whatever adjusting steps and footwork you need to get into the best position for your shot but again minimise these.

Walking and running are the most efficient movements but use side steps by all means, just don't try to cover the whole court this way.

When trying to improve your game, don't forget about your squash movement – it is not the same thing as being able to run well.

Don't run long miles to build up your stamina and then expect to float like a butterfly on court. Practise using efficient squash movement in your: court sprints, shuttles, solo and practice games, ghosting and skipping. In practice isolate and work on the movement patterns you would like to use in a game and concentrate on these.

FOOTWORK

The best players play their best shots frequently because they are usually in the best place for the shot. If you are not in the best place, if you are awkwardly positioned, stretched, overreaching or cramped, the shot is less likely to be effective. A few classy players seem to be able just to step into each shot but most of us need to adjust our positions to get this just right – part of this adjustment is with the knees and part with the feet. Use little adjusting steps that will allow your last stride to the ball to be a comfortable length; dance back and forward and side to side to get the best positioning possible.

Skipping is excellent for footwork. Some of my pupils have also tap-danced. Practise on your toes, adjusting your position for each shot and using little movement exercises to warm up and develop footwork dexterity – try bouncing side to side, stepping back and forth over a line and bouncing from the ball of the front foot to the back and so on. Practise fast-stroking sequences with the racket, stepping in and out of shots and turning.

RECOVERY

Our heroic efforts in squash go into retrieving the ball but then there is a slight tendency to rest on our laurels. Don't. You can only stop twice in a squash rally – when you are hitting the ball and when you are on the T. To give yourself the best chance of retrieving the ball you want always to aim to be ready on the T. Push back from your shots and try to make your recovery smooth and economical, even leisurely if you want, just be back ready at the T before your opponent hits. If you are not there you have been caught out of position and you will have left an opening that an opponent can take advantage of.

From the front run backwards tripping smoothly and turning the head to see an opponent's shot preparation. This backwards recovery allows a sudden change of direction forward again. (Sometimes we can use a boast to wrong-foot a player who turns when running backwards.) This is an important idea in your recovery. Move in such a way as to be able to change direction, taking small, evenly balanced steps that will allow a sudden, darting movement in an unexpected direction.

From the back walk. Yes walk! But walk quickly. Trot a little if you are not going to make the T in time and run only in emergencies. (Rushing doesn't facilitate composure and changing direction.)

PUSH BACK

Don't dawdle if you want to recover the T before your opponent strikes. As you are finishing the stroke push back to the T. Take that up and away movement at the end of a stroke and transfer it into a pushing back movement.

From the front push back from a bent knee position. From the back, step up out of the shot at the end of the follow-through and towards the T (or towards the half court line if you have hit straight), turning at the same time.

Don't let this movement interfere with your shot but make it almost one flowing movement.

Recovery will be slower if you run through the ball, have to push back off the wall, hit and move forward or cramp the stroke. Brake and brace in a strong stance that not only gives balance and a good position for a variety of options, but also gives the ability to push back towards the T immediately.

PRACTISING MOVEMENT

Be aware of your movement, how well you anticipate, get ready, take off, move, recover and push back. Do activities to improve it, especially in the preparation phase of your programme and incorporate squash movements into your fitness programme. Concentrate on movement when practising and in practice games.

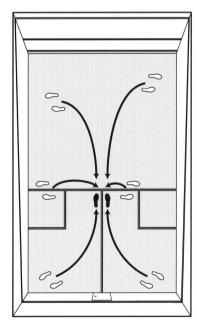

Fig 25
Recovery

Push back to the T after your shot. The rules give your opponent the right of direct access to the ball which means that sometimes you are obliged to circle back to the T to avoid interference

Plate 30 –
Del Harris still perfectly
balanced pushing back in
recovery from his shot and
watching at the same time

Fig 26 (opposite)
Ghosting

Skipping

This is an ideal movement exercise which can be used at different rates to build speed, stamina and to warm up. Skip in trainers on a sprung floor or carpet. Use all the different skips you can to build up different routines, even using the take-off astride and double skips.

Ghosting

Ghosting uses simulated squash movement and strokes with the racket but without the ball to practise movement and build endurance. This is a method developed by Jonah Barrington and is used by many top players. Lisa Opie the first British woman to win the British Open for thirty years in 1991 says: 'When you first attempt ghosting, try the movements slowly and precisely, getting them right from the start. When you have them mastered, then you can speed up. The key thing to remember is to push back from your shot on to the

back foot and recover quickly for the next.'

Start each routine from the T. Practise the ready position, crouching as if you don't know which direction you will move in; the take-off; preparing for the shot as you move; the stance; pushing back; recovering and preparing for the next shot.

Lisa adds words of caution: 'Initially, be careful to stay in position throughout your shots. Don't pull away too quickly. You must be still for the shot and then push back as quickly as possible to regain prime position on the T. Pushing back is not easy when you have been forced to play an awkward shot. But with practice you will soon be getting out of the shot as quickly as possible.'

Here is the series of ghosting routines that Lisa uses. Work for thirty seconds on, thirty off at maximum speed. Lisa does ten to fifteen sets. This could be built up to a minute at maximum speed for anaerobic endurance and longer intervals, say six sets of two to three minutes for aerobic endurance.

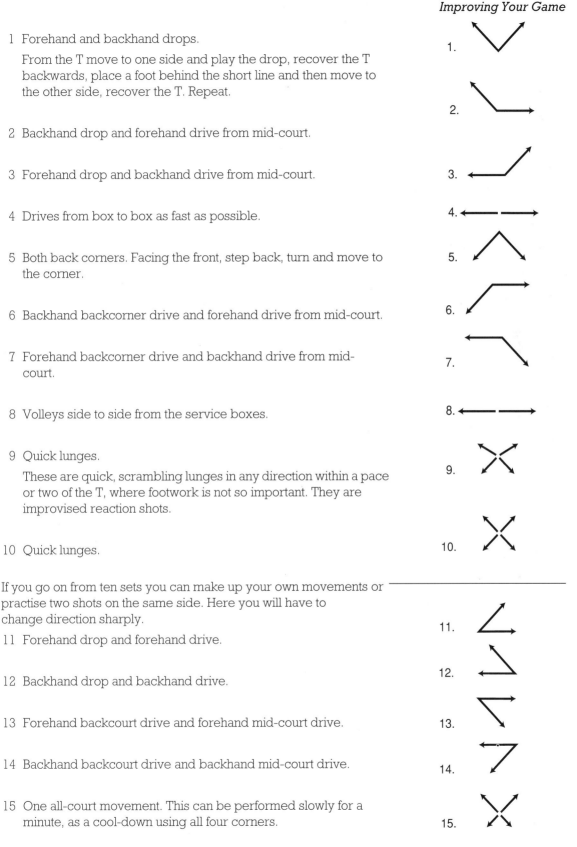

1 Forehand and backhand drops.

   From the T move to one side and play the drop, recover the T backwards, place a foot behind the short line and then move to the other side, recover the T. Repeat.

2 Backhand drop and forehand drive from mid-court.

3 Forehand drop and backhand drive from mid-court.

4 Drives from box to box as fast as possible.

5 Both back corners. Facing the front, step back, turn and move to the corner.

6 Backhand backcorner drive and forehand drive from mid-court.

7 Forehand backcorner drive and backhand drive from mid-court.

8 Volleys side to side from the service boxes.

9 Quick lunges.

   These are quick, scrambling lunges in any direction within a pace or two of the T, where footwork is not so important. They are improvised reaction shots.

10 Quick lunges.

If you go on from ten sets you can make up your own movements or practise two shots on the same side. Here you will have to change direction sharply.

11 Forehand drop and forehand drive.

12 Backhand drop and backhand drive.

13 Forehand backcourt drive and forehand mid-court drive.

14 Backhand backcourt drive and backhand mid-court drive.

15 One all-court movement. This can be performed slowly for a minute, as a cool-down using all four corners.

Plate 31 –
Shuttle running on court is one of the main
fitness activities for anaerobic squash fitness

Shuttles

Shuttle running on court is one of the activities we use to build anaerobic endurance. There is no reason why different movement exercises cannot be used for this as long as they can be produced at maximum. *See* page 79.

Incorporate some of the following movements into your court shuttle running.

Lengths
These can include: 1 forward running; 2 forward running to the front, backwards to the short line, turning and forward again to the back; 3 forward running to the front, backward to the short line, forward again to the front and forward to the back wall.

Jansher in his court-length running practises a long bounding stride that gets him down the court in five strides.

Widths
These include: sidesteps and lunging each side of the court or lunging either side from the T.

T to Corners
Running from the T can include the ready position, take-off, turning and recovery used in a game: 1 run from a ready position to the front corners and backwards to the T; 2 run to all four corners.

Lunging
This can easily be performed as an exercise off court and is the main area where local muscle endurance is required on court, that is, for braking and pushing back. Practise this from a ready position. Work in sets of between twenty to fifty gradually building up the numbers.

Practise from a ready position incorporating lunges in different directions in both open and closed stances and off both feet. Use as interval training or incorporate in circuits.

Stations
Squash movement can be incorporated into shuttle running from the T to different stations around the court. This is similar to ghosting but without the racket.

When working with a partner, one player can call the number of a station or point and provide change of direction practice by changing the command (and station) when a player is in full flight.

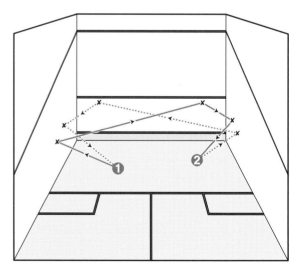

Fig 27
Solo Movement Practice

Solo frontcourt boasting is an ideal
movement practise

Solo Practice

Force yourself to move your feet and give yourself time to do this in your solo practices with the ball. Step back from and into your shots. Don't just stand and hit back to yourself. Incorporate practices that allow movement. The corner and double corner exercises are useful for footwork.

One excellent solo movement exercise that can be used as a shuttle substitute is solo boasting. In the front court boast high so the ball lands on the floor and rebounds off the opposite side. Boast alternate sides. Start at twenty and build up the numbers. Use the shuttle intervals. Practise different footwork. Initially it may be useful to experiment with a faster ball.

Pairs Practice

Pairs practice gives you the opportunity to practise both shots and movement. When practising concentrate on one thing at a time. Gradually build up the amount of movement so that you are practising moving into and out of position, and if the exercise allows, work from the T. Work like a dancer learning steps, gradually getting them smoother, faster and more efficient. Don't rush around, allow yourself time to concentrate on your movement. The basic boast and straight drive practice is excellent for movement but also try the two shot exercise below, where **A** drops and drives; and **B** drives and boasts.

This allows full and comfortable movement to and from the T and gives you the opportunity to concentrate and work on all the movement elements.

A drops to himself and straight drives pushing back from the shot, turns to watch while recovering smoothly to a ready position on the T and prepares to take off again to the opposite corner.

B drives straight and boasts, pulling out of the boast and stepping back towards the T in one movement. Walking briskly or trotting to a ready position, he watches ready to move to the opposite side. (**B** also has the option of practising his recovery via the short line which he would have to do if he played straight in a game.)

Try to incorporate the basic elements of movement into your pairs practice and allow time for movement to and recovery from the T in at least some practices. Extend the above exercise so that **A** can randomly hit straight or crosscourt; or **B** can intercept on the volley; or play either a drop or boast.

Practice games

Playing easier practice games will give you the chance to concentrate on movement without the pressure of having to win a match. Practise the movement elements and see if you can recover a ready position before your opponent plays his shots.

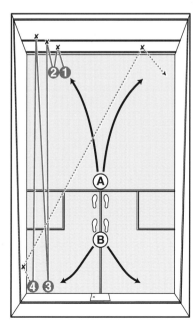

Fig 28
Pairs Movement Practice

1 Player **A** straight drops
and then,
2 straight drives before
recovering backwards to
a ready position on the T.
3 Player **B** moves from a
ready position on the T,
straight drives, and
4 boasts before
returning to a ready
position

FITNESS

Squash is tiring. Part of the point of the game is that it is a good workout. When we tire, we slow, and we are beaten by opponents' shots more frequently, we struggle to get to more shots, play weaker returns, mishit and make mistakes. Because we are tired we take more risks and tend to make tactical errors. When we tire we find it hard to get to the ball early and to pressurise our opponents. Being slower in our recovery, we leave gaps that opponents can take advantage of to pressurise and move us.

The speed with which you can recover the ball and the endurance to sustain this action without lapsing into all the problems of tiredness are crucial to your success at squash and dependent on your fitness level. The endurance required is both the aerobic endurance of the middle-distance runner and the anaerobic endurance of the 400 metre runner; the speed is like that of the sprinter; but also required are the strength and power of the jumper to jump and lunge, the flexibility and agility of the gymnast to twist and stretch and the footwork of the dancer to turn and change direction.

Playing hard squash two or three times a week will develop these abilities but the ambitious player will train to improve them and to overcome any weaknesses so that he can get an edge over his opponents and be able to survive at a higher level.

As with your overall game, select what you need to do to improve your fitness, work on the activities in cycles as explained in the chapter on Planning, (page 140). Give yourself tests at the start of a period of fitness training and then again at the end. For example, if running, time yourself over a measured course.

Don't, however, assume all your problems are due to lack of fitness. Balance your fitness and squash training and balance out the type of fitness activities you do.

AEROBIC ENDURANCE

Distance running is the ideal activity to build aerobic endurance, your base level fitness. Cycling at the right level is as good, longer interval training can be used, skipping can build aerobic endurance and is excellent for footwork, while rowing and swimming substitutes can be used, especially if injured or if building endurance off season.

An aerobic fitness programme should be the first part of your build-up in the off season lasting for a period of six to eight weeks.

Running
Whether distance running or running on a machine, start slowly and gradually build up your runs to over twenty, perhaps thirty minutes. Beginners should start jogging on alternate days (even walking and jogging) for five minutes and gradually build up times. Wear trainers with well-cushioned soles. Progress to a hard pace at about 90 per cent effort.

A competitive player should aim at a pace of six to seven minutes a mile to cover three and a half miles in twenty minutes, with a club player starting at more comfortable levels and taking longer to build up. When trying to build up aerobic fitness run at least three times a week.

Cycling
On an exercise bike build up to twenty minutes' continuous cycling.

Skipping
Start slowly with short periods of skipping and build up to twenty minutes at a rate of 130 heartbeats per minute using different skipping steps. Another skipping regime is to skip in batches of 1000 in a time of seven and a half minutes. You can build up to two or three sets.

Others
Varied paced running (called Fartlek or speed play) incorporates continuous running and jogging with bursts of speed over various distances and therefore incorporates both aerobic and anaerobic fitness. Interval track running building up to six repeats of runs of 400-800 metres will also build aerobic endurance.

If an injury stops you playing or running, stamina can often be maintained by other activities such as swimming at a good pace building up to thirty minutes, or working out on a rowing machine or climbing machine in the gym.

ANAEROBIC FITNESS
The energy that is used for intense bursts of action lasting from ten seconds to two minutes is mostly anaerobic. This crucial energy source for squash

players is best trained by interval methods. This involves periods of high-intensity exercise followed by rest during which time the waste products such as lactic acid are removed allowing a further burst of activity. Sprinting or shuttle running on court is usually used, but skipping, cycling, hill running, a series of conditioning exercises or any very hard exercise can also be tried.

Start your intervals at six sets of thirty seconds and gradually build up the number and length of each interval.

Individual differences in physiology demand different work and rest periods but it is important that intervals should be at maximum, so don't extend your time if the work rate is going to drop off.

Dr Craig Sharp says that muscular people are better off working nearer the thirty seconds on thirty seconds off level, while those on the slim side are better nearer the one minute on, one minute off level. A good average figure is forty-five seconds on with forty-five seconds rest, although it is probably easier to set numbers of court lengths, for example, sixteen or twenty.

When building up your fitness concentrate on this for between four to eight weeks with two, perhaps three, shuttle sessions a week. One to two shuttle sessions a week after this cycle will help you to maintain fitness.

Shuttles

Running lengths of the court is a simple activity. A good runner will cover sixteen lengths in forty-five seconds or twenty lengths in a minute with an equal period of rest. Shuttle sessions can be fitted in at the end of a practice session or practice game. (Not before as you will be leg weary when practising your skills.) Alternatively shuttle running can be carried out in a gym or suitable area outside.

The starting point will depend on a player's fitness. If you are just easing into the game, try four lengths the first week then five the following week and gradually increase by one each week until you have reached ten. (Try to complete two sessions a week.) Ten sets would be a good level for the club player to aim at although top professionals may build up to twenty sets.

The rest between shuttles should be active with jogging or at least walking. This will help to disperse the lactic acid. Warm down and stretch the legs after shuttle running and allow at least one day between sessions.

Running lengths of the court is the simplest shuttle exercise but there are many variations as discussed in the Movement section, including the ghosted movements discussed on page 74. Below Simon Parke explains how he does this.

Parke's Session

Former World Junior Champion Simon Parke explains how he organises his shuttle or ghosting session.

In the mornings I practise and in the afternoons I go down to the club for a game and often follow this with a ghosting session, a workout in the gym or with a sharp run. I do the ghosting two or three times a week, even if I'm tired. If you're going to try ghosting, don't overdo it but if you're keen and can fit in two sessions a week, it will really help your fitness and movement. I use it because it doesn't drain you like running and you can get through it quickly – it simulates squash and trains you both aerobically and anaerobically.

This is my ghosting sequence:

Work	Rest
6 x 1 minute on	1 minute rest
6 x 45 seconds on	45 seconds rest
6 x 30 seconds on	30 seconds rest

When ghosting, think of the movement, get your feet right. Always start from the T and move in an arc up and down the middle so you're not too close to the ball. Prepare as you move.

Backtrack to the T from the front then turn. Use six positions to move to, one on each side in the front, middle and back, reaching down for the imaginary drive and up for the volley. Move through the T between shots.

Two ghosting sessions a week would make you a lot fitter, but do try to get some practice in and play hard matches against someone better than yourself. Hard games are the best way to improve.

Plate 32 –
Simon Parke in a ghosting routine practises his
movement and builds his fitness alone on court

Skipping

Skipping can be substituted for shuttle runs if done on a similar basis of thirty seconds fast skipping and thirty seconds rest, eight to twelve times. Fast skipping should be at about 180 skips a minute alternating the feet.

SPEED

Speed on a squash court involves more than just quick muscle movements – there are a whole range of abilities involved from how you read the game, anticipate, react and when you take off. It is improving these abilities that will improve your rate of getting to the ball. Dr Craig Sharp says that these abilities are equivalent to a sprinter beating the gun, except that in squash it is quite legal. As well as improving your leg speed, work on improving your ability to recover the ball by developing the speed habits discussed in the Movement section.

Leg speed can be improved using speed shuttles, sprints, skipping and plyometrics, but before you start these complete two to four weeks of simple leg strengthening work. Once completed you can then start on your speed programme choosing from a menu of these four components: 1 speed shuttle running; 2 sprinting; 3 fast skipping; and 4 plyometrics.

Either speed shuttles or sprints are essential components of this programme, that is, skipping and plyometrics should not form the only elements. The mix could involve, for example, speed shuttles and skipping, speed shuttles and plyometrics or sprinting and plyometrics.

All these programmes demand a good warmup, good shoes and a good floor surface. Speed is quality work and should not be very tiring. Stop immediately when you feel the quality decline. Speed training should be in the first part of the training session, not at the end when you are tired.

Your speed programme should be for four to eight weeks before a main competition but can continue through a competitive phase as it should not be physically tiring.

Leg Strengthening Programme

Using multigym equipment concentrate on stations that exercise the quads, hamstrings and calf muscles. To develop strength use heavy loads and low repetitions, ten is a good number. Choose a load with which you can just complete a set of ten, with ten seconds between each. Complete each movement as fast as you can. Repeat this set five to ten minutes later and possibly a third time.

Carry out this programme three times a week. Use some upper bodywork alternating this with the lower exercises.

Speed Shuttles

Court shuttles and those in a gym or other suitable area should be movements carried out at maximum speed for about ten seconds followed by fifty seconds' rest. Do sets of six, and progress to two sets with ten minutes' rest between.

For court shuttles you can: 1 sprint court lengths (say four); 2 run from a ready position on the T to the corners; 3 take several quick steps from the T and return to repeat in another direction. You can invent various movement patterns but these should all be carried out at maximum intensity.

Sprints

On a track, on short grass or in a sports hall make two marks twenty metres apart. Warm up thoroughly and sprint as fast as possible between the marks decelerating to a walk after the second. Repeat after thirty seconds and complete six repeats or until quality drops. Then stop or rest ten minutes and complete another set. On an oval track several sets of sprints' marks can be set out.

Skipping

Skipping to develop speed should be at an alternating leg rate of 180 skips per minute for thirty seconds, with two minutes' rest and as many quality repetitions as one can do, (say six to ten).

Don't skip on a hard surface, use carpet or a sprung floor and a heavy rope like the leather ropes that boxers use.

Plyometrics

This training, originally developed for jumping events, uses various forms of rebound jumping to develop speed, of which depth jumping and bench bounding are useful for squash players.

It involves loading the muscles at speed. The down phase of the jump provides the load and the immediate fast take-off the speed. This maximises the use of 'fast' muscle fibres and provides a training effect.

Adopt a cautious approach when using plyometrics as, if overdone, it may cause injury of muscles and tendons. Use appropriate landing surfaces and shoes. Start with a short session once a week, gradually increasing the length and number of sets and the weekly frequency. Players with a tendency to Achilles tendon problems should avoid plyometrics and skipping.

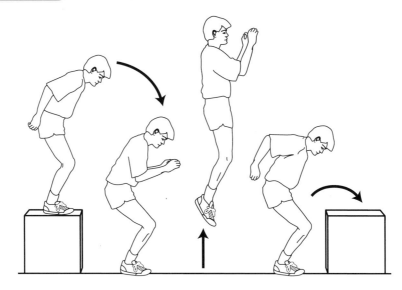

Fig 29
Depth jumping

Jump down from the box,
immediately rebound as high
as possible, then jump/step on
to the other box

Fig 30
Bench bounding

Using a gymnasium bench,
stand on one end and jump
down and up, progressing
along the bench

Depth Jumping

For this you will need two stable stools, boxes or chairs about sixteen inches high placed at a suitable distance apart on a soft surface such as carpet. In explaining the manoeuvre Craig Sharp says you jump down from one and immediately rebound as high as possible, then jump/step on to the other chair, turn and repeat the movement after pausing to gain balance. A set of ten such jumps should be done followed by a few minutes' rest. The number of sets should be determined by the quality of the jumping. Once it begins to deteriorate noticeably, stop.

Bench Bounding

Use a gymnasium-type bench, about ten to twelve inches high, stand at one end with your feet together, then jump down, feet astride, and back up on to the bench, progressing along it in a continuous kangaroo fashion to the end. The number of sets should be determined by maintenance of quality.

Racket Speed

Like a boxer, the squash player needs the ability to read and react, fast feet and one other skill of the noble art – fast hands. So often we see beginners struggle to the ball but are then unable to execute a stroke in the limited time the ball stays in the impact zone.

Racket speed, like anticipation and leg speed, can be developed – much of it depending on preparation. Take your shoulder round for the shot early, take the racket directly (not on some loopy path) to the backswing position and have this ready before you arrive and before you need to swing. If you don't, in pressurised situations you may be there but be unable to hit the ball or you may be late on to it and mistime the shot. Adapt the size of your swing when under pressure – the smaller the swing the more likely you are to connect.

Practise this fast preparation and racket work with the following exercises. Note that your technique will break down at a certain level of pressure. Start with good technique and control and then extend this into the pressured area trying to maintain this control and technique while developing your speed with the racket.

Reflex Drives

Using good technique start with controlled drives to the service box and gradually move forward, increasing the pace until you are driving hard and low in front of the short line.

This is not easy. Use a compact swing and fast preparation.

Reflex Volleys

Halfway between the short line and front wall, volley straight and gradually increase the pace until you are volleying as fast as possible and the technique is almost breaking down. Rest and relax the wrist frequently – you will feel it.

Alternating Reflex Volleys

Standing halfway between the T and front wall, alternate forehand and backhand volleys building up the pace while gradually moving forward.

FLEXIBILITY

Flexibility allows your movement to be smooth and rhythmic as opposed to stiff and awkward. Being flexible allows you to twist and reach in difficult positions, helps you maintain balance and reduces the chance of an injury.

Basic Stretches

Stretching is an important part of the warm-up and the basic stretches should be carried out before every squash – and fitness-training session. Stretching is again important in the cool-down and will help alleviate any stiffness felt after a match or training session.

Stretch before and after every match and training session and make time once or twice a week for an extended stretching session.

Before stretching, warm up using the warm-up and loosening exercises on pages 158–160. Breathe naturally while stretching. After completing the first easy stretches, re-stretch slightly further and feel the slight tension again. Hold the tension for ten to thirty seconds, after which it should ease off slightly.

The basic stretches are in the Warm-Up section of Chapter 9: Match Preparation. The stretches overleaf are additional stretches for your extended stretching session.

Further Stretches

Fig 31
Further Stretches

Sitting Quads
Sit with your right leg bent and your right heel just to the outside of your right hip. Bend your left leg and place the sole of your left foot to the inside of your right thigh. Use your hands behind you for support and lean slowly back until you feel a light stretch. Do not let your knee lift off the floor. Hold for twenty seconds. Repeat for the other leg.

Sitting Quads

Hamstrings
To stretch the hamstrings one leg at a time sit with the right leg out straight in front, bend the left leg and place the sole of your foot against the inner thigh of your right leg. Bend forward again from the hips keeping your back straight and your head up, slide your hands slowly down to grasp your leg or ankle. Hold the tension for fifteen to twenty seconds and repeat on the other leg.

Hamstrings

Inside leg
To stretch the inside of your raised leg, keep the raised leg straight on a bench, turn your body so that the foot you are standing on is parallel to the bench. Slowly bend sideways towards your raised leg until you feel a stretch on the inside of your upper leg. Hold for fifteen to twenty seconds.

Inside leg

Hamstring and lower back
Lie on your back, try to keep your head on the floor and pull your knee towards your chest. If you pull the knee towards your opposite shoulder you should feel a light stretch on the hamstring and the outside of your hip. Hold for twenty seconds, relax and repeat on the other leg.

This stretch also helps to relax the lower back.

Hamstring
and
lower back

Front of hip, groin and hamstring
Move your right leg forward until your knee is directly over the ankle. Put your left leg back until your knee is touching the floor. Your left ankle should be extended. Keep your feet in this position and slowly lower your hip until you feel a good stretch at the front of your hip and a light stretch in your groin and hamstring. Hold for fifteen seconds, relax then repeat on the other leg.

Front of hip,
groin and
hamstring

Lower back and hip
Lie on your back, legs bent and soles of your feet resting comfortably on the floor. Stretch your arms out sideways, palms of your hands downwards. This will keep your shoulders flat on the floor. Lift your right leg over your left leg and use it to pull your left leg towards the floor until you feel a good stretch in your lower back and the side of your hip. Keep your head on the floor. Hold for twenty seconds.

Lower back and
hip

Back Stretch

1 On a soft surface sit with your legs bent and wrap your arms around your knees to hold them against your chest. Tuck your chin into your chest and roll gently backwards and forwards six times. Control your movements and you should stretch the muscles along your spine.

As you roll back the sixth time, support your hips with your hands and take your legs completely over your head to touch your toes to the ground. With practice you will be able to straighten your legs. This will help to stretch your hamstrings and improve the stretch on your lower back. After holding this stretch briefly, place your hands directly behind your knees for support and roll gently forward keeping your knees bent as you lower yourself.

2 Lie on your stomach, arms bent and held close to your sides with your hands palm down under your shoulders. Lift your head and push your arms straight to arch your back. Hold for fifteen seconds.

Lie on your back with your legs out straight and your arms stretched out sideways at right angles to your body. Lift one leg straight in the air then swing it down sideways over your other leg to touch the floor with your foot. Your outstretched arms will help to keep your shoulders on the ground allowing your trunk to twist. Hold for fifteen seconds, then repeat for the other side.

Side of upper body

Stand with your feet shoulder width apart, knees very slightly bent. Place your left hand on your hip, extend your right hand over your head and bend slowly from the waist to your left. This will stretch the muscles along your right side from your hips to your right arm. Hold for fifteen seconds. Do not bend forward. Repeat for the other side.

Upper and lower back and hips

Sit with your right leg out straight in front, bend your left leg and cross it over to rest your left foot against the outside of your right knee. Use your right elbow placed against the outside of your left knee to keep your leg stationary as you turn your trunk towards your left. Hold for ten seconds, repeat on the other side.

Shoulders and arms

Standing with your arms above your head, with your palms facing upwards and your fingers interlocked, push your arms up and slightly back until you feel a good stretch in your arms and shoulders. Hold for fifteen seconds.

With your arms at shoulder height, fingers interlocked and palms facing away from the body, extend your arms forward until you feel the stretch in your shoulders, arms, hands and fingers. Hold for fifteen seconds.

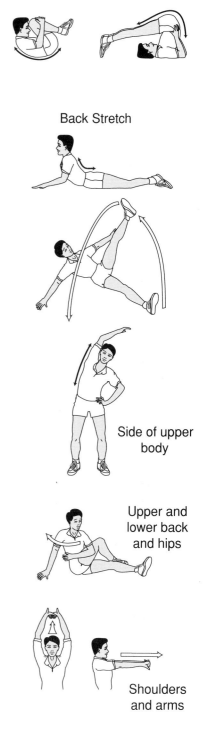

Back Stretch

Side of upper body

Upper and lower back and hips

Shoulders and arms

Triceps

With both arms overhead, hold the elbow of your right arm with your left hand and gently pull your right elbow behind your head until you feel a light stretch in the back of your arm. Hold for fifteen seconds then repeat on the other side.

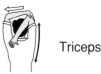

Triceps

Neck

1 Sit or stand, arms behind you and clasp your right wrist with your left hand. Lean your head sideways towards your left shoulder and at the same time use your left hand to pull your right arm across behind your back. This will stretch the side of your neck and the top of your shoulder. Hold for ten seconds, change hands over and repeat for the other side.

Neck

2 Sit or stand, gently bend your head forward to touch your breast-bone, then slowly lift your chin and tilt your head back as far as it will go. Repeat very slowly several times. Turn your head to the left until you feel a light tension, then using your right hand gently push your head a little further to the left, hold for five seconds, relax and repeat for the other side.

Complete your neck exercises by slowly rotating your head through a full range of movements in both directions.

PACING YOURSELF

This idea may seem a little out of place here when we are discussing Movement and Fitness. But what often is put down to poor fitness can be attributed to the inability of players to pace themselves through matches, vary the pace and relieve pressure.

Squash is usually the best of five. It's no use starting off on a long-distance run with a 400-metre sprint and then finding your legs dead. Spend your fuel wisely, not rashly. Choose when it's to your advantage to expend more energy and run faster, hit harder and move quickly. Do this when you can pressurise your opponent more than yourself. When pressurised yourself, relieve the pressure with lobs. Vary the pace in your game by playing both hard and soft shots in rallies so that you are working within the limits of your fitness. A match ebbs and flows and most good players will hold something in reserve.

Play shots that will allow you to pace yourself through a rally and a match. If you are puffed and under pressure, slow the rally and game down.

If your opponent is tiring, hit hard, speed up play and apply pressure.

THE SHOTS

If you have good basic control you can improve your shots by: improving the technique you use to play them by; clarifying your 'target area' (*see* Playing Squash, page 26); 'lining up the ball' better (*see* Basic Control, page 65); developing variations of placement and pace; grooving the shots so that they are more consistent; practising them in moving and pressurised situations so that you can play them more quickly, consistently and powerfully from a greater range of positions.

If you have only a vague idea of your target area it is impossible for your shots to be very precise. Technique is best worked on with a coach but with good basic control much of it can be done by yourself. In the end it is the accuracy and consistency of your shots that count and you will be able to judge this by your results.

Matches, when you are focused on the physical effort of getting to the ball and on match play, are poor places to practise shots. They are best practised out of the match situation in solo and pairs practice and to some extent in practice games. It is sensible when considering Your Game to select your relatively weaker shots to practise. Also practise your winning shots. They form only a small proportion of the overall shots you play so you need to spend extra time developing and grooving them. Often practice time is limited, so much can be achieved in practice games – here the more clearly your aims are defined the better. At times in practice games you can put winning aside and use the game to concentrate on particular shots and aspects of your play.

STRAIGHT DRIVES

To play the straight drive you need to impact with the ball just behind the right angle your racket makes with the side wall. To do this you need to be facing the side, since you use a side-on hitting action across your body in squash. The problem with the straight drive is that we tend to move straight to the ball, not to a position at the side of it, and hence to impact with it in front of the right angle (when moving forward) bringing the ball out from the side as a loose shot.

Take a *path* for the straight drive so that on

Plate 33 –
Jason Nicolle facing the side, positions for the
straight drive. He is well balanced, a comfortable distance from the ball with his racket
making an approximate right angle with the side

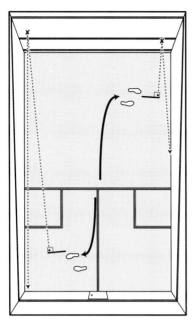

Fig 32
Forehand Straight Drive

For the straight drive take a path that allows you to position yourself facing the side wall with the ball between your position and the wall. Take the ball behind the right angle your racket makes with the side wall so you fade the ball into the side

impact you are in a *position* facing the side with the ball between you and the side wall. From here everything else is easy.

Forehand
From the front court in a closed stance, (or in an open stance with hips twisted to the side), impact with the ball just behind the knee. Hold your body steady while you swing through with shoulders parallel to the side. Let the swing come down and then up on the ball with an open racket face so that you can use the height of the front wall to get length.

In the back court, move to the side and parallel with the ball, leaving room for a side-on swing. Try to take up a stance evenly balanced on both feet or use a backfoot stance.

Backhand
On the backhand it is again important to be side on,

in a closed stance facing the side wall. Here the shoulder is in front of the body and the impact point is in front of the leading foot. It is especially important on the backhand to concentrate on the shoulder turn as there is a tendency for the body to be slightly front on which restricts a full backswing.

Variations
With the straight drive you have a whole range of paces from the kill (where you cut down on the ball) and the low drive, to the straight lob. Use all of these different heights and paces, and vary the angle into the side depending on whether your aim is to beat an opponent's volley, provide a clinger in the back or fade the ball in on a dying length so that it won't bounce back into the court.

IMPROVING YOUR STRAIGHT DRIVE
Improve your straight drive and the overall tightness of your game by using the boast and drive exercise to practise straight drives from the front court and solo driving to practise from the back court. Also *see* the Backcorners section on page 108.

Solo Practice
Use the basic technique practices (page 66) to improve your straight hitting and technique. Develop rhythm out from the side but then move in closer, practising getting the ball as tight as possible. From the back, once rhythm has been established, see if you can hit the side behind the service box or play a clinger on the rebound off the back. Groove the basic shots and then practise variations, taking the ball before and after the back to practise varying the length; practise varying the pace by mixing hard, medium and high, soft drives.

Pairs Practice
Practising straight driving from the front is best done in pairs.
1 *Feed and Drive*
Player **A** feeds from behind for Player **B** to straight drive. **B** at first can concentrate on technique and rhythm, then groove his stroke into the target area, playing with the height to get length and the angle of impact to get it tight.

2 *Boast and Drive*
Here **A** in front, straight drives and **B** behind boasts.

A must position up and around to the side of the ball. This is an excellent exercise to practise straight driving and moving, where **A** can concentrate on preparation, technique, target areas and variations. Once a rhythm has been established it is useful for **A** to concentrate firstly on length, even on over length and secondly on getting the ball tight.

3 Drop and Drive; and Boast
In this practice **A**, dropping and driving in the front court, gets the opportunity to feed himself an easier set-up for the drive.

Condition Game
A drives to the area behind the service box; **B** boasts below cut line.

Practice Games
Play some easier practice games where you concentrate on straight drives. Against easier opponents you may be able to play almost exclusively straight and perhaps limit yourself to one attacking shot, the straight drop. Think how much better and tighter your straight driving would be after you have played several games like this.

CROSSCOURTS
The crosscourt and boast are the two loosest shots in squash. The problem with the crosscourt is that when it is out from the wall it can present an easy target for an opponent's volley. (There is only one place it can be on the side.) The problem with the lower crosscourt that beats the volley is that it lands short and you may not get an opponent out of the middle with it unless you can play it before he has recovered position. The crosscourt needs to be wide to beat the intercept but not so wide that it rebounds back into the court. Often it is over-played, allowing it to be predicted (really an opponent regularly needs to be given the problem of deciding whether a shot is going to be straight or crosscourt) and too often it drifts through the middle. Use the side walls when you crosscourt. Have the ball reach them safely before an opponent reaches the ball.

From the Front Court
The crosscourt is played out in front of the body. Take up a stance facing the front corners. Step and

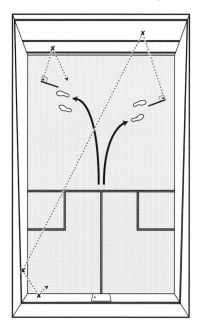

Fig 33
Crosscourt

For the crosscourt take the ball out in front of the body, more towards the front corner than the side where the straight drive is struck.
The path to the crosscourt position is more directly to the ball

point your toe into the corner. This gives the position for the crosscourt which is easily reached on a direct path from the T. As on the straight drive, take the forehand just behind the line with the knee, and the backhand just in front.

Work with a partner or coach who feeds or boasts from behind so that you can practise crosscourts targeting the side, floor and back in the back corner. When this is grooved in, practice dying length crosscourts for the floor, side and floor or back.

From the Back Court
The impact point of the crosscourt needs to be out in front of the body to get an angle across the court, so in taking a path to position yourself you need to move to the side and slightly behind the ball – not so easy when moving backwards to a ball travelling down the court. If you don't do this it is likely your attempts at crosscourting before the back

will not be wide enough, and hence you will allow an opponent to intercept.

From the back corners you need to position to the side and select balls to crosscourt that rebound a little past you, allowing enough angle to reach the opposite side wall. If you can't get in this position, don't crosscourt.

The crosscourt has the advantage of not rebounding fully back into the court from the back corners but first you have to get it past your opponent. Position yourself so you can do this.

Variations

Again you have a full range of paces on the crosscourt. Use high, wide crosscourts to give recovery time; full-length crosscourts to force an opponent right round the back corner to dig it off the back wall; hard, dying length crosscourts to the floor behind the service box and low crosscourts to die early, when an opponent is out of position.

Take care from the back to get width and try some high, wide crosscourt lobs.

Use extra width to beat a volley when you are committed to the crosscourt and an opponent is forward threatening an intercept. Get the ball into the side before he can volley it.

IMPROVING YOUR CROSSCOURT

The crosscourt from the front court is most easily practised in pairs with the standard boast and crosscourt practice. This is an important practice and even those who get away with the minimum of practising should be familiar with this exercise and be able to groove in their crosscourts during a practice session. If they don't, it is not going to get any better in a game. A little practice can be gained when put forward in the knock-up or from a self-feed short.

The crosscourt from the back court is rarely practised diligently enough but the knock-up and an extended knock-up practice are easy and convenient exercises if aims are clarified.

Plate 34 –
This crosscourt drive from Jahangir Khan is a fine study in power. See how he has braced as he powers the ball through. His stance for the crosscourt is a little more open to the front than for the straight drive and he is taking the ball out in front of his body

Solo Practice
Solo Crosscourt from the Back Corners
Here you play several straight-length drives and pick the ball to crosscourt (that is one that rebounds enough) for the opposite side, floor and back. Then move across to recover this ball, (after one or two bounces), and repeat on the other side.

Pairs Practice
1 *Boast and Crosscourt*
A frontcourt crosscourts; **B** backcourt boasts. This basic exercise is excellent practice at both grooving the crosscourt and recovering the ball from the back corner. Step back from each crosscourt to practise at least recovery from the shot and part of your recovery to the T. Prepare your racket early and hold your body steady as you swing across it. Concentrate on one target area at a time and groove in your shot. First, groove in a medium-paced shot for the side wall and floor to drop off the back to force a boast. Next target the floor behind the service box, side and back; and then practise the high and wide crosscourt.

2 *Knock-up*
Use the knock-up to practise crosscourts, targeting the side, floor and back, both high and wide, and low and hard.

Feed several straight drives for length and pick a ball that comes off the back enough to get an angle on to the opposite wall for a partner to repeat on the other side.

This exercise can almost develop into a game with one player **A** crosscourting from the back (off his own straight drive) and the other **B** on the T trying to intercept with a straight volley if it is slightly loose. **A** tries to get it past **B** for the side, floor, back (or floor, side, back) to force a boast.

3 *Drop and Crosscourt; Straight and Boast*
Here **A** practises his crosscourt by feeding a drop and then crosscourting. This exercise where **B** volleys or drives straight and then boasts gives **A** more recovery time which should be used to recover the T.

4 *A alternates Straight and Crosscourt Drives*
Here **A** alternates straight and crosscourt drives; **B** boasts.

Condition Game

Backcourt game in which crosscourts must hit the side wall on the full.

Practice Game

Play a practice game looking for opportunities to crosscourt. This is easier once an opponent is back off the T. One of the things you will be doing is trying to force the boast, then, if your self-imposed rules allow, you will straight drop.

LOB

Underestimated and underrated, the lob allows you to put your game into the third dimension – height, the first two being length and width - to use all of the fifteen-foot front wall and to play a game with a full range of paces.

Technically a lob is very simple. Bounce the ball up and down on your racket. Have your racket come under the ball and hit up on it. This is what you do when lobbing. Lower your backswing so that you can get under the ball easily, open the face and come up on the ball with the short swing that will allow you touch. If the ball is low you may need a very low backswing and a flick – generally, however, a firmer wrist action will give more control.

Use the open stance on the forehand, especially if playing under pressure.

Variations

The standard lob is targeted high on the side wall behind the service box, to drop and die on the back. This can be played high to go over an opponent and drop below the out-of-court line or lower and wider to pass an opponent with width.

When playing an excellent volleyer or in a pressure situation where control is difficult and lobbing conventionally could risk playing the ball out of court, the cling lob can be a useful alternative. Play this very high to go over an opponent and attempt to rebound it off the back wall on the full to cling. This shot will give you time to recover and although it may sometimes present an easier backcorner shot for an opponent, this is better than hitting out or presenting a volleying opportunity. You have at least survived and can fight for control of the rally on the next shot.

Improving your Lob
Pairs Practice

1 Lob and Boast

This can be incorporated into the Crosscourt and Boast exercise or practised separately.

2 Drop and Lob; Straight and Boast

3 Lob and Volley Boast (or Crosscourt Volley Nick)

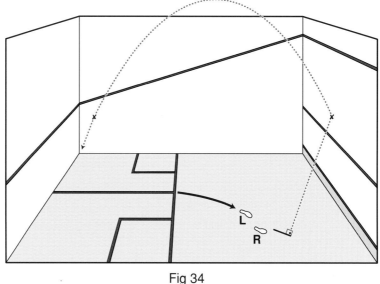

Fig 34
For this lob the player has used a direct path to the ball and an
open stance

Plate 35 –
This lob shot is a fine example of poise and
balance. Note how the player has got down
to the ball and how the open racket is
coming up under it

Condition Game

Front/back game.

Practice Games

Play a normal game where you concentrate on
lobbing. Often it is a good time to practise lobbing,
or your 'lob and drop' game when you have
finished playing a match and are playing a few
friendly games afterwards.

A self-imposed rule could be to lob every time
you are under pressure or every time an opponent
plays a short shot.

LOW DRIVES

Low drives are pressure shots, kills and attacking
shots. They may not get an opponent out of position but if he doesn't reach the shot quickly he will
be beaten. If he does get to the ball the pace of shot
may make it difficult for him to 'time' and 'line up'
the reply, forcing a mistimed or loose shot.

When to play these pressure and attacking
shots is important. It is discussed in Match Play
(page 163).

Try to get low drives, which are often hit
crosscourt, low across the floor, to die on or before
the side. If they rebound back into the court before
the back, they are losing pace and rebounding
back an opponent's way. If you can get on to a ball
early before an opponent has recovered you will
have a gap to punch the ball into at a narrower
angle so that it won't rebound.

Low drives will pass an opponent and die near the back or behind the service box. (Dying length drives die on the back.)

Kills die short before the short line or in the service box. To kill take your racket high and swing down diagonally, cutting across the back of the ball. This cutting action and the downward trajectory of the shot, if taken high, will pull the ball down off the front wall to die short in the court.

These two things, the cutting action and the downward trajectory, are used to a greater or lesser degree in both shots but the technique is best practised in the kill.

The low drives and kills provide only one chance to recover from them, whereas a length may pro- vide two or three (before the side, before the back and after the back), and a dying length may pro- vide two (before the side and after the side).

IMPROVING LOW DRIVES AND KILLS

Practise the kill from high, soft feeds, taking the ball high and grooving the diagonally cutting action so that whenever an opportunity to play it occurs it can be dispatched quickly and smoothly.

Solo Practice

From outside the service box, feed high and soft to the short line, kill straight to cling and quickly recover to repeat. Keep feeding until you have the right ball to kill.

Use the corner exercise to feed high, soft balls to kill down into the opposite nick.

Pairs Practice

Ask a partner to feed from behind for straight or crosscourt kills.

Plate 36 –
An easy ball sitting up in the front of the court gives the striker the opportunity to come down on the ball for a low drive

SERVICE

The serve is your chance to take charge of a rally, dominate the T and give your opponent a problem. You will want your serve to beat an opponent's volley, push him into the back corner and, like the crosscourt, force a boast. To do this you will develop a basic serve but it is useful to have a range of serves you can try out on an opponent to surprise and, like a spin bowler, probe for weaknesses.

From the Right Box

For this standing crosscourt take up a position facing the front corner, start with a low backswing, an open racket face and lift the ball high on to the front wall to land high on the side wall behind the service box and drop into the corner. Subtle changes of position will allow you to play with the horizontal angle of the shot. Adjust the serve back and forth, up and down, until you have it just right. This will need a little practice. Don't rush it. Once you have a workable routine, repeat it and groove the action.

As you pull out of the serve, sidestep quickly to the T and turn to watch your opponent (rather than follow the ball) as you do so.

Plate 37 –
A backhand serve from the right box allows the server easy access to the T and early visibility of his opponent

Fig 35
Stand facing the front corner, aim 2ft to the right of the imaginary centre line. Lift the ball high to hit the side, floor and back

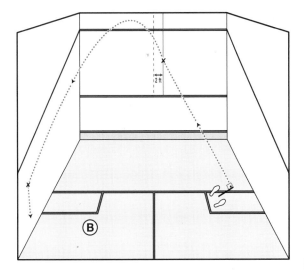

From the Left Box

Face the opposite side and step along the service line as you serve. Because of the narrow angle of this serve you will need to aim further to the right on the wall than you did from the right box. Often this serve is aimed lower and firmer to reach the side without the risk of going out and to ensure that you beat the forehand volley.

Variations

Lob

The standard or semi-lob serve above can easily be moved up the wall to drop down into the back corner. The danger, of course, is that it can land out of court. Minimise this risk by gradually moving up the wall or hitting high for a cling lob.

Backhand

For the right-hander from the right box this allows quick entry to and from the T and sends the ball at a narrower angle closer to the side. Step along the short line.

Smash

A hard, tennis-type serve smashed at targets low on the side, on the floor, or to the nick behind the service box. This needs to be hard enough to carry to the back.

Bodyline

This serve can be played awkwardly into an opponent's body on an approximate line with the shoulders, soft to die on the back, hard to unsettle or, as Jahangir did, directly for the backwall nick.

IMPROVING YOUR SERVE

The serve can be practised solo with a set of six to ten serves interspersed with another practice such as driving during which the ball is warmed. But a serve is easiest practised with a partner.

1 Practise serving to and receiving from a partner with ten or so serves each.

2 Play a serving and receiving condition game. This can be with the receiver winning a point if he can return the serve to the area behind the service box and the server winning one if he doesn't.

3 Three-shot game. This is similar to the above exercise but this time the server can intercept and receives a point if he does so successfully.

4 Consistent practice on the serve can be organised using other practice exercises which can be started with the serve. In condition and practice games the same player can serve every time (even from the same box) to give some sustained practice at serving. Scoring, of course, would be American-style.

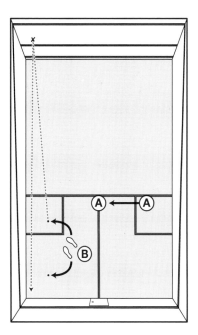

Fig 36 *(left)*
The receiving position is a position we move from. To return straight, away from the server who is taking control of the T, move to the side of the ball

Plate 38 *– (right)*
A loose serve allows the receiver to position quickly to the side of the ball and power it down the wall for dying length on the volley

RETURN OF SERVE

The return of service and the backcorner problem are the graveyards for beginners. This is because they have not yet developed the skills to handle this area easily. Your return of serve too depends on your volley and on your ability to straight drive and boast from the back corners. Develop and improve these important skills.

The standard return of serve is straight back down the wall for length, with occasional crosscourts wide to pass the server. If the opportunity presents and you have consistent skills for it, you may attack, especially on the volley, but you must be aware that your opponent is mid-court and in a reasonable position to reach it.

Attack the serve but be aware of what has happened with this before. Attacking here can be a good way to waste points and is often the first sign of a lapse in concentration or control.

When receiving you are in a defensive position and your first priority is to get your opponent back and to win the T.

To receive a serve stand about a racket length behind the back corner of the service box, toes facing the front corner and head turned to study the server. Study his position, racket and the ball.

The receiving position is a place you move from. Don't go directly to the ball on the volley or you will tend to hit crosscourt or bring it out from the side. From the receiving position move to the side of the ball for straight shots.

Variations

These variations are your main options when receiving a serve. Consider them according to preference.

1 The first question you will ask yourself is: 'Can I attack this serve?' Be cautious, this is a defensive situation but if the opportunity is there and the match situation is not crucial you may attempt it. Attack with a:
  1 straight volley drop or kill;
  2 the volley reverse angle, especially on the backhand;
  3 volley crosscourt nick.
(N.B. Be aware of your opponent's likely speed to the front and ability to counter, before returning serve with drops or attacking volleys. Low drives and kills are not advised unless it has been a very weak serve.)

2 Having resisted any temptation to attack, look to volley. Play these straight or crosscourt hard for dying length. Dying length can give an opponent the opportunity to take the ball early so you must be in a position from which to recover easily.

3 If the volley is difficult, play straight and tight for full length or wide and deep for safety and to create recovery time.

4 If you leave the volley option, straight drive for good length or wide to pass the receiver.

5 Try not to leave a situation where you have to boast but if you do, quickly recover the T so you can cover an opponent's straight drop.

IMPROVING YOUR RETURN OF SERVE
Solo Practice

1 Stand behind the service box and practise straight volleys. See how many you can do.

2 Straight drive from the back corners.

Pairs Practice
Drop and Crosscourt; Straight and Boast
This exercise allows you to practise volleying straight off the crosscourt, a similar angle and shot to the serve. Volley after the ball has hit the wall on a wide crosscourt or lob, and practise straight drives off a crosscourt from the back. This is an excellent exercise to practise many of the skills required in receiving a serve.

Games
As with serving you can use the serving and receiving game, the three shots game, and practise receiving while a partner practises serving in practices and practice games.

THE VOLLEY
Volley to stop the ball going into the back, to keep the T, to catch an opponent out of position, to apply pressure and to attack. The player who volleys at the right time gains all these advantages. Improving your volley is simple – it is the easiest of shots to practise.

Adapt your swing to a short, punching action with a firm wrist for the basic volley. The ball is travelling faster than off a bounce, so an early and short racket preparation is crucial. When practising volleys snap the backswing back early and pause. At the very least the racket needs to be ready a split second before you want to hit. Use a firm controlled and short follow-through, punching down the line of the shot.

Open up this basic volley swing with a shoulder turn when more power is needed and time allows. Work more volleys into your game by becoming more familiar with it in practice and practice games; set up straight rallies where you look to volley as you move back to the T; become familiar with the volley combinations and practise attacking volleys so that you can confidently take advantage of openings. Study opponents as discussed in the Movement section, anticipate, move early and get the advantages of volleying in your game.

Variations

Defensive Volley
It can be an advantage to volley from behind but this shot has dangers and you must go for length and width. Use an open face, the height of the front wall and push up on the ball.

Volley Lob
Brilliantly played by Lisa Opie, the volley lob taken early is a difficult shot for her opponents to intercept. It gives Lisa the T and her opponent a dying ball in the back. Use a short swing, open face and touch.

Pressure Volley
From the middle of the court you don't need the time a full-length shot gives you to recover the T,

so punch these volleying opportunities for dying length or low and hard when you can. Ideally hit away from your opponent, punching crosscourts straight and straight shots across the court.

Smash
Overhead on the forehand use an overarm throwing action, like a tennis serve. When an opponent is behind use this to go for the nick both straight and crosscourt when set up, but also use it to volley deep past an opponent.

This is an easy shot to practise off high feeds to the short line and off the corner volley exercise.

Volley Drop
Ideally use an open face and a downward cutting action that will take the pace off the ball and which brakes through or just after impact. Practise these straight from the service-box area and look for opportunities to play them in your game off weak crosscourts from the back.

Often when an opportunity pops up a quick push will do, with the ball almost bouncing off the racket to the front.

Volley Kill
Swing hard, cutting down on the ball in a diagonal path to the nick or low to die.

Volley Boast
Play as for the boast letting the ball in between your position and the side. Use a short swing, braking on impact. Look for opportunities to volley boast straight shots from behind.

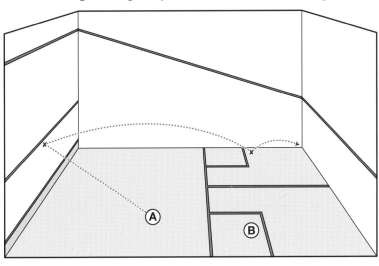

Fig 37
Pressure Volley

Player **A** seizes the opportunity to volley away from **B** who has been slow to recover the T. **A** pulls the ball short for dying length so that **B** can not return it after it rebounds off the back wall

IMPROVING YOUR VOLLEY
Solo
1 Straight Volley
Face the side and practise volleying straight to yourself with good preparation and a short, firm swing. Use your feet for each shot and line it up. As you get better, gradually move down the court.

2 Corner Volleys
From just in front of the short line, volley forehand crosscourt to hit the front, then side and rebound back into the middle for a backhand volley crosscourt front, side and so on.

Build up speed and rhythm as you get better.

3 Attacking Volleys
Attacking volley drops and kills, straight and crosscourt for the nick can be practised off straight feeds to the short line or angled balls from the corner exercise.

Pairs
1 Volley Across
Stand behind the short line and volley crosscourt to each other. How many can you do? Gradually build up the pace. Next alternate volleys, one straight to yourself then one across for your partner to repeat.

2 Crosscourts and Volley
From opposite back corners players drive straight and select balls to crosscourt for their partners standing near the T to attempt to intercept straight, and repeat.

3 Crosscourts and Straight Volley Drops
A on the short line, feeds across to **B** (on the short line) to volley drop or kill straight and then returns a feed for **A** to repeat.

4 Circling and Volleying
A and **B** straight drive, circling in the back corners, volleying any loose balls.

5 Drop and Crosscourt; Volley Straight and Boast
A drops and crosscourts for **B** to straight volley and boast.

Condition Games
1 Crosscourt Volley Games
A volleys across to the opposite back quarter trying to beat **B** who volleys across trying to beat **A**.

2 Volley Circling Games
Both players drive and volley down one side to, for example, the areas behind the service box or the short line.

Practice Games
Practise your volleys in friendly games where you emphasise volleying by taking every opportunity you can to volley. One game you can play uses the rule that if the ball is allowed to hit the back wall you lose the point. After this, volleying in your game will seem easy.

THE DROP
The drop shot is responsible for more winners than any other shot in the game. It is a simple shot that is often made overly complex.

When Jahangir and Jansher Khan played in the semifinal of the World Open in 1987 they played 146 rallies, 34 lets, and 2,616 shots – of these 10 per cent, that is one out of every ten, were drops. In your game you may only play a handful of drops but their accuracy and consistency may be the most vital element of all. The importance of the drop and its relatively low use in matches means that it really needs extra practice.

The drop is a soft shot that drops into the front corners. To hit slowly you need to move your racket slowly through the impact area (or to cut through it), and to 'time' this slow-moving swing it needs to be short. Keep your drop simple, use an open face, a firm wrist for control and a short, pushing swing with the forearm. Bend down and take the ball in front of the body. This will help you to aim the shot.

Stand close to the front and pat the ball against the wall. Now turn this pat side on and using a short, horizontal swing with an open face lift the ball above the tin. Snap the racket back into a low backswing so it is waiting and ready to lift the next ball above the tin.

Plate 39 –
The compact swing of the volley, early preparation and eye on the ball

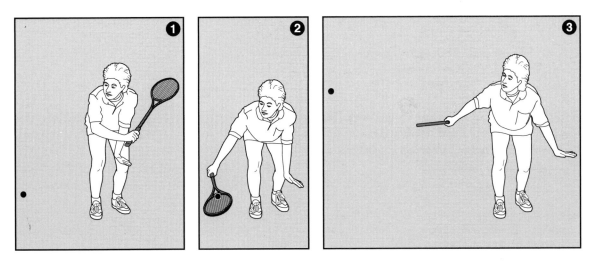

Fig 38
The Cutting Exercise

Use a short horizontal swing with an open face and practise cutting the ball just above the tin.
1 The short, open-faced backswing
2 Impact. Cutting through the ball with an open racket
3 The compact follow-through that gives touch

Now try this touch exercise above, cutting the ball by applying backspin or underspin with your open racket and build up the speed a little.

We use these two techniques 'touch' and 'cut' on the drop. The basic touch or floating drop is soft and dies in the corner. Often from a fuller swing we brake the swing through the impact zone to apply more touch. On the quicker cut drop, spin pulls the ball down off the front wall.

Play straight drops to cling, crosscourt drops for the nick and little fading drops to die on the second bounce before the side.

Disguise and deception can be added after you have mastered the basic shots, but don't let these spoil your basic control.

Variations
Straight Drop
The straight drop off the boast is one of the classic combinations in the game. To play this move up to the side of the ball so that you can get an angle in towards the side wall. At times you will have to use a long reach and hold the wrist back so that you get an appropriate angle.

If there is enough angle, play the ball to bounce and cling. Even if it is a little high and your opponent gets there, if the ball is clinging to the side at the moment of impact, it will be very effective. If you have enough angle, say the width of the service box, aim for the nick.

The straight drop is the most frequently played as it is tighter, safer and less likely to leave you out of position than the crosscourt.

Plate 40 –
Jahangir seizes the opportunity to cut down a backhand straight drop against Ross Norman. Note how he has held himself steady, played the ball in front to assist his aim, and pushed the racket head through the ball

Crosscourt Drop

Take the ball for a crosscourt drop high if you can and cut down on it for the nick. Be careful you don't leave yourself out of position and open to a straight drop or drive reply. With the right ball, the crosscourt drop allows a fuller swing that allows the option of driving, a smooth cutting action across the body and a comfortable open stance. It is an excellent winning shot when grooved and carefully selected.

Cut

Put cut on your drops when you can, but especially when the ball is high. Cutting allows you to play the ball more quickly without imparting all the force of the impact into the trajectory.

Top Spin

There are a whole variety of drops to be experimented with – the only rule is use what works. A top spin or half-volley type of action can be well disguised and can take an opponent by surprise. It is also taken very early on the bounce and deprives your opponent of time.

Deception

Shape for a full drive and suddenly brake your swing just to touch the ball, shape to play straight and at the last moment after your opponent has already moved flick across, shape to hit across and hold the wrist back to push straight. For more on deception *see* page 155.

From the Back

The general rule is not to drop from the back or from behind your opponent, but if the opportunity presents itself when your opponent is tired or back off the T and you have an easy ball, it can be well worth having it in your game if used carefully. Don't lapse into playing the shot randomly but select opportunities carefully and monitor the results carefully.

Improving your drop
Solo Practice

1 *Touch Exercise*
Position close to the front in a side-on position and with a firm wrist lift the ball softly just above the tin repeatedly.

2 *Cutting Exercise*
As above, with a quick, cutting action.

3 *Straight Drop*
Stand outside the service box and drive several times to warm the ball then feed straight and drop to cling. Repeat. Gradually introduce more cut.

4 *Crosscourt Drop*
Stand just in from off the T and use the corner exercise to warm the ball and then feed high and soft for a drop to cut down crosscourt to the opposite nick.

Pairs Practice

1 *Drop and Drive; Boast: Drop and Drive; Straight and Boast*
Here you can practise the important drop of the boast combination in a moving situation.

2 **A** *Feeds;* **B** *Drops*
There are many feeding routines which players can take turns with. **A** in the front feeds straight to the service box for **B** to straight drop. **A** in the front feeds crosscourt to behind the short line for **B** to crosscourt drop. **A** feeds both straight and crosscourt for **B** to practise straight and crosscourt drops in a moving situation. **A** moves side to side to feed a variety of balls for **B** to straight drop. **A** drives straight for length for **B** to straight drop.

3 *Drop and Crosscourt; Straight and Boast*

Condition Games

1 *Short Game*
Any short in the front half.
2 *Front/ Back game*
3 *Back Game plus Drop*
4 *Tactical Rule*
A must drop off the boast; or must only drop or lob off boast, or can only drop when in front of an opponent.

Practice Game

Serious matches are poor places to practise drops. Overplay them in friendly or practice games for practice in a match situation. Sometimes, especially if your opponent is the weaker player, you could emphasise playing them by extending rallies for practice with them.

Plate 41 –
For the boast, let the ball come past the impact point for the straight drive and turn it into the wall

BOASTS AND ANGLES

Having walls for squash has the marvellous advantage of keeping the ball in, and allowing second and third attempts to recover it. This encourages rallies and lets us play a highly skilled, tactical game, while having a good workout. The walls are useful for ricocheting the ball into the court at various angles, to outmanoeuvre opponents and help us to recover the ball from difficult positions.

The boast is both an attacking and defensive shot. Overplay it and you easily let an opponent into the front court. Ideally its use should be restricted to when an opponent is back off the T and to occasions when a player has no other option. This latter situation should be rare and one of the abilities ambitious players are continually trying to develop is to drive straight from the back and avoid being forced to boast.

With both boasts it is important to recover the T quickly and to be able to cover the possibility of an opponent straight dropping or playing an angle.

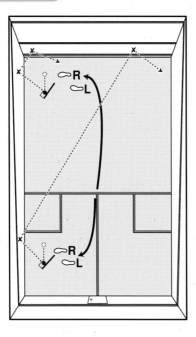

Fig 39
Boasts and Angles

To play boasts or angles,
shape for a straight drive and
then let the ball come past the
straight drive impact point and
turn it into the side

From the attacking boast go beyond just recovering and actively follow up, looking to seize the opportunity to volley. Try to volley straight for dying length off a weaker crosscourt.

Variations

Boast
The standard boast, taken before the back and played to die on the opposite side wall, is similar to the basic straight drive with a slight change in position. Shape as for a straight drive, but let the ball come through and past the straight drive impact point. Swivel back a little with toes, knees and hips so the trunk is facing back and turn the swing into the side. If the ball is tight to the wall you may have to brake the swing immediately after impact or run along the side of the ball.

Use a compact swing when you boast so you have good control and can feel the pace of the ball.

Practise the boast in a variety of positions and learn to take it early on the bounce so you can pressurise an opponent when he is out of position. Use the boast to move opponents. Practise shaping the same way for some boasts and drives, so creating the option of being able to play both from the same position.

Learn all the variations and especially in practice games seize the opportunity to play them but don't overdo it and become a 'loose boaster'.

Backcorner Boast
From the back corners a player has a number of options of pace on the boast and two target areas – the faded boast (that is played so that the second bounce dies in the nick or on the side) and the nick boast (sometimes called the three-wall boast, where the shot is played to rebound into the opposite nick). *See* Backcorners, pages 108–111.

Angle
Also called frontcorner boast or trickle boast.

In the front, shape as for a drive, let the ball come back and turn it into the side so that it just rebounds around the corner. Holding the wrist back a little will angle the racket face to the wall.

The angle is usually a touch shot but it can be played firmly as it will lose pace off both walls. It is easy to disguise and should be mixed in with straight drops, drives and crosscourts to maintain the element of surprise.

Volley Boast
Position as for a straight volley and let the ball come back. On the forehand the wrist must be held back. On the backhand turn the trunk and let the ball go past enough so that you can get an appropriate angle into the side. Use a compact swing and touch to get the ball to die.

Reverse Angle

This is a simple shot that can be easily and quickly executed. Stand behind the ball facing the front (more open than a crosscourt position) and hit firmly across your body aiming for the side wall close to the front. Rebound the ball off the side so that it comes across the front wall at a sharp angle staying close to the front.

This is a particularly effective shot from loose balls that bounce in the middle because it holds an opponent out of position, can be taken early on the bounce and can be dispatched quickly.

Practise from different positions around the court so that you can catch your opponents out when the situation feels right. Use sparingly.

The reverse angle from the back, especially on the forehand, is a nice surprise shot. Top Australian Liz Irving uses it frequently and at crucial times to pick up vital points. Make sure the ball comes out enough from the back to allow you the appropriate angle.

On the return of serve, especially on the backhand, the volley reverse angle is an excellent option when disposing of a loose ball. You are well positioned for it, it can be played early, quickly and it moves away from the server.

Backwall Boast

This recovery shot, which rebounds off the back wall and lobs over to the front, is called the backwall boast (I prefer the backwall lob as a name). It is a last-ditch option for a ball that has passed you and which won't come off the back. Try to move parallel to the ball, make sure you get right under it and hit up firmly on it across your body so that the ball travels on a diagonal path and rebounds near the opposite side wall, hopefully to cling.

IMPROVING YOUR BOASTS
Solo Practice

The boast is best practised in pairs but it can be learnt and improved from the back by throwing the ball off the back wall and boasting, then with straight driving and boasting. The attacking boast can be practised following several straight drives, retrieved with straight drives on the opposite side and repeated. The front corner boasting exercise is excellent practice for speed, movement and technique.

Pairs Practice

1 *Boast and Drive*
A boasts from the back and **B** drives. Here it is best if **A** concentrates on one type of boast at a time and gets that grooved in.

2 *Attacking Boasts and Drives*
Here **A** drives to the service box (or drives or kills low) so that **B** can practise taking the ball in a position from which he would want to use the attacking boast in a game.

3 ***A** Drops and Drives; **B** Drives and Boasts*
Here **A** is practising the straight drop off the boast combination. This gives **B** time to practise pulling out of the boast, smoothly recovering a ready position on the T and to practise the path from the T to position for the shot.

4 *Drive and Volley Boast*
A frontcourt straight drives high and **B** on the short line volley boasts on alternate sides.

5 *Boast and Crosscourt*
A crosscourts, targeting the side, floor and back for **B** to boast back.

Condition Games

1 *Boast and Drive*
A straight drives to the area behind the service box (or short line) and **B** boasts (below the cut line).

2 ***A** Boasts or Volley Boasts; **B** Drives*
B straight drives to the area behind the short line (of service box) and **A** Boasts or Volley Boasts.

3 *Circling and Boasting or Volley Boasting*
Both **A** and **B** can drive straight (alternatively they could be allowed to drive or volley) to the area behind the service box and both can boast or volley boast (off a straight shot).

Practice Games

Set up straight rallies in practice games and look for short balls to boast and loose balls to volley boast. Follow up on these with straight volleys. Limit yourself to this pattern and you will have an excellent workout on the boast and much practice on when to play it.

BACKCORNERS

When you are in the back and when your opponent has the T, you will be in a situation where he can quickly and easily take advantage of any short shots or loose boasts. Boasting will move him short but will leave you out of position and will not give you control of the rally.

From the back corners try to put your opponent in the back so that you can win the T and from this position look for opportunities to attack, move and pressurise. Win the T with straight length. This is the first option to look for. If you cannot get behind the ball enough to hit it straight, boast and then cover your opponent's options by quickly recovering the T.

Choose to boast from the back only if you have special reasons: for example, when your opponent is watching the front wall; when he is back off the T; when he is on his heels or in a poor ready position; when he is tired; when he is slow to the front; to surprise an opponent or break up a long rally; when your opponent is having difficulty changing direction and you can wrong-foot him as he back-pedals from the front.

So, you can boast from the back but don't do it because it is the easy option, first look to straight drive to win the T and only boast if this is difficult.

Path and Position

When you journey to the back corners it may not be immediately obvious which shot you will be playing, so position for both, look for the straight drive, but if the ball doesn't come far enough off the back, boast.

One of the backcorner problems is that players tend to take a direct path to the ball and play it from a position that doesn't allow them to get behind it enough to hit straight. Hence, through poor positioning a player is forced to boast more frequently than necessary and so let his opponent into the front court. Another problem that compounds this propensity to boast at the wrong time is the old-fashioned idea of leading with the front foot. This puts the body in a position for the boast and makes straight shots and crosscourts difficult.

From the T, take a path down to the side of the ball. If the ball is going to rebound off the side, allow room for this.

To boast take up a position facing the back with the ball between you and the corner. If the ball

rebounds enough for a straight drive move back a little and swivel to the side. If the ball only rebounds a little from the back, face the back more and position well to the side as if you are trying to get around behind the ball.

Stance

A backcorner stance with toes to the corner and weight evenly balanced on both feet in a semisquat gives good balance, allows you to get right down under the ball and allows you to reach a wide range of impact points by bending your knees and swivelling on your feet.

When under pressure you can also use the backfoot stance, stepping down parallel to the ball.

One of the advantages of the backcorner stance is that it allows the body to swivel easily on the knees and hips. As you move to the corner let your body face the back and turn your shoulders with the racket preparation.

Swing

If the ball bounces far enough out from the back you can use a full swing for the straight drive, crosscourt and boast. Often on the more difficult shots you will use a compact or short swing. If the ball is low and you want to hit it high and straight, use a low backswing and an open racket face so that you can get under it. Swing down and up,

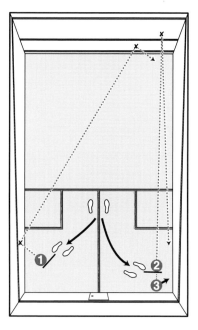

Plate 42 – *(right)*
Toes into the back corners, shoulders around and trunk twisted to the back, Jahangir prepares to drive from the back corner

Fig 40 *(left)*
Backcorners

1 Do not move directly to a ball in a back corner. This will put you in a position where you will always have to boast.
2 Move down and to the side of the ball and look to play straight.
3 Try to position so that you have the option of straight driving or boasting

down under the back knee and up through the ball. A high backswing when the ball is dying at your toes is not useful. Sometimes with the low swing you can use an upward flick of the wrist. A corresponding movement in behind the ball with the butt and arm can propel even the most difficult ball straight.

On these balls you may like to experiment with a short grip, sliding it up to the top of the handle.

Recovery

Recovery is crucial from the back. The most basic tactical thing players do is try to get their opponents in the back corners and then play shots before they can recover the T. Push back from your backcorner stance as you come out of the shot, step back towards the T (or the half-court line) and walk, trot or run to recover it before your opponent strikes.

Variations

Straight Drive

Take up a position to the side of the ball and impact with it between yourself and the side. Angle the drive in to cling to the side behind the service box. Lifting the ball high will give you recovery time but it must be tight to beat an opponent's volley. If the ball sits up off the back wall and recovery is going to be easy, this may allow a dying length drive or even a kill.

Boast

Face the corner and lift the boast into the side, to rebound into the front corner and die on or before the side. Play with the angle back and forward along the side wall until you can get the ball to die.

Often players hit the boast too hard from the back and it ricochets around the corners. Initially use touch and when you can get the ball to die build up the pace. Practise both the dying (two-wall) and nick (three-wall) boasts from the back. For the nick boast hit hard and at a sharper angle so that the ball rebounds directly off the front into the opposite nick.

Crosscourt

Crosscourting from the back is a necessary variation otherwise your play will be very predictable, but it is an option which must be selected carefully – you must pass your opponent with width or power.

Take up a position as for a straight drive and select balls that come far enough out from the back for you to get behind so that you can rebound the ball into the opposite side wall. Crosscourts from the back which are too narrow and give opponents volleying opportunities, occur because the player has selected a ball that has not rebounded enough or because he has positioned too much at the ball and not behind it.

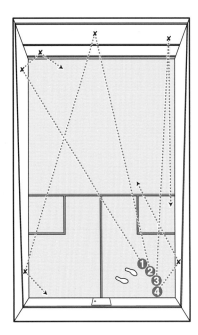

Fig 41
1 The Reverse Angle
2 Crosscourt
3 Straight Drive
4 Boast

Reverse Angle

The reverse angle is a useful surprise option if used sparingly. Select balls that rebound well out from the back and step in well behind the ball while still disguising the shot as a crosscourt.

Skid Boast

The skid boast is a useful variation on a warm court and can be used to break up an opponent's rallying. Position further behind the ball than for a boast.

Drops and Kills

These can be useful against tiring or slow opponents and on a cold court – use sparingly. Concentrate on the straight drop but try crosscourts for the opposite nick and deceptive, fading crosscourt drops.

Try these later in matches but be prepared to give them up immediately if not to your advantage – monitor carefully.

IMPROVING YOUR BACKCORNER PLAY
Solo Practice

1 *Straight Drives*

When driving straight initially start out practising from the side walls, so you can develop a rhythm, then move in tight. Lift the ball above the cut line.

When learning, from here initially you can start with single shots, throwing the ball off the back and driving straight. Consider using a faster ball.

Once you have established good control and rhythm on the straight drive you can vary the pace (one soft, one medium, one hard), the height (one high, one low) and the length (taking one before the back and one after).

2 *Straight and Crosscourt*

The crosscourt from the back can be practised solo by straight driving and then selecting an appropriate ball to crosscourt for the side, floor and back. Repeat on the other side after one or two bounces. Also try the crosscourt lob.

3 *Variations*

Straight drive, develop a rhythm and then select appropriate balls to reverse angle, drop and kill.

Pairs Practice

1 *Boast and Drive*

A straight drives from the front; **B** boasts.

2 *A Drops and Drives; B Boasts*

This exercise gives **B** time to recover the T, to practise the path to the corner and positioning.

3 *A Drops and Drives; B Straight Drives and Boasts*

Here **B** practises straight driving from the back. Try this before Exercise 6.

4 *A Drops, B Drives, A Drives, B Boasts, A Drops*

Here the players are moving up and down the court to retrieve from the back corners. There are many variations on this exercise with or without the drop. Add as many straight drives from the back as you wish.

5 *Crosscourt and Boast*

A crosscourts from the front and **B** boasts from the back corners.

6 *Circling*

A and **B** straight drive for length and circle back to the T via the half-court line.

Condition Games

1 *Circling*

A and **B** straight drive to the area behind the service box, losing points when they fail to return the ball to this area. (An alternative area is behind the short line.)

2 *Straight and Crosscourt Drives*

A and **B** straight drive to the area behind the service box and crosscourt to the area behind the short line. (Areas and conditions can be varied. A rule can be established that crosscourts must hit the side on the full.)

3 *Backcourt Game*

A and **B** play any shots behind the short line.

Practice Games

To improve your backcorner shots in practice games you can concentrate on just one of the shots and extend the rallies to get practice with this. For example, concentrate on playing mainly straight drives or on crosscourting frequently.

Plate 43 –
Attacking: Jansher Khan picks up a short ball to play a drop when his opponent is trapped out of position

TACTICS

Playing the right shot at the right time is simple from the gallery – we can easily see the openings when a player is out of position, the foolishness of hitting back to an opponent and the shots that leave a player out of position.

In a match we are doing everything at once and cannot sit back and treat squash purely as a tactical battle with time to marshall our best resources, plan, think and calculate our best moves. There are only split seconds at our disposal and as well as the tactical battle we have the physical one of recovering the ball, the technical one of executing shots under pressure and the mental one of concentration. Improving tactics in a match situation is difficult with all this going on.

To improve your tactics it is important to have a clear understanding of the basic tactical rules (see pages 28–30) and to recognise when things go

Plate 44 – *(left)*
Jahangir Khan is early on to a loose ball
from Qamar Zaman and hits it hard to
apply pressure

Plate 45 – *(below)*
Hit away from your opponent

wrong tactically (Tactical Errors page 14). Learn from your mistakes. First recognise these errors and then resolve to overcome them.

The problem with tactical rules is that they can seem very distant and theoretical when you have to make immediate decisions on selecting a shot, pace and target. What we need to do then is to practise these tactics so that we are familiar with them and to apply them to specific situations. Just as we practise shots we can select and practise particular tactics or tactical shot combinations, become familiar with them and then work them into our game.

Firstly learn the ten basic tactical rules:
1 Defence first, wins the T with length and width;
2 Vary the pace to create time to recover the T;
3 Pressurise opponents by taking opportunities to take the ball early and hit hard;
4 Volley to dominate the middle and apply pressure;

5 Positional play is used to hit the ball away from an opponent when openings occur;
6 Attack when an opponent is out of position and you have an easy ball;
7 T recovery and domination control the game;
8 Return to defence to tighten your game and move in and out of defence to make attacking, pressure and positional plays;
9 Rally to set up opportunities for winners and to force errors;
10 Match play is where you adapt your tactics to an opponent's strengths and weaknesses.

Become familiar with the four main types of play: *defence* where you are driving your opponent into the back and winning the T; *pressure* where you take the ball early before an opponent has recovered the T; *positional play* where you look for openings to move an opponent; and *attack* where you seize openings to play winners.

Plate 46 –
Combinations: volley drop the
loose crosscourt from behind

In a game you are using all these, so become familiar with each in isolation and then put them together.

Become familiar with the different paces of shot you can use and the different paces of game you can play.

Become familiar with the basic shot combinations.

Combinations
Combinations of shot are standard moves that aid decision making.

1 *Keep it Straight*
When in doubt keep it straight. Straight shots are tighter and the automatic safety choice. Only vary your shots when you have a good reason.

2 *Return Service Straight*
Make this an automatic response. Keep the ball away from your opponent.

3 *Look for Opportunities to Crosscourt*
Use crosscourts when you have the opportunity to pass an opponent and to play shots that will die in the back rather than bounce out.

4 *Lob to Create Time*
Whenever you are under pressure, lob. This will create the time you need. Make this an automatic response.

5 *Volley Away from an Opponent*
Volley straight from an opponent's crosscourt.

Volley crosscourt off an opponent's straight shot if you can get the angle. Try to play away from your opponent and use dying width and length when your opponent is out of position.

6 *Volley Drop the Loose Crosscourt*
The best positional play moves your opponent over the diagonal. Look for opportunities to volley drop loose crosscourts when your opponent is behind.

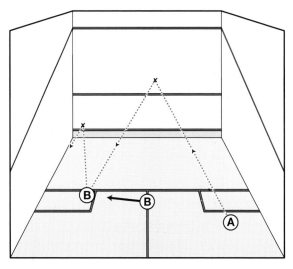

Fig 42
Volley Drop the Loose Crosscourt

Player **A** plays a loose crosscourt and
B steps in and volley drops straight,
away from **A**

Plate 47 –
Combinations: drop off the
boast

7 Volley Boast the Loose Straight Ball
Hang in to the side when your opponent is forced to play straight and move him over the diagonal.

8 Straight Drop the Short Crosscourt
Look for short crosscourts to straight drop. As soon as this occurs this opportunity should be your automatic response. However, there are two questions you must ask yourself, quickly before you decide to attack: 'Do I have an easy ball?'; and 'Is my opponent out of position?'

9 Boast the Short Ball
When your opponent is behind and his straight shot has landed short, boast to move him over the diagonal. The boast is a working shot.

10 Drop off the Boast
Force your opponent to boast out off the back and counter with a straight drop.

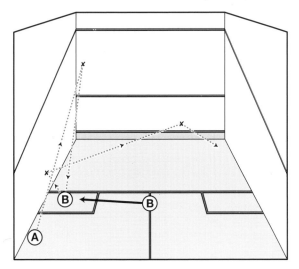

Fig 43
Volley Boast the Loose Straight Ball

Player **A** plays a loose straight drive which **B** seizes on to volley boast, thus moving the ball away from **A**

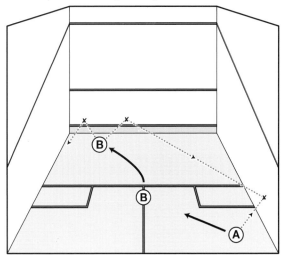

Fig 44
Player **A** boasts when **B** is in a good position on the T. **B** is quickly on to the ball and straight drops before **A** has recovered position

IMPROVING YOUR TACTICS
Combinations

1 Keep it Straight

Practise this using the boast and drive exercise; the practice where **A** drives, **B** drives (from the back), **A** boasts, **B** drives, **A** drives, **B** boasts etc; the circling exercises; the straight condition games; the straight drive and volley condition games and the side game.

If you have a coach, ask him to feed randomly for you to practise straight driving on both sides. In practice games concentrate on straight shots whether eliminating boasts and crosscourts or rarely playing them. This will straighten up your game.

2 Return of Service

Practise this with the serve and return game (*see* page 96). In a condition or practice game one player can serve permanently and one receive to give extended practice receiving.

3 Look for Opportunities to Crosscourt

Practise this with the boast and crosscourt exercises; the practice where **A** drops and crosscourts, and **B** plays straight and boasts; and where **A** alternates frontcourt straight and crosscourt drives, while **B** boasts.

Practise from the back by hitting across and attempting to hit the side, floor and back. Your partner repeats from the other side. Extend this practice with your partner who can intercept a loose crosscourt with a straight volley while working from the T.

Practice a straight and crosscourt condition game (both players concentrate on driving straight or crosscourt to the area behind the service box or short line); the Front/Back game; a Backcourt game (one rule that can be used here is that crosscourts must hit the side).

In practice games continually look for opportunities to pass your opponent with crosscourts. If you are not getting it past, hit wider, vary the pace of the crosscourts or use more straight shots.

4 Lob to Create Time

Practise the boast and lob exercise; and work with a coach where he is pressurising you with three-corner feeding (one backcorner and both frontcorners), so you can practise lobbing under pressure or picking drives and lobs.

Use the Front/Back game where all shots from the front are lobs or play a game where all short shots (or all boasts or drops or all the shots where you are under pressure) have to be lobbed. Play a practice game where you emphasise lobs and certainly lob when under pressure. With a coach adjudicating you can make this a rule. If you don't lob when under pressure you lose the point, whatever happens.

This draconian type of tactical rule can be used in many practice games to help eliminate tactical errors.

5 Volley Away from an Opponent

A feeds crosscourt from behind for **B** to volley straight and feeds straight for **B** to volley.

Play a condition game where straight drives must land behind the service box but volleys, either straight or crosscourt, can land behind the short line.

6 Volley Drop of a Loose Crosscourt

A behind feeds crosscourt for **B** on the T to volley drop straight and then drive.

In practice games keep the ball straight and deep and look for loose crosscourts to volley drop. Play a back game where the only short shot allowed is a volley drop off a crosscourt.

7 Volley Boast the Loose Straight Ball

Practise the volley boast and drive exercise and use a condition game where each player concentrates on straight driving to the area behind the service box and on volley boasting.

In practice games keep it mainly straight and look for opportunities to hang in to the side and volley.

8 Straight Drop the Short Crosscourt

Play practice games and look for crosscourt shots that are short to crosscourt.

9 Boast the Short Straight Ball

When practising boasting and driving, practise some attacking boasts by having your partner drive to the service box and practise boasting before the back. Play a condition game where you can drive to the area behind the short line or boast before the back.

116

In practice games drive straight, keep opponents behind and look for opportunities to boast short balls.

10 *Drop of the Boast*
Practise the exercise where **A** drops and drives while **B** hits straight and boasts (page 77); and the exercise where **A** drops and crosscourts and **B** hits straight and boasts (page 91).

In practice games look for opportunities to crosscourt deep and force the boast so that you can attack with the straight drop.

Margin for Error
Practice
Vary the height you play the ball above the tin of the attacking shots you play, so that you minimise the risk of making an error. Practise this simple idea. In solo practice when practising drops and attacking volleys, count the number of shots you can play without a mistake. In pairs practice when boasting and driving and when being fed drops (have a partner feed to you randomly all over the court for you to drop straight), use a margin of error and count the number played without a mistake.

To practise the consistency of attacking shots in a game situation make the boast and drive exercise into a game and practise the Front/Back game.

Condition Games
High Game
All shots above the cut line. This is useful to practise using the height of the front wall for length.

Back Game
All shots behind the short line. This condition game emphasises defensive play and volleys. Here you try to force weak balls and mistakes with tight length and dying length as well as volleying to keep the T.

Back Game and Short Shot
As above, but with one or more short shots. Here you emphasise defensive play plus select the opportunity for one attacking shot.

Front/Back Game
A plays to the front court and **B** to the back court. Here **A** is concentrating on attacking and volleying

without making errors and **B** concentrates on good length and width so as not to give **A** opportunities.

Middle Game
With a line drawn between the short line and front all shots must land in front of this and behind the service box. This is useful for practising tight squash of good length without any loose shots in the middle.

Side Game
A game down one side within the width of the service box. This is a good condition game to practise playing straight and to help tighten up.

Front Game
A game where both players just play soft shots in the front court.

Practice Games
As with the shots you want to develop, tactics can be practised in practice games.

Start by concentrating on one thing at a time. Make this idea as clear as possible. It may be to: practise rallying straight; play the tightest defensive game you can; play the lob and drop game; vary the pace and concentration on high straight tight drives; dominate the middle and volley everything you can; move your opponent; concentrate on following up on attacking shots and intercepting; practice combinations; pressurise your opponent with hard low drives; and many more.

Try playing practice games where you just concentrate on one of the game types – defensive, pressure, positional or attacking – so you become more familiar with them.

Play a game concentrating on defence where you pick up on loose balls immediately and don't give your opponent any opportunities. Play a pressure game, volleying, taking the ball early and driving hard to excess, so that you are quite familiar with, and are improving, this type of play by concentrating almost exclusively on it. Play a game where you are practising some or all of the combinations and looking to move your opponent at every opportunity. Practise your attacking game by playing shots at every opportunity and against weaker opponents, concentrate much more on the front court while using a margin of error so that you don't make mistakes.

Next concentrate on the defensive game and one other of the game types. Practise keeping this defensive base to your game and picking the right time to move into either pressure, positional play or attack. Take one step at a time. In match play you will want to mix all four in varying quantities to counter your opponents' differing abilities.

Become familiar with the ten tactical rules, the four game types, the ten combinations and the differing paces you can use – you can do all this in

Plate 48 – *(right)*
Rodney Martin concentrates intently as he approaches the ball

your practice games. Matches are difficult places to learn.

Improve your tactics in practice games and then you will have the tactical weapons to use in match play.

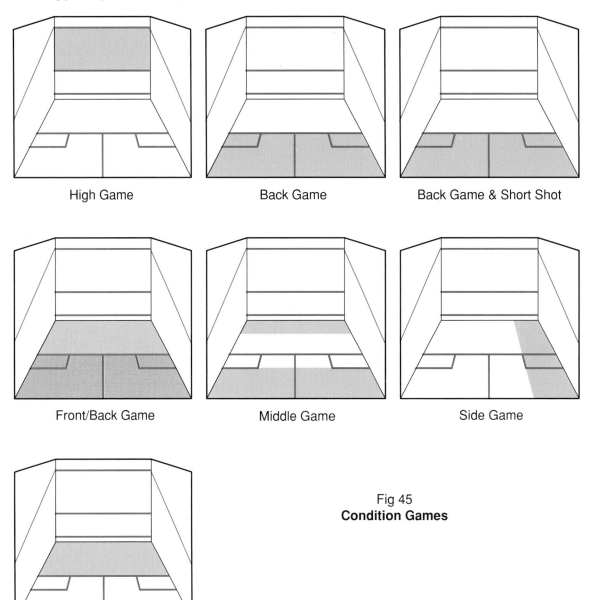

High Game

Back Game

Back Game & Short Shot

Front/Back Game

Middle Game

Side Game

Front Game

Fig 45
Condition Games

THINKING

Why do we play well some days and on others disastrously? Why do we play well in practice but in matches all sorts of fears creep in and we end up rushing and mistiming shots?

Our mental performances fluctuate and it often seems that we are the victims of a game of chance. 'Just not my day,' we say.

But we don't have to be victims. Mental skills can be learned and practised. You can take charge of your thinking on court. It can be improved.

First let us look at the mental approach of the best players, then at what it would be like to play our best in any situation. You can learn to control your anxiety, to concentrate better, keep your confidence up and learn the danger areas to look out for in your game. In the troubleshooting guide we show you how to take a positive approach to your game.

MENTAL TOUGHNESS

James E. Loehr in his book *Mental Toughness Training for Sports* lists the skills of a mentally tough player, skills that can be learned. The mentally tough player is characterised as being:

Self-motivated and self-directed – he doesn't need to be pushed, shoved or forced from the outside. His direction comes from within;

Positive and realistic – he is not a complainer, a criticiser or a fault-finder. He is a builder focused on success and what is possible;

In control of his emotions – uncontrolled emotions have unfortunate results. Bad refereeing, stupid mistakes, obnoxious opponents, poor playing conditions represent powerful triggers for negative emotion. Anger, frustration and fear must be controlled;

Calm and relaxed under fire – he doesn't avoid pressure but is challenged by it. He is at his best when the pressure is on and the odds are against him;

Highly energetic and ready for action – he is capable of getting himself pumped up and energised for playing his best, no matter how he feels or how bad or meaningless the situation is;

Determined – he is relentless in the pursuit of his goals. Setbacks are taken in his stride as he inches his way further forward;

Mentally alert and focused – he is capable of long and intensive periods of total concentration. He is capable of tuning in to what's important and tuning out what's not, whether there is no pressure or great pressure;

Doggedly self-confident – he displays a nearly unshatterable sense of confidence and belief in himself and in his ability to perform well;

Fully responsible – he takes full responsibility for his own actions. There are no excuses. He is fully aware that his destiny as an athlete is in his own hands.

These are the mental ingredients that many top players exhibit and which you can aspire to. They have been listed to give you a clear idea of the ingredients in mental toughness, not as a rather frightening list which you will fail to match up to but so that you know which way you can move in order to improve your performance mentally.

PLAYING YOUR BEST

To perform your best, focus on playing your best rather than winning or losing. Fears of winning and losing matches can lead to muscle tightness, anxiety and poor concentration.

Plate 49 –
Jahangir under pressure but confident and relishing the contest

To play your best you will need to overcome the things that stop you playing your best such as nerves, poor concentration and lack of confidence. But before we consider these let's look at a state called peak performance. Professor Sanderson of Liverpool John Moore's University, a noted writer on squash psychology, calls this an apparent 'altered state of consciousness in which the individual can do no wrong'. It is the time when everything seems to go right, when the ball is as big as a football and the nicks like canyons. Loehr calls this state your Ideal Performance State (IPS) and sees twelve ingredients in it.

The ideal mental climate for you to perform well in will be:

● where you feel relaxed and loose
● when you feel a sense of calmness and quiet inside
● when you feel no anxiety or nervousness
● when you feel charged with high energy
● when you feel optimistic and positive
● when you feel a genuine sense of fun and enjoyment in your play
● when your performance feels effortless
● when you feel automatic and spontaneous in your play
● when you feel mentally alert
● when you feel mentally focused and tuned in
● when you feel highly self-confident
● when you feel in control of yourself

One of the techniques Loehr uses to make people aware of how their inner world affects their performance is to have them evaluate their mental performance and results with the objective of developing control over their IPS. He lists twelve ingredients, and then adds two more (i.e. thirteen and fourteen) performance criteria. Firstly he suggests you fill in the chart, (using the first twelve questions), for your imagined Finest Hour, then your Worst Hour and after that you monitor your performances regularly (using all fourteen questions), so that you start tuning into your 'inner world' and see how this affects your performances. (For example, by circling the number one of the first item, you would be indicating you felt very relaxed; the three, moderately relaxed; and the five would mean your muscles felt very tight.)

1	Muscles relaxed	1 2 3 4 5	Muscles tight
2	Calm and quiet	1 2 3 4 5	Fast and frantic
3	Low anxiety	1 2 3 4 5	High anxiety
4	High energy	1 2 3 4 5	Low energy
5	Positive	1 2 3 4 5	Negative
6	Highly enjoyable	1 2 3 4 5	Unenjoyable
7	Effortless	1 2 3 4 5	Great effort
8	Automatic	1 2 3 4 5	Deliberate
9	Confident	1 2 3 4 5	Not confident
10	Alert	1 2 3 4 5	Dull
11	In control	1 2 3 4 5	Out of control
12	Focused	1 2 3 4 5	Unfocused
13	Played well	1 2 3 4 5	Played poorly
14	Positive energy	1 2 3 4 5	Negative energy

Increased awareness will enable you to determine when this IPS state is present, when it is not and what is missing.

PSYCHING UP OR DOWN?

Psyching up for competition, that is, developing short-term motivation, is needed when a player is underaroused and needs to raise his arousal level to the most appropriate to perform his best. If overpsyched or nervous he will need psyching down.

Most players have at times succumbed to nerves which have spoilt if not destroyed their games. Using unsublte psyching-up techniques here can be counterproductive.

Anxiety can be triggered by threat, the most common of which is the perception of threat to winning. Setting appropriate goals, those of playing well, can alleviate much of this threat.

Individuals vary in what works for them and some experimentation is useful. Below are a few tips on psyching up. *See* also the chapter on Match Preparation (pages 156–62).

Psyching-Up Tips

1 Create a positive attitude and an eagerness to play.

2 Inspiration and motivation can be gained by identifying with an admired player.

3 Try watching top squash players on video before playing a match.

4 Use audio tapes. (*See* Controlling Anxiety below.)

5 Verbalisation. Use positive self-statements such as 'You are going to play well'.

6 Use positive mental imagery. (*see* Visualisation on page 126.)

CONTROLLING ANXIETY

Top players have a high tolerance to stress, often using and channelling it positively, but for most players it leads to anxiety, that is, where you become anxious and start worrying about your ability to cope.

Excess anxiety affects us in two ways. It can make us worried and affect our decision-making, lead to defeatist thoughts, loss of concentration and confidence, a decrease of tactical awareness, and frustration, and is often accompanied by counterproductive aggression. It can also affect us physiologically, noticeable in symptoms like a racing heart, sweating, the urge to go to the toilet, a dry mouth and nausea. This produces muscular tension, tiring us and affecting our technique and timing. As Sanderson says 'anxiety can cause irrational thought processes and dissipation of energy'.

So anxiety affects performance. To maintain performance we can either reduce anxiety or increase stress tolerance. The anxiety, of course, results from the perception of our ability to cope, not our actual ability to play. Change your perception of the stress and you can remove the anxiety. Finding the right technique to reducing anxiety may need some experimentation.

Action

1 Pre-match put yourself in situations where you feel relaxed. These will vary from individual to individual: perhaps being sociable with a friend or alternatively being by yourself.

2 Know what you are going to do when you go on court. Develop a game plan, (*see* Match Play, page 167), use a knock-up check list, (*see* Match Preparation, page 161), and use a playing-in period.

3 Using audio tapes with either inspirational messages, inspirational music, relaxing music, relaxation procedures or reminders.

4 Learning to relax. Employing relaxation techniques can help to block anxiety. Try inducing muscular relaxation. Progressive muscular relaxation can help but not immediately before play.

5 Use deep breathing. First consciously relax the arms, neck and shoulders before focusing on your abdominal muscles. Inhale slowly through your nose, allowing your stomach to expand; hold for a few seconds, whilst maintaining relaxation in your upper body. Exhale slowly through your mouth and feel your muscles relax. Repeat the cycle a couple of times.

Plate 50 –
Anxiety often hinders performance

6 Use thought-stopping. By stopping negative thoughts you may turn self-defeating anxiety into positive action. Learn this technique by concentrating on a negative thought, for example, 'I'm playing badly' and immediately use a trigger to stop it by shouting 'Stop' or 'No' to yourself or even using an action such as slapping your leg.

Negative thoughts are self-defeating.

7 Improve your self-confidence or more specifically your squash confidence through hard work. This is a buffer against anxiety.

8 Develop the art of positive thinking and learn to substitute positive thoughts for negative ones. (*See* Troubleshooting on page 126).

9 Set achievable and appropriate goals. (*See* Planning: Goal Setting on page 140.)

10 Use imagery to give a positive image of yourself performing successfully.

11 Overlearn: practise twice as much as you think you need to so that your skill is reliable under competitive stress.

12 Competition training is where players are gradually desensitised to harmful stimuli in sport – for example, crowd noise, poor referees, belligerent opponents etc. Don't always practise in ideal conditions with ideal partners.

Advice given to anxious players needs to be sensitive and perceptive.

CONFIDENCE

The extent to which individuals believe in their ability to be successful at squash has a marked effect on success. The converse of this is seen in a player who loses confidence and succumbs to the self-defeating prophecy of not believing that he can be successful.

Research has shown that winning players tend to be those whose self-confidence is focused on performing well rather than those who are overly concerned with the outcome. The message to players is to concentrate on the task and enjoy it. The result will take care of itself.

Action

1 Confidence is based on hard work, knowing you have done the background work to perform well. Not only does practice make perfect but practice makes confident.

2 Good players are confident because they work to overcome their deficiencies

3 In a match begin as you intend to go on and keep up this momentum.

4 Express your thoughts positively in terms of what you will do, not what you won't do.

5 Think positively and think in terms of successful outcomes. Don't say to yourself 'Don't hit the tin' say 'Aim higher'.

6 Set appropriate and achievable goals. Success breeds confidence.

7 Use positive self-statements: 'I can do it.'

8 Imagine yourself performing well. (*See* Visualisation on page 126.)

CONCENTRATION

Good concentration, that is, giving full attention to the task, is one of the vital elements for success in squash. Concentration is disrupted by psychological stress, that is, a perceived threat – usually the threat of losing.

Good concentrators are stress tolerant, able to ignore pressures such as poor referees, noisy spectators and poor court conditions. Poor concentrators go to pieces and may even imagine conspiracies against them.

Loehr puts it like this: 'Focusing on winning or losing the external contest too frequently leads to performance paralysis. Fears of winning and losing quickly lead to muscle tightness, excessive anxiety and poor concentration. Focusing on "doing the very best you can" and on "winning the contest with yourself" rarely leads to such performance problems.'

Sanderson says a player should wrap himself in a 'cocoon of concentration keeping the mind free from irrelevant thought and maintaining a positive approach throughout the fluctuating fortunes of the match'.

There are two ideas that are very useful in aiding concentration. One is having appropriate tactical ideas to focus on and the other is to be aware of danger areas where concentration can be lost. It is not much use concentrating intently on, say, winning points as early as possible if your opponent is playing a very tight game and you are making mistakes.

Action

1 Prepare for your matches to minimise the chances of becoming preoccupied with minor irritations and distractions.

2 Use the knock-up to establish your match concentration.

3 Be aware of the danger areas where you could lose concentration and any personal tendencies you have to lose it. For example, you may lapse when you are well up and be unable to get your concentration back, or after you have got back to 2 games all or 8 points all from being well down. Forewarned is forearmed.

4 Concentrate on the next rally. Make a habit of switching to the next rally and of focusing on your match play check list (*see* page 173).

5 Practise concentration in concentration training games where one player deliberately tries to distract another using verbal abuse or bad refereeing decisions or when hostile crowd noise is used.

Danger Areas

Be particularly aware of the areas where you can lose concentration – where an event or incident can result in a lapse. There are many areas where this can happen, from despondency over the loss of another point to a disruptive incident on court. Here are some examples:

1 The loss of a point. (You feel despondent.)
2 Making a mistake. (You feel despondent.)
3 Opponent hits a classy winning shot. (You lose confidence.)
4 Opponent hits a lucky shot. (You feel things are against you.)

5 You hit an exciting winner. (You become over-confident.)
6 After a long tiring rally. (You seek easy points.)
7 After a hard rally for your opponent. (You feel as if you have already won and play rashly.)
8 After a good lead. (You feel you are going to win anyway and stop focusing on key tactics.)
9 On game or match ball. (You feel you have won.)
10 After recovering to 8 points all or 2 games all. (Having reached the immediate goal you relax.)
11 A refereeing decision goes against you. (You focus on the injustice rather than the next rally.)
12 Your opponent is disruptive. He blocks and barges. (You focus on your opponent's tactics rather than your tactics to avoid this problem.)
13 Any situation in which you become emotional on court.
14 Any delaying situation such as a ball breaking or an injury.

These are some of the danger areas that could remove your attention from the immediate task and lead to a lapse in concentration.

Make a list of areas where you have lost concentration or could lose concentration and when this occurs in a match. Use these as a signal to refocus on key tactical ideas. (*See* Check list in Match Play, page 173.) Use the break between rallies for this. Use different tactical emphasis on serving and receiving. (*See* Match Play on page 173.)

I must refocus on the next rally and on my key tactical ideas after these danger areas:

1 ....
....

2 ....
....

3 ....
....

4 ....
....

5 ....
....

VISUALISATION

'Visualisation is where you imagine yourself playing really well,' says Sanderson, and adds that it 'recreates images from successful matches and mentally rehearses shots and strategies in a variety of match situations. With practice your imagery will become more vivid and, providing you concentrate on creating positive mental images, it could be very beneficial just prior to or even during a match.'

Loehr calls it: 'the process of creating pictures or images in your mind. Whereas language is thinking in words, visualisation is thinking in pictures. Very simply, it is the use of imagination, "seeing" with the "mind's eye". It is a dramatically effective training technique for translating mental desires into physical performance.'

Visualisation simulates conditions of competitive play and allows you to rehearse specific tactics. It is a learned skill and can be performed in two ways. Subjective visualisation is where you imagine yourself actually performing with the muscles activating as in a physical performance. This is excellent practice for skills. Objective visualisation is where you see yourself as though you are watching a movie of yourself.

Practise visualisation using all your senses to make vivid mental images. Mentally rehearse techniques and tactics; replace successful mental images for failure images; rehearse helpful mental and emotional responses to difficult situations; work daily to change negative self-defeating images into positive and constructive ones.

Loehr suggests establishing a regular visualisation practice routine when you are relaxed and quiet. Many short sessions (approximately five minutes each) are much better than one or two long sessions.

MENTAL TROUBLESHOOTING

One of the main things you can do to improve your thinking on court and about your game is to reduce negative attitudes and replace these with positive ones. Be aware of your inner voice and as soon as there is a negative thought shout 'Stop' with your inner voice and replace the negative thought with something positive and constructive.

Constantly repeat the right attitudes and give yourself frequent written and recorded reminders.

Replace these negative attitudes

This is all going wrong.

Winning is everything. I hate losing. I will be a failure and look bad.

Mistakes can't be tolerated and I am not going to make them. I'm going to get really upset with myself if I make a mistake.

Other people are putting all this pressure on me. I've no control over it and it is not helping my game.

I'm tired. I'm finished. I was better than him when I was fresh but now I've had it.

My opponent is just too good in the air. I'm going to get thrashed.

I'm going to win this match love, love and love.

I can't play the drop.

Damn. I've just lost another point. I need to get a point quickly.

This is hopeless.

I've got three games to win this match now I am two up. I should win it.

Thank God I've got back to 2 games all. That was a killer.

That was an appalling decision. It is so unfair. I feel like giving up. It's no use. I'll show him how angry I am by smashing the ball hard just above the tin.

I'm always weak in the back corners.

I'm always a slow starter.

Don't hit the tin.

I hate this court. I lost on it last time.

With these positive ones.

I can do it.

I am going to concentrate on playing to the best of my ability. Being obsessed with winning is self-defeating.

I am going to minimise my mistakes and when I make one I'm going to learn from it.

Pressure is something that I put on myself. Really I don't see the situation as a threat but as an exciting personal challenge.

I'm tired but so is he. I really made him work in the first game. He's going to slow more as we go on. I just need to pace myself for a bit and not show I'm breathless.

I can play tighter so that he can't volley. Keep it straight and tight, angling in the ball where he wants to volley.

I'm going to keep my opponent down to a minimum number of points.

'Stop.' I'll drop safely when he's right back.

I'm receiving so I need to take care. Right! I'll put my opponent right in the back.

Keep trying; you can win.

Concentrate on pressing home your advantage. Keep playing well.

Good! Now make that effort count. I'm going to play as well as that in the fifth.

Damn! There is nothing I can do about it except win this next rally. Come on get this return deep and really tight. That's it.

I've practised this, put in the work and I feel much better about it.

I'm going to get control in the knock-up and keep it in the game.

I am going to attack with good margins when my opponent is behind.

Last time was an off-day. This is a different opponent, it is the same for both of us and I know the conditions this time.

Practising

We have said it before, but it is worth saying again – matches are poor places to improve technique, shots and movement. In matches you don't have time to think whether you are in the best place for a shot, or to concentrate on grooving a swing, nor do you have the luxury of persevering with a shot that is not quite right. You are focusing instead on getting the ball back, on winning points, on handling the pressure and to do this you do what is familiar.

Squash development goes in spurts and plateaus. When you reach a plateau, more of the same is unlikely to lift you to another level. Improving particular aspects of Your Game will and you can only achieve this through practice.

Taking the skills you want to improve out of a match situation to where you can concentrate exclusively on them gives you the best opportunity for improving them. The best players practise. Not always well, not always systematically, but they practise. If you want to excel at squash, practising is one of the main things you can do. Practice can lift your game beyond its present limitations.

One of the problems of practising is what we call, the novices' problem. 'I've practised it,' they say, 'and it is better in practice, but I still can't do it in a game.' The short answer, is 'more practice then' but there can be a massive gulf in pressure between what we can achieve in a static, unpressurised practice situation and during a match. The more complete answer is to take this improved skill and practise it in moving, in competitive and in game situations. Then it will be more ready to be used in matches. This we do with pairs practice, condition games and practice games.

Practise to improve your technique. This will give you greater accuracy and consistency in your shots. Practise your shots. Groove them so that you are comfortable with them in a match situation. Practise your movement so that it is smooth and economical.

Practice time is often limited. This is why it is important to focus on what is really crucial to your game. As always it is best to take a long-term approach and concentrate on specific practices at different times of the season. We will cover this further in Programming on page 144. Make special times to practise, but do grab the opportunities for little practice sessions (especially on your winners) when you can.

Plan your practice sessions. Don't go on court with a partner, run through a few vague practices and end up playing a game. Work out what you want to improve, the practices you will use, how the session will be structured and then timetable it. Write it down.

Balance out your practice sessions between solo practice, pairs practice, condition games and practice games. If possible, over a period of time, progress through these four practice types with each practice.

Make your practice time count and don't just go through the motions. Remember it is 'perfect practice that makes perfect'.

Here are some ideas that will help you practise well.

Targets

Work out where you want the ball to land. Use physical targets (chalk lines, paper, racket covers).

Line up the ball

Eliminate casual shots. Try to be in position with

your racket prepared and waiting for the ball to get to just the right point before you hit.

Feedback
Look where your shots are landing and work out how you can adjust each stroke to be more accurate.

Front Wall
Calculate where on the front wall you need to aim your shot. Use simple up and down, back and forth terms.

Feel
As well as analysing your shots get a feel for your swing, body position, balance and movement.

Rhythm
Search and work for a rhythm in your shots but don't expect it all the time.

Start Easily
Start easily taking one thing at a time and making adjustments.

Progression
Once you have shots under control, build up the pace and pressure.

SOLO PRACTICE

Solo practice is ideal for developing technique, shots and grooving winners.

One of the main areas of the game that sets a player's standard is the back corners and this is something easily practised solo (*see* page 111).

As we have said, the practice of winning shots in matches is very limited and every player should spend some time, however briefly, running through these and grooving them in.

If something is not working well in your game, solo practice is the first place you can try and work it out.

Practices
Technique practices are covered on page 66 and shot practices are covered in the Shots Section of Improving Your Game.

YOUR PRACTICE SEQUENCE
Build practice sequences starting with technique and lining up the ball, before moving on to shots of increased difficulty. Design sequences that fit around a theme and balance static and moving practices so that you don't get tired too early and are still practising for quality at the end. Write your sequences down using the technique and shot

Plate 51 –
Chris Dittmar works alone on court perfecting his shots

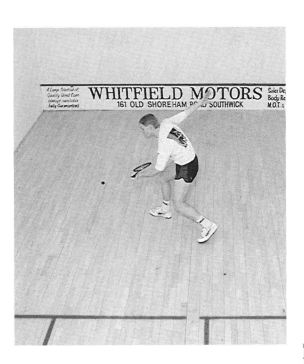

practices discussed in earlier sections or from the suggested sequence below. Develop your own practices, extend those already mentioned, use feeding shots to set up the ball for shot practices.

- Below are examples of practices that could fit into your practice sequence. This sequence would allow you to develop technique, drives and shots. You may prefer initially to concentrate on either drops or volleys but when you are quite familiar with these, using them will be an ideal way to improve.

- Don't attempt all parts of each practice. Build to those most appropriate and work on them.

- Some players will benefit from using a faster dot ball, especially in cold weather and in the back corners. Use the continuous exercises, corner, double corner, volley corner, driving and volley exercises to warm the ball when necessary.

- Test yourself on suitable exercises and set targets to aim for.

- Always start with the first two exercises before moving on.

- Where appropriate complete each exercise on the forehand and backhand.

A SOLO SESSION

1 Service-Box Drives
Start your solo practice session by driving to the service box and checking out the parts of your technique in turn. Try to step back from and into each shot, preparing and pausing before you hit. Build up the pace from all above the cut line, to one above, one below, to all below.

2 Backcorner Drives
First, practise out from the side wall in the back, to get into a rhythm and then see how tightly you can play your drives.

Once this is established you can practise variations of pace and length. For example, one hard, one medium, one soft; and taking one shot before the back and one after.

Also practise crosscourts from the back, pick-ing a ball that comes out from the back a little more to crosscourt for the side, floor, back and repeat after several straight drives from the other side.

3 Drive and Drop
Drive feed to the service box and straight drop. Use some cut, allow several inches margin of error and play to cling.

4 Straight Volley
Practise at a comfortable distance from the front wall, use a short swing, prepare your racket and volley straight continuously. After developing a rhythm try moving back and forth and even crosscourt to volley straight on the other side.

As you get better, move back down the court and see how many shots you can do continuously behind the short line or the back of the service box.

5 Straight Volley Drops
Stand a comfortable distance from the front wall, (just behind the short line), set up a high feed and volley drop. Use a side-on action and cut across the ball with a firm, short swing. Move back as you progress.

6 Corner Exercise
Standing on the short line hit a forehand crosscourt to hit the front and side walls and to rebound into the middle, then a backhand crosscourt front/side, forehand crosscourt front/side and so on. Develop a rhythm.

7 Corner Exercise and Drop
As above, then feed front/side for a crosscourt drop aimed for the nick, (not too hard) feed again and repeat. Use the corner exercise and high boasts to feed appropriate balls. Repeat on back-hand.

8 Volley Corner Exercise and Drops
Use the volley corner exercise to feed balls front/side for crosscourt volley drops and nicks. Concentrate first on one side and then on the other.

10 Cutting Exercise
An excellent exercise for developing touch and confidence on the cutting action used on drops. Position close to the front, crouch and lift the ball just above the tin with a soft, side-on cutting action.

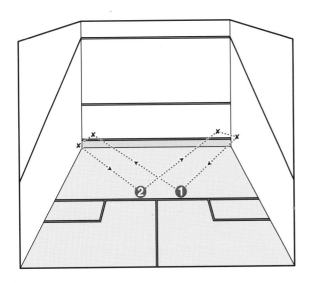

Fig 46
The Corner Exercise

1 Forehand crosscourt front/side to rebound in the middle
2 Backhand crosscourt front/side

11 *Double Corner Exercise*
A control exercise which is also excellent for footwork and positioning. Forehand crosscourt front/side, backhand straight front/side, backhand crosscourt front/side, forehand straight front/side, and so on.

12 *Alternating Volleys*
Stand halfway between the T and the front wall. Alternate forehand and backhand volleys hit directly to the front and to return directly. Move closer for shorter, sharper shots.

PRACTISING ATTACKING SHOTS

Make opportunities to practise your winners. Do this for two reasons: firstly to groove your winners and bring them up to scratch; secondly to develop them.

It is best to plan special practice sessions, but take opportunities when they arise – even a short practice before a game or at the end of a match when warm, on drops and attacking volleys for instance, can make a lot of difference to your accuracy and consistency, not to mention your confidence.

Concentrate on one shot at a time, grooving it in and then move on. Remember to spend time on the ones you are not so good at.

Concentrate on exercises 3, 5, 7, 9 and 10 and use exercises 6, 8 and 11 to warm the ball and to keep feeding it.

Near the end of a session on practising winners use a greater variety of shots, even introducing some kills and boasts, more movement, disguise and deception. Perhaps play a little game with yourself in the front court.

PAIRS PRACTICE

In pairs practice you are grooving and moving. In the end you must be able to move quickly to position for your shots and pairs practice allows you to practise this. Shots that you have practised and controlled in the stationary solo practices can now be practised moving.

Pairs practice also allows a greater range of shots to be practised. The straight drive, crosscourt and lob from the front court and the boast are all difficult to practise solo, so these are the important exercises to practise when in pairs.

You will need to pace yourself through a practice session, and bearing this in mind, try to use the movement you would wish to use in a game. If you can, recover and take off from the T but if time doesn't allow, practise pushing back from your shots and using footwork in adjusting your position.

Practices

Movement (page77)	**A** boasts, **B** straight dives **A** drops and straight drives; **B** straight drives and boasts **A** boasts; **B** straight drops; **A** straight drives; **B** boasts **A** boasts; **B** straight drops; **A** crosscourts; **B** boasts **A** boasts; **B** crosscourts; **A** straight volleys; **B** boasts
Straight Drives (page 88)	**A** feeds; **B** straight drives **A** boasts; **B** straight drives **A** drops and drives; **B** boasts **A** alternates straight and crosscourt drives; **B** boasts
Crosscourts (page 91)	**A** crosscourts; **B** boasts **A** alternates straight and crosscourt drives; **B** boasts **A** straight drives and crosscourts; **B** repeats **A** drops and crosscourts; **B** straight drives and boasts **A** drops and crosscourts; **B** straight volleys and boasts
Lob (page 92)	**A** lobs; **B** boasts **A** drops and lobs; **B** straight volleys and boasts **A** lobs; **B** volley boasts **A** lobs; **B** volleys drops crosscourt (or straight volleys and volley drops)
Low Drives (page 94)	**A** feeds from behind for **B** to straight kill **A** feeds crosscourt for **B** to crosscourt kill **A** feeds for **B** to straight kill and crosscourt **A** straight drives low and hard; **B** plays attacking boast

Feeding

All shots can be practised feeding the ball for a partner. Start your feeding by giving your partner the easiest possible shot, often a high, soft feed. To do this use a short swing or pushing action and an open racket face. (Many feeding exercises break down because the feeder is inexperienced, unlike a coach who makes it look easy.)

Once a rhythm is established in the exercise the feed can be made more difficult. Do this progressively. Incorporate movement into the exercise and remember a player will need time for this. Take turns at feeding.

Examples of feeding exercises:

1 From the front feed to the service box for straight drops.
2 Feed short and to the service box for straight drops.
3 Feed anywhere in the court for straight drops (i.e. both sides).
4 From the front feed straight lobs for volley drops.
5 Feed straight for both drops and volley drops.
6 Feed crosscourt lobs for crosscourt volley drops.

Practices

Service (page 96)	**A** serves; **B** straight returns behind service box
Return of Serve (page 98)	**A** serves; **B** straight returns behind service box. **A** drops and crosscourts; **B** straight drives and boasts **A** drops and crosscourts; **B** straight volleys and boasts
Volley (page 101)	**A** feeds from behind for **B** to straight volley **A** and **B** crosscourt volley to each other **A** crosscourts; **B** straight volleys, straight drives and crosscourts; **A** straight volleys and so on **A** feeds a crosscourt from behind; **B** straight volley drops and straight drives; **A** feeds **A** and **B** circle in the back corners driving and volleying. **A** drops and crosscourts; **B** straight volleys and boasts
Drop (page 104)	**A** straight feeds to the service box for **B** to drop. **A** straight feeds, short and long for **B** to drop **A** straight drops and drives; **B** boasts
Boasts (page 107)	**A** boasts; **B** straight drives. **A** plays attacking boast; **B** kills and drives low. **A** drops and drives; **B** straight drives and boasts **A** straight drives; **B** volley boasts
Backcorners (page 111)	Circling. **A** and **B** straight drive from the back **A** drops and crosscourts; **B** straight drives and boasts **A** straight drives; **B** straight drives (from the back); **A** boasts; **B** straight drives; **A** straight drives; **B** boasts

YOUR PAIRS PRACTICE SEQUENCE

Try to plan and timetable your pairs practice session. Write it down even if it is in shorthand. Be clear about what you want to do, what you want to get out of each of the exercises and communicate this to your partner.

At the start of each session take time to work on technique and line up the ball before moving on to shots. Ease your way in using the driving and moving exercises at the start of your session and get the basic shots grooved in before moving on. Use the pairs practices above and finish each session with a little condition game or a practice game. Design your sessions around a theme.

A useful structure is to divide a pairs practice session into three parts:

    A Technique and basic drives
    B Shots and movement
    C Variations, feeding, condition games and fitness

The section, Your Pairs Practice Session is an example of how you can organise and select practices for your practice sessions but there are many alternatives and you should adapt this to your needs. Add from the practices above and design further practices of your own.

A PAIRS PRACTICE SESSION

This section provides the structure and practices for your pairs practice sessions. Make a decision as to which exercises you will do at the start of each session. Over a period of time try to achieve some sort of overall balance between exercises. Adapt the structure and practices to your needs and the time you have available.

Section A starts you easily and co-operatively. Spend long enough on each exercise to get into a rhythm with your technique and movement and to get your strokes grooved in. These are the basic practices that can be used before any game or practice and form the basis of your pairs practice session. Section A will take approximately twenty to thirty minutes.

Section B is the shot section and will take approximately twenty to thirty minutes.

Section C allows you to practise shots in a competitive situation. Allow ten minutes.

Section A _____

Do at least one exercise from each practice group in Section A.

1 Knock-Up

(i) Technique Practice. Try as a target area the intersection of the service-box line with the short line. Step back from each ball, move your feet, get in the best position, prepare for your shots and groove your swing.

(ii) Use the Knock-Up Check List (page 161).

2 Boast and Drive

(i) Length: **A** drives for length; **B** boasts.

(ii) **A** plays low drives and kills; **B** plays attacking boasts.

Plate 52 –
Jansher Khan and Ross Norman practise hitting straight length in the circling exercise

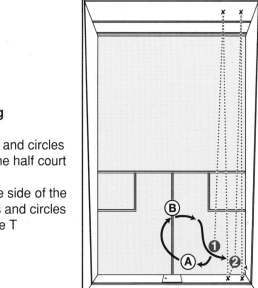

Fig 47
Circling

1 A straight drives and circles back to the T via the half court line
2 B moves in to the side of the ball, straight drives and circles back to the T

3 Boast and Crosscourt/Lob
(i) **A** crosscourts to hit the side, floor and back; **B** boasts to get the ball to die on the second bounce or for the nick.
(ii) **A** Lobs; **B** boasts.
(iii)**A** alternates straight and crosscourt drives; **B** boasts.

4 Boast, Drop and Drive
(i) **A** straight drops and drives; **B** boasts.
(ii) **A** drops and drives; **B** straight drives and boasts. This allows time for both players to concentrate on movement and recovering the T.
(iii) **A** drops and crosscourt drives **B** straight drives and boasts.

Section B
Pick two to five exercises to practise.

1 Circling (Straight drives and volleys)
(i) **A** and **B** straight drive for length.
(ii) Condition game driving into the area behind the service box.
(iii) Driving and volleying. As for (i) but both players looking to volley as much as possible.
(iv) Condition game – driving and volleying. Driving to the area behind the service box and volleying to the area behind the short line.

2 Two Shot Exercise
(i) Crosscourts from back. **A** feeds several length drives to himself and picks one to crosscourt (target: side, floor, back); **B** repeats from the opposite side.
(ii) **A** drops and crosscourts/lobs; **B** straight volleys and boasts.

3 Drops and Volley Drops
(i) Feeding for straight drops. **A** feeds from the front alternating short and long feeds (that is, to and in front of the service box) for **B** to drop straight.
(ii) Feeding for volley drops. From the front, **A** feeds high for **B** to volley drop.
(iii) Feeding for the drop and volley drop. **A** feeds high for the volley drop and short for the drop.
(iv) Crosscourt and volley drop. From behind **A** feeds crosscourt for **B** to volley drop and straight drive.
(v) **A** boasts, **B** drops, **A** drives, **B** boast etc.
(vi) A straight drives, **B** alternates boasts and drops.

4 Volleying
(i) Volleying across. Standing on the short line, players volley across to each other.
(ii) **A** crosscourts, **B** straight volleys, **A** boasts, **B** crosscourts, etc.

(iii) Volley boasts: fast. **A** straight drives several feet from the wall and gradually builds up pace; **B** volley boasts.

(iv) Volley boasts: tight. **A** straight drives and straight lobs, **B** volley boasts.

5 Kills

From behind **A** feeds high and soft for **B** to kill straight.

Section C

Play one or two games (condition games).

1 Volley Game

A and **B** in the backcourt volley across. They win points by landing the ball in the opposite back quarter, and lose points if they miss it.

2 Front/Back Game

A can play any shot to the back, **B** any shot to the front.

3 Backcourt Game

Both players can only use the back of the court.

4 Backcourt Game plus Crosscourt Rule

As for 3 except crosscourts must hit the side on the full.

5 Backcourt Game plus Boast and Volley Boasts

As for 3 and 4 but allowing boasts and volley boasts. (It is often a good rule not to allow a boast off a boast.)

6 Straight Drives plus Boasts and Volley Boasts.

Both players can straight drive to the area behind the service-box, boast and volley boast.

7 Backcourt plus Drops.

As for 3 and 4 but allowing drops (plus volley drops).

8 Front Game

Only soft shots are allowed in the front quarter or half off the court.

9 Drives and Volleys

Both **A** and **B** can drive straight or across to the area behind the service-box, volley straight or across the area behind the short line.

10 Side Game

Any shot is allowed down one side and within the service-box width.

ROSS NORMAN'S PERSONAL PRACTICE ROUTINE

Ross Norman, the former World Champion and the man who ended Jahangir Khan's long, unbeaten run explains his personal routine.

Practising with a partner is an important part of my training programme and it's something that club players should do. If you can't play shots consistently in practice, don't expect to do it in a game.

I use a small group of six exercises when doing a pairs session and sometimes just pick out a few to practice. I've found that these are the ones that work for me and I concentrate on doing them well.

1 **Boast and Drive** This is the most important and basic pairs routine in the game. When I practise this I think 'corners'. Try to get the ball right back, forcing your opponent to take it off the wall and, initially, don't worry if you are hitting overlength. Try to get into a rhythm. If you have only got five minutes, this is the practice to try.

2 **Drop and Crosscourt; Drive and Boast** One of the important parts of my game is to be able to hit good length from anywhere on court. It's also important to be able to hit straight from the back where too many club players go for the easy option of a boast and put themselves out of position. With this practice, where my partner is at the front straight dropping and then crosscourting, I have to decide whether to take the ball before the side and back walls or whether to wait for it to come off. This is an excellent exercise for practising length from a difficult situation.

3 **Crosscourt, Volley Drop; Crosscourt, Volley Drop** I stand on or at the short line and feed a crosscourt for my partner to straight volley drop (or volley kill) and feed crosscourt back for me to volley drop. Generally, I build up to hit these crosscourts quite hard and this is good reflex work. Here we practise the attack-

ing opportunity that a loose crosscourt provides.

4 Drop, Crosscourt; Straight Volley, Boast
This exercise gives excellent practice at intercepting crosscourts with a straight volley. Step back towards the T and allow a little room to approach the shot. Get the ball into the back. Initially you may want to let it bounce twice. If you are rushed, hit higher and use a short swing.

5 Feed and Drop From the front feed to the service box but vary the feeds so your partner is not static and is working more like in a game. Extend with feeds for crosscourt and straight drops to the same corner.

6 Feed and Volley Drop You can do this both crosscourt and straight. Again use the time with a partner to vary the feeds. You can easily practise static feeding alone.

I don't hit a lot of shots in a game but when I do they have got to be accurate. They also have to be consistent and to do that I have to practise. That's why I try to fit these last two practices into my pairs sequence.

If you don't practise, you'll find that you just haven't got time to work out what to do in a game when you are in trouble. If you are used to correcting problems in practice, then it's a lot easier to do it in a game. If you haven't been working them out in practice, you won't have time to think about it in a match.

CONDITION GAMES

Condition Games help to bridge the gap between improving skills in practice and improving them in matches. They take pairs practices and make them into competitive games so that shots are practised in a competitive situation. These games place special conditions on parts of the whole game so that concentration is focused on these and with this concentrated practice, the skills involved improve. This focus of concentration on part of the game is useful for developing tactics as well as skills.

The rules or conditions of condition games can restrict play to particular areas, shots or tactics. Make these workable and initially not too complex.

For example, we can take the standard boast and drive practice and restrict **A**'s straight drives to the area behind the service box (or short line), or allow both straight and crosscourt shots to this area. **B**'s boasts must be above the tin and below the cut line.

Scoring should be simple, a point a rally is easiest, and games short, say to six or nine points.

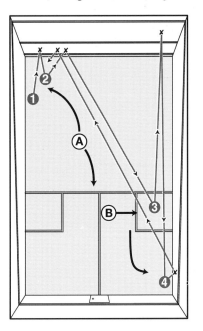

Fig 48
**Drop, Crosscourt,
Straight Volley, Boast**

1 A drops straight then,
2, crosscourts for **B**,
3, to volley straight and then,
4, boast. **A** drops again and
the exercise continues

The easiest option on serving is just to hit the ball off and allow receiving it to be declined if it is too difficult.

A wide range of condition games can be developed. Those used in this book are outlined on pages 117 and 136.

Two players can, of course, play with different conditions, the stronger with more restrictions, or one player can play a normal game and his opponent a condition game.

Plate 53 –
Lionel Robberds, who is World Champion Michelle Martin's uncle and coach, feeds her from behind as they work on grooving her shots before the British Open final

PRACTICE GAMES

Once your shots have been improved by solo practice, pairs practice and condition games it is time to get used to playing them in a game situation. Practice games allow you to do this by allowing concentrated practice at shots, tactics and game types. They are the chance to concentrate on particular parts of your game and styles of play without the pressure of having to concentrate totally on winning.

For example, you may forgo other attacking opportunities and concentrate on trying to set up opportunities to drop. You may play many more drops than would be tactically astute in a match, but this would be excellent practice at improving the drop in your game.

You may wish to develop your volleying, so in a practice game you concentrate on volleying at every opportunity, taking risks and overplaying the shot. Perhaps you will play a game where you try not to let the ball get past you.

In practice games you may forgo winning opportunities so that you can set up the situation you want to practise. Select good rallying opponents and organise games where you are in control and where winning is probably not an issue.

PRACTICE GAME ACTIVITIES

Practice games can provide practice in a number of areas.

Shots

Perhaps against an easier opponent you could play hundreds of drops in a practice game, where in a serious match you would be much more circumspect.

You may, for example, concentrate on volleys, length, lobs, boasts or straight drives and, by concentrating on particular shots, receive extended practice with them in a game situation.

Weaknesses

There may be areas of your game that are weak and that you avoid or shield in a match. A back corner or front corner, or a side from which you always crosscourt. Work at overcoming these in practice games.

Setting up rallies

One of the things you will want to do in matches is to be in control of the rallies. Work out the standard rally patterns you want to play.

For example: (1) it's quite common to set up long, straight rallies on the backhand and then look for opportunities to volley or crosscourt; (2) use hard, straight rallies with bursts of low, hard crosscourts to work a slower opponent; (3) long, slow rallies and lobs.

Combinations

Concentrate on particular combinations of shots so that these become quite familiar. The drop off the boast is a standard attacking combination. Look for this opportunity and set it up by playing and selecting opportunities to crosscourt that will force a boast.

Initially pick one or two combinations to concentrate on at a time. Try, for example: boasting the short straight ball played from the back; volley dropping straight off a loose crosscourt from behind; or volley boasting the loose straight ball.

Tactics

Eliminate particular tactical errors and develop countermoves in these situations. For example, lob every time you are stretched in the front. In a match you would be trying to win some of these points and play different alternatives; you would not choose to lob every time but practice like this could give you more practice at tactical lobbing than ten matches.

Game types

Practise types of games – defensive, attacking, pressure, slow and volley so that you are quite familiar with these and will be able to play them in matches.

For example, concentrate almost exclusively on defence, play most shots to the back court, vary the pace and frustrate your opponent by pinning him in the back court and by not making mistakes.

It is best to make clear decisions about what you want to do before you play. To get the best out of practice games, discipline and concentration are necessary. For those who hate structured practice, practice games are not an alternative to these but they are a useful way to learn. For the players who have chosen to use solo and pairs practice to improve, this is the step that will allow you to use these improved skills in matches.

Planning

Having stepped through the chapters in this book – Playing Squash, Your Game, Improving Your Game and Practising – you will have been able to make an assessment of what standard you have reached, where you would like to go with Your Game and have plenty of ideas on how to get there.

If you seriously want to improve, there are two further things you need to do before rushing into action. Firstly you need to set some goals and secondly organise a programme.

You may already have some goals but they are probably vague – the more realistic, specific and worthwhile you can make these, the more chance you have of fulfilling them.

You already have a programme although you may not recognise it as such. If you make a list of everything you did in your squash training for, say, the last six months what would it add up to? If we looked back on it would there be a sensible build-up to a time when you wanted to play well, a balance of different activities (fitness, practising and playing), different phases where you could concentrate on specific aspects of your game, or is it just a list of short-term day-to-day events? Think ahead. If you want to lift your standard it may take a little time. One practice will not make you play better, but twenty will. One run will not help but after six weeks of running three times a week you will be fitter. To lift your game, set some goals and plan a programme.

GOAL SETTING

Squash players, like most sportsmen, have dreams and ideas of what they would like to achieve. We will call these long-term aims. They may be career

aims or aims for a particular season. Perhaps it is to be World Champion; to get in the world top ten; represent your club, county or country; win the club or country championships, or your section of it, or perhaps this year it is to reach the quarter-finals; maybe it is to get in a team above the one you are in now; to work your way up to a higher position on the ladder or in the league; and so on. These types of aims inspire us over the long term.

What squash players are not so good at is breaking down these long-term aims into intermediate and short-term goals – this is what we do in goal setting. How well we create realistic steps in this process is important in helping us to achieve these longer-term aims. Achieving intermediate and short-term goals is vital in helping to maintain self-confidence and motivation while working towards long-term aims.

There are many examples of goal setting aiding sportsmen. John Naber, the 1976 Olympic Gold Medallist in the 100 metres backstroke calculated that he would have to reduce his best time by four seconds to be good enough to win an Olympic Gold Medal. This massive reduction he broke down into one second a year, 1/10 of a second per month, 1/300 of a second per day and 1/1200 of a second per hour of training. Finally he considered this goal of 1/1200 of a second per hour and argued that from the time he began to blink his eyes to the moment his eyelids touched was 5/1200 of a second. He then believed he could improve by the required amount in an hour and set about working towards his long-term aim and he won the Gold Medal.

If the steps in your goal setting are small and realistic there is more chance of building on success.

TWO TYPES OF GOAL

There are two main types of goal – product and process orientated goals.

Product orientated goals establish some end product. These can be either expressed in terms of outcome such as winning a tournament, or in performance terms like completing ten sets of court sprints, or running three miles in under twenty minutes. Product orientated goals are best for setting long-term aims and intermediate goals.

Process goals focus attention on aspects of performance. These may, for example, be getting back to the T before an opponent hits the ball, hitting length to rebound off the back, taking every opportunity to volley or always watching the ball. Process orientated goals are best for short-term goals and where skill is a factor.

Goal setting is a well-researched area and the subject of an excellent tape and booklet by the National Coaching Foundation. Let's look at some key points they consider in setting the goals.

Ten Key Points on Setting Goals

1 Break down long-term aims into intermediate and short-term goals.

2 Goals can be either product or process orientated.

3 If you don't set process orientated short-term goals, work out strategies that will help you to achieve your product orientated goals.

4 Set goals for training and competition.

5 Set target dates by which goals are to be achieved.

6 Set goals which are realistic and worthwhile. These should be difficult but accepted by the player (not imposed).

7 Set positive not negative goals.

8 Product orientated goals are good for enhancing concentration.

9 Feedback on your goal achievement is essential. Positive feedback enhances self-confidence and motivation, whilst negative feedback strongly suggests that the goal should be reassessed and altered.

Measured feedback can easily be given from practice sessions.

10 Use goal setting as a means of restructuring negative statements which you make about yourself or your performance.

Plate 54 –
Process goals focus attention on aspects of performance, for example, watching the ball

PLANNING A SET OF GOALS

Here is one method of planning a set of training goals used by the National Coaching Foundation. Try this, adapt it and experiment to find a way that suits you.

1 Write down three long-term aims in order of importance for this season and label them A, B and C. Make one or two of them about developing a new skill.

2 Write down three realistic and worthwhile intermediate goals which will lead to A and which can be achieved in the next month or so. Label these A1, A2, and A3.

3 Write down one realistic and worthwhile intermediate goal which will lead to B and label it B1. Leave C for now.

4 For intermediate goal A1, determine three short-term goals or courses of action which you can complete this week and which will help you to achieve intermediate goal A1. Select two for short-term goals for A2, and one for intermediate goal B1.

EXAMPLE GOAL SET

Long-Term Aim	Goals for the Next Month	Goals and Courses of Action for This Week
A Improve my game to first-team standard	**A1** Tighten up my game	**A1. 1** Complete two solo sessions of at least half an hour each on straight and crosscourt drives
		A1. 2 Play two easier practice games concentrating on setting up rallies and emphasising the defensive game
		A1. 3 In match play recognise loose shots and correct immediately
	A2 Improve my tactics, so that I am playing the right shot at the right time	**A2. 1** Read the section on tactics in Improving Your Game and plan a series of condition and practice games
		A2. 2 Play two practice games and discipline myself only to play short when my opponent is behind me
	A3 Practise my attacking play	
B Get fit enough for first-team standard.	**B1** Start a court shuttle programme	**B1. 1** Complete two court sprint sessions of six sets of 45-second sprints
C Win a B grade tournament		

Check your Goal Plan

Ask these questions about each aim or goal:

1 Does it set a specific target?
2 Is this target independent of other people?
3 Is it measurable?
4 Can you realistically expect to achieve it in the time available?
5 Will you be excited and satisfied when you achieve it?

Evaluate Your Goal Achievement

1 At the end of each week evaluate your goal achievement over the week, reconsider your goals for the month and adjust appropriately.

2 At the end of each month evaluate your goal achievement over the month, reconsider your goals for the season and adjust appropriately.

3 At the end of each season evaluate progress over the whole season and establish new aims for next season or year.

4 Try not to adjust goals at other times.

YOUR GOALS

Long-Term Aim	Goals for the Next Month	Goals and Courses of Action for This Week
A	A1	A1. 1
		A1. 2
		A1. 3
	A2	A2. 1
		A2. 2
	A3	
B	B1	B1. 1
C		

PROGRAMMING

Your programme is a plan of the activities you have selected to use to reach your long-term aims. Planning is important so you can think ahead and work out where you are going in the long term rather than getting excited, depressed or bogged down in day-to-day activities.

Select activities that will work for your particular needs. Work on weaknesses. This needs discipline and advice.

Think long term. Take time out from competition and from seeking immediate results. If you only seek immediate results you will be continually doing the same thing and finding it hard to get to a new level. Trying something once or twice may not have any impact on your skills or game. You may even get worse. Practise it twenty times and you could well have considerable or dramatic improvement. Twenty times would be twice a week for ten weeks. If you lack stamina, start running daily; in one week you will be tired, in six weeks you will be fitter. Progress your training. Start with something you can be successful at and then progress it.

Balance your training. In the end it must provide the correct balance between practice and play, between squash and fitness training and between work and rest.

Motivate yourself by setting achievable targets and also rewards for doing well. Don't overtrain. It will lead to boredom and less intense effort. Don't just go through the motions.

Peaking

With experience you will know what works for you. What are the conditions and what training precedes playing your best squash? How can you get everything together so you have your best performances in all areas? It is unlikely that you will walk on court after a summer's fitness training and play your best squash. How much practice do you need to get all your shots grooved? Which speed training sharpens you up? How much competition will you need?

Squash Programme

Your squash programme should balance out and progress through solo practice, pairs practice, practice games and matches. Firstly work on your technique and skill; then develop your shots and movement; practise these in practice games and then they will be ready for matches.

Fitness Programme

Build up your fitness by concentrating as you did with skills on areas where you are weaker. In your programme first work on strength and aerobic endurance, then anaerobic endurance followed by speed.

Rest

Rest is important after major competitions to replenish energy reserves, to provide a mental break (so you will be mentally fresh later for playing and training) and to reassess your programme.

Use an active rest indulging in non-squash activities that will help to maintain your fitness.

The professional in training should have one rest day a week, a three-day break once a month and perhaps one week off every three months.

The Season

It is unlikely (and not necessarily desirable) that the squash year or squash season will be a build-up to just one major competition (as it can be for an athlete) or competition period.

Your season then will be divided into segments covering periods of competition, the build-up to these and short rests. Careful selection of competitions to provide peaking targets as well as time for basic training towards long-term aims is the professional player's problem.

The Training Cycle

We can't do everything at once so what we try to do is concentrate on particular aspects of training at a time, build this area to a new level and then maintain it at that level while focusing on a new area. (Maintaining your fitness with only a slight drop in level will only take one third the effort of building up fitness.) Once built up, fitness may be topped up with a shorter period of foundation training or a shorter training cycle.

The times given below for each phase are examples only and must be adapted to the player's needs and circumstances.

THE TRAINING CYCLE DIVIDES INTO FOUR PARTS

Foundation (six weeks)	*Fitness* The focus here is on basic fitness, that is, building up aerobic endurance and strength, with a little muscular endurance work. This is the time to concentrate on any specific weaknesses in strength or movement. Main activities: running and gym work.	*Squash* This non-competitive phase is ideal to concentrate on technique, skills, developing shots and for working on problem areas. Work with a coach on developing suitable practices and routines. Play at least one game a week to keep up with it but concentrate on solo practice. Main activities: friendly games and solo practice.
Preparation (six weeks)	Still work on improving aerobic endurance but emphasis now moves to anaerobic endurance, that is, shuttle running, with some circuit work to build muscular endurance. Main activities: running, shuttles, circuits.	Continue with technique and shot development by solo practice but now is the time to emphasise work on shots while moving. Also practise starting to construct rallies with condition games and practice games. Main activities: solo and pairs practice, condition and practice games.
Early Competition (four weeks)	Maintain aerobic, anaerobic and muscular endurance, with some running, shuttle running and circuits. Emphasis now moves to speed and movement. Main activities: speed shuttles.	Emphasis now is on getting the shots you have improved with solo and pairs practice into your game. Concentrate mainly on playing. Play practice games as well as matches but maintain skills with solo and pairs practices. Main activities: games plus solo and pairs practices.
Competition (four weeks)	Maintenance of all fitness elements. Emphasis on speed before important events with appropriate rests. Main activities: running, shuttles and speed shuttle.	Emphasis now on match play. Tactical and mental preparation. Preparing for main matches. Don't overdo hard matches. Practise to maintain grooved shots. Main activities: hard matches, easy games, solo and pairs practices.

SAMPLE 20-WEEK TRAINING PROGRAMME

Week	Run	Weights	Exercises	Shuttles	Speed Shuttles	Matches	Solo	Pairs Practice
1	3	2	2			1	2+	
2	3	2	2			1	2+	
3	3+	2	2			1	3+	
4	4+	2	2			1	3+	
5	4	1	1			1	2	
6	4	1	1			1	2	
7	3	1	1	1		1	1	1
8	3	1	1	1		1	1	1
9	2	1	1	2		1	1	2
10	2	1	1	2		1	1	2
11	2	1	1	3		1	1	3
12	2	1	1	3		1	1	3
13	1+	1	1	2	2	2	1	2
14	1+	1	1	2	2	2	1	2
15	1+	1	1	2	2	2	1	2
16	1+	1	1	2	2	2	1	2
17	1			1	1	3	1	1
18	1			1	1	3	1	1
19	1			1	1	3	1	1
20	1			1	1	3	1	1

TRAINING ACTIVITIES

Squash

Solo Practice

Develop a solo practice sequence that concentrates on your weaknesses and loose areas. Also work on the techniques, skills and shots that you want to develop. Start with technique and rhythmic hitting, then concentrate on length drives and variations on these and then move on to shots. See the sections on: Player Profile (page 33) and the Ten Things I Need to Improve On (page35); Basic Control (page 52); and A Solo Session (page 130).

Pairs Practice

Develop a pairs sequence and write down the exercises before going on court. Try to groove shots into a target area and then increase pressure and movement. *See* Pairs Practice Sequence (page 133).

Practice Games

Play easier games where the emphasis is not on winning but on developing aspects of your game. Often this will be the shots and movement you have practised in solo and pairs practice. *See* Practice Games (page 139).

Matches

Vary matches between hard, medium and easy matches. Select types of matches, opponents, and conditions. *See* Match Play (page 163).

Fitness

Running

Gradually build up to continuous running for twenty to thirty minutes at 75 to 90 per cent effort. Keep times. Competitive players will reach three to three-and-a-half miles in twenty minutes. Club players will take longer. *See* Fitness Activities (page 78).

Weights

Work on specific weaknesses to develop leg strength and improve overall strength levels. For leg strengthening work on fixed weights concentrating especially on exercises that work the quads, hamstrings and calves. Work with fairly heavy loads and limited repetitions (say ten). Rest for several minutes between sets and attempt three sets. *See* Leg Strength Programme (page 81).

Exercises

Build muscular endurance with conditioning exercises after play or practice. Use squat jumps, press-ups, back arches and sit-ups.

Shuttles

Sprint court lengths working between thirty and forty-five seconds with similar rest periods. Build up the number of sets from six to twelve. *See* Anaerobic Fitness (pages 78–79) and Shuttles (page 76).

Speed shuttles

Work at maximum for ten to fifteen seconds with approximately fifty seconds rest. Use court lengths for shadow movement. Ten sets or two sets of six with ten minutes' rest in between. *See* Speed (page 81).

PLANNING YOUR TRAINING PROGRAMME

1 Calendar of competitions

Work out and write down the competitions you will be entering. When do you want to peak? Work backwards from there.

2 Phases

Your programme fits into four major blocks of time, each with a different emphasis and purpose. When adapting the programme, try to keep this general structure.

3 Records

Keep a diary of your training and times. Compare these with your programme and your goals. Keep records of your fitness tests. Compare scores

YOUR TRAINING PROGRAMME

Week		Fitness Activities					Squash Activities			
Week	Date						Solo Practice	Pairs. Practice	Practice Games	Matches

before and after training.

4 Adapt

Adapt the programme content and format of the example below to your individual needs. Substitute activities and adjust periods so that you concentrate your training time in key areas and build up to play your best when you want to.

Example of a Weekly Training Schedule

This is an example of an actual training programme used by a professional player in the foundation stages. The professional player wanting to improve will often schedule two sessions, occasionally three, a day. The club player may only be able to schedule one but don't overlook early morning workouts and practice times at lunch time.

DAY	A.M.	P.M.	EVENING
M	Pairs (2hrs)	Aerobic (1hr)	
T	Solo (2hrs)		Hard Play (2hrs)
W	Aerobic (1hr)	Pairs (2hrs)	
Th	Pairs (2hr)	Solo/Easy Play (1.5hr)	Gym. Strength (1.5hr)
F	Solo (1.5hr)	Med/Hard Play (2hr)	Aerobic (1hr)
S		FREE DAY	
S	Solo (1.5hr)	Easy Play (1.5hr)	Circuits Gym (1.25hr)

N.B. Times include warm-up, cool-down and stretching times

FITNESS AND SQUASH ACTIVITIES

M	
T	
W	
Th	
F	
S	
S	

Your Weekly Training Schedule

Allow one rest day a week, alternate hard and easier days, allow time for warming-up and cooling-down. Combine sessions, for example: solo practice followed by court sprints and then stretching; pairs practice followed by a practice game; a match followed by conditioning exercises. Don't try to do too much. Work hard on the day but don't get overtired so that this tiredness compounds and you are going into matches or training sessions drained.

Reaching a New Level

Having long-term aims and a well-organised programme are very important in trying to reach a new level in your game but they are not the only things to do. Organise the right level of competition for yourself. (This will depend on your individual needs.) Here are the six basic things you should do.

1 *Get Fit for the Next Level*

Get fit so that you can play and survive in the level above your own. To play at this level you will have to work harder to get the ball back and rally. If you are playing a better player you will have to be fitter than him to survive.

2 *Play Better Players*

Playing better players is a learning experience, not an ego trip. Organise these games.

3 *Advice and Coaching*

Seek advice on what you are doing and how you can do it better. A professional coach is the best person. When you play better players ask their advice on your game, your strengths and weakness and what you should do.

4 *Set yourself for some Matches*

Play competitive matches where you are trying to get everything together and give your best.

5 *Practice*

Practise to improve technique and shots

6 *Learn from your Defeats*

Don't waste the valuable lessons in every defeat. Don't make excuses. Learn from your defeats and resolve to do better.

Advanced Shots and Techniques

Advanced players do the basic things better, so it is important to focus your energies on improving these and not kidding yourself that a few fancy shots will lift your level. That said, advanced shots and techniques can give you the edge over a player of similar ability. Work at improving the quality and developing the range of your attacking shots – they are your point earners. Take the attitude towards your game that it is developing and that you can learn new tricks. Watch other players and learn. Experiment.

SPIN

CUT

Cutting the ball has three advantages. Firstly it allows you to play the ball quickly and firmly while taking the pace off it – not all the energy of the impact goes into propelling the ball. Secondly the downward cutting action allows you to take drops early. And thirdly it imparts backspin which pulls the ball downward off the front wall allowing a greater margin for error above the tin.

Use cut on drops, especially when the ball is high, on volley drops and kills.

To practise cutting the ball, stand close to the front wall and stroke the ball just above the tin to yourself. Practise your stance and footwork, use a firm wrist, a short swing, and a low backswing that comes under the ball and lifts it above the tin.

Now introduce spin by cutting down more on the back and under the ball. Whip your racket back early, have it waiting ready for the strike and gradually build up speed.

TOP SPIN

Top spin is used on the idiosyncratic top spin drop and the opportunist half volley. On the drop, the extended follow-through of the top spin action can add deception and fool the inattentive. Use the half volley to take the ball early when an opponent is out of position, depriving him of the recovery time he would have had as the ball slowed over the bounce.

Plate 55 –
Jahangir Khan, open racket face poised high, about to cut down on the ball

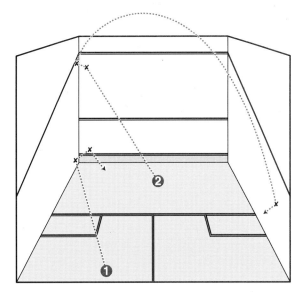

Fig 49
1 Long Angle
2 Corkscrew

NEW ANGLES

SKID BOAST

The skid boast, really a type of lob, is useful if your opponent is well up the court as it can be played high over his head to rebound at a sharp and awkward angle in the back. It is especially useful if your opponent is hanging into the side threatening a volley.

Attempt this skid boast only with a hot ball on a warm court and on a ball that has rebounded well out from the back.

Get behind the ball and hit upward hard at an angle where the ball just skims the side and rebounds high off the front to hit the side before the opposite back corner.

This can be practised with a player on either side of the court driving straight. Select the right ball and skid boast crosscourt for a partner to repeat on the other side.

HARD ANGLE

This is a similar shot to the skid boast, but played at a lower angle and hard into the side very close to the front. It comes back at a very narrow angle down the court, catching an opponent by surprise. A specialist shot played by Australians Tristan Nancarrow and Brett Martin.

LONG ANGLE

Played from a ball rebounding off the back wall, this is a soft angle played down the wall to hit the side near the front and rebound around the corner. The narrow and awkward angle of rebound can catch out opponents.

CORKSCREW

From centre court in front of the short line, hit up high and hard to rebound the ball off the front, close to the side so that it flies off the side high overhead crosscourt to the back corner.

The spin of these impacts can rebound the ball at right angles to the side and if well judged it can be rolled along the back wall for an unplayable winner.

VARIATIONS

To play shots that opponents can't get, we are continually looking to provide unexpected problems. Once a player is familiar with what we are dishing up, anticipating, reading, taking off, moving and recovering the ball, then working out the best counter shots is easy for him. As soon as this happens, and preferably before it happens, it is time to disguise, deceive and introduce new shots – if you have the option.

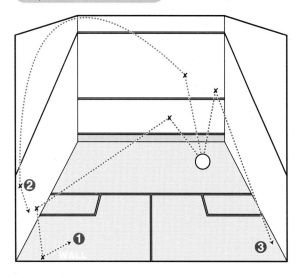

Fig 50 *(above)*
The three main defensive options from
the front court:
1 the crosscourt drive,
2 the lob,
3 the straight drive

Fig 51 *(below)*
We have many attacking variations in
the front court. The three main options are:
1 the straight and crosscourt drop,
2 straight and crosscourt kills,
3 angles

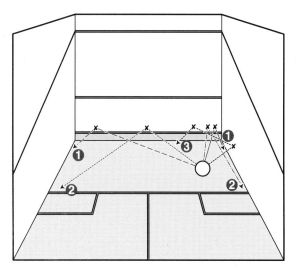

Part of this ability to come up with different options is to position so that you can play a variety of shots. For example, from the front court you can position for either a straight or crosscourt shot (that is, take up a compromise position between the straight shot position facing the side and the crosscourt position facing the corner) and mix these two shots to catch out your opponent. Perhaps from the forehand side you will mainly crosscourt and suddenly whip one straight. From the backhand you may hit straight and suddenly play a crosscourt or play a mix of both.

FRONT COURT
From the front court you have three main defensive options, the crosscourt drive, straight drive and lob. If you are under pressure you will choose one of these. If you are able to keep these three options open (this is not always possible or desirable), your opponent will not be able to anticipate your shot until you have hit it and so must wait or indeed recover from the direction he was anticipating, change direction and retrieve. (A good example of this is in the back court where an opponent looks as if he has been forced to boast but manages to get the ball straight and catches out an opponent already on his way to the front.)

Often you will be able to position and prepare for all three shots and if there is no pressure advantage in taking the ball early you can prepare and pause before selecting your option.

As well as the three main defence options, there are three main attacking variations – the straight drop, angle and kill. Often you will choose these when your opponent is under some degree of pressure.

When you go to the front, take a path and position so that you have these variations available. Lull your opponent into a sense of security as to what to expect and then surprise with a new variation or mix them and keep him guessing.

These are the basic shots but there are many more. Generally it is best to keep to the basics and use the more advanced variations to surprise so that your game doesn't become over elaborate. Still learn all the variations you can. Use little wrist flicks to take the ball crosscourt to die on the second bounce or aim crosscourt for the nick. Cut kill the ball straight for the nick, or play a surprise reverse angle.

Discover and practise as many variations as you can and use the full range of paces.

MID-COURT

From the mid-court there are a full range of options, which is why we try not to give our opponents this advantage by avoiding hitting the ball to this area.

Attacking opportunities may present themselves for the boast, reverse angle, straight and crosscourt drops and kills. Opportunities to pressurise opponents with low and dying length drives can be considered as the T is easily recoverable. And there are the three defensive options. Position and prepare so that you have all these options available.

BACK COURT

Back court is basically a defensive situation where you will choose to straight drive, crosscourt drive, perhaps crosscourt lob and only boast if forced to or if there is a special opportunity.

The back corners can be a very limiting place (which is one reason we try to put opponents there) but having even the limited variations of straight, crosscourt and perhaps the boast can be useful so that play does not become predictable.

Attacking from the back should be used sparingly but can be a useful points winner when you catch out an opponent. If successful it can be done again.

Practise and especially develop the straight drops which can be played tight but there are also the options of crosscourt drops, kills, low drives, reverse angles and skid boasts, all of which should be used sparingly.

Plate 56 –
Simon Parke lines up the ball.
From this position he has a number of options.
He has some disguise on his shot as he has
positioned to allow both the straight drive and
crosscourt shots

DISGUISE

One important squash idea closely related to that of variations is disguise. We disguise our shots by shaping the same way for a number of shot variations. That is, we use the same positions, stance and racket preparation.

Don't worry about disguise to the extent of letting it stop you playing your best shots. It is a useful idea especially when playing unexpected variations and when you have time, as your opponent won't know what shot you are playing until it is played.

It can be practised easily with the pairs exercises where (i) **A** alternates straight and crosscourt drives and **B** boasts; and (ii) where **A** drops and drives, (that is, **A** shapes for a drive and drops) and **B** straight drives and boasts. (Here **B** shapes to play either a straight shot or boast.)

DECEPTION

Deception is where we show one shot and then play another. Unlike disguise, where we position for several shots, in deception we try to make it very obvious which shot we are showing and lure an opponent into moving early for it. So a little delay between the show shot and the actual shot is necessary. Our opponent sees the shot, moves or at least transfers his weight and then we change the show shot into one going in the other direction.

Don't be afraid to delay deceptive shots. Give time for your opponent to run the wrong way. The magic of deception is conjured with the wrist but is not too difficult. You probably have your favour-

ites. Collect a few more. Study other players and try out their shots in practice and practice games. The more ways you have of winning points the more likely you are to win them.

The first two of the following deceptions can be practised with the exercise where **A** alternates straight and crosscourt drives and **B** boasts or better still in the front/back game.

SHAPE TO DRIVE STRAIGHT

Exaggerate the position to the side, turn your shoulder, angle your bottom around to the front and wait for the ball. From behind, everything says straight, but as the swing comes down and through, the wrist flicks the ball crosscourt. Keep the body positioned for the straight shot until the end of the stroke or after it.

SHAPE FOR THE CROSSCOURT

Facing forward and keeping the ball in front, swing through for the crosscourt, swing your body a little and then hold back the racket head letting the ball come through and play straight.

SHAPE TO DRIVE AND PLAY SHORT

Shaping to drive, throwing an opponent back on his heels and then playing short is easiest with the angle. Shape to straight drive, let the ball come back a little, swing through as for a straight drive and turn the shot into the side for an angle. The angle can be played a little quicker and with a fuller swing than the drop.

The disguised full swing for a drop must suddenly be braked through or just before impact to allow touch. This is something you can practise easily on the drop and drive, and boast exercise.

Plate 57 –
The games most deceptive player,
the brilliant Australian Brett Martin,
demonstrates one shot with his body
positioning and uses his wrist to play another

Match Preparation

M any matches you could win are often lost before you go on court. At times things just seem to go wrong, you are not at your best and afterwards it is easy to see it wasn't your day. Excuses are easy. Outside events had conspired to defeat you or you just didn't feel right. You may know players whose off-days are every-day occurrences.

Now imagine that things go right for you. Your programme, however informal, has turned out right and you have played and practised enough before the match but not so much that you are tired. Physically you are fresh.

You have eaten well and stocked up on energy without overeating and arrive at the courts well hydrated. The day has gone as comfortably as you could arrange it and without any major hassle. You arrive at the courts relaxed and unencumbered by worries. You know who you are going to play, you have thought about his strengths and weaknesses and you have planned how you will play.

You have organised yourself to arrive early, have all the necessary equipment and spares ready and may even have briefed your coach or a supporter who could advise you between games.

At the club you change early and start preparing mentally. You visualise yourself playing well, build up your confidence and are keenly awaiting the battle even if there is a little nervousness.

You warm up thoroughly, warming, loosening and stretching and even playing a few shadow strikes. You are completely loosened up. Mentally you start focusing concentration on your game plan, and visualise an excellent knock-up.

In the knock-up (warm-up as it is called erroneously in the rules – the warm-up is off court), you have a check list and run through the basic shots and groove them in. You have started studying your opponent, picking out which shots are about to come up. Now when the racket is spun you are ready to play, ready to play your best. When you go on court you are mentally and physically ready to play, not just ready to warm up.

We have all met players who are always late; who have something else on their minds; who had a big lunch or a few drinks; who were tired after yesterday's match or who haven't played for a week; who had a hassling meeting just before play; never warm up; always lose the first game; etc, etc.

If you want to excel at squash and play your best, then prepare to play your best. If you don't want to excel at squash, don't prepare, you will have the self-deluding comfort of another prearranged excuse that it just wasn't your day.

Prepare to play your best. Make it your day. Let's look at what you can do.

PROGRAMMING

You can't run through a whole squash programme a day or two before a match but you can avoid programming mistakes. Your programming build-up should include some matches but then rest on the day or two before a match, with some light court work, perhaps a practice game or practices to groove in your shots, especially your winners. Professional players always practise with a light workout in the morning before their afternoon or evening matches.

Don't train heavily before a match and expect to be fresh enough to play your best.

DIET

Eat sensibly so that the energy books are balanced and make sure that if you have had to play a hard match (say the night before) you have taken in enough food before the next one. Eat as soon as you can after the last match.

On the day, you want digestion to be completed before play and you should eat no later than two hours, preferably four, before play to allow time for food to leave the stomach. (For high-fat foods this takes two to four hours and for carbohydrates between one and two hours.) Prepare meals that feel right but do take in sufficient carbohydrates. The content of the last meal before a match is not crucial but avoid sugary snacks. Caffeine (preferably taken in the form of filtered or percolated coffee or alternatively cola, instant coffee or tea) taken forty-five minutes before play can, however, be useful.

FLUIDS

A squash player can lose up to two or three pints of sweat an hour and it is not possible to absorb fluid from the intestine as fast as it is lost in sweat.

Therefore players should arrive for matches well hydrated and should drink half a pint or so of water or diluted juice before the start. Between a game, a player should drink not more than a quarter of a pint of water. This is all a strenuously exercising body can absorb every fifteen minutes. (For exercise of two hours or less, it is loss of fluid rather than loss of electrolytes or energy which is the initial limiting factor.) Water or a still, weak electrolytic drink is best, not a soft or carbonated drink.

In a tournament situation it is vital to replace fluid as soon as possible after the match to give adequate time for replacement before the next match. At the end of each day's play it is important to replace the salts lost, mainly by adding a little salt to the evening meal and by having fruits or fruit juice with it.

ON THE DAY

Organise your day so that you don't have any disruptive influences, especially near match time, so that transport is assured and leave a little extra time for any emergencies. Arrive early.

PREPLANNING

Try to find out who your opponent is and how he plays so that you can plan how you would like to play the match. (*See* Game Plan page 167.) Consciously work out an adaptable plan to counter your opponent's strengths and attack any weaknesses.

Use a little caution in your planning. Players have been caught out having arrived at the courts with the expectation of playing one opponent, only to find that this is wrong and the change has thrown them.

EQUIPMENT

Prepare and pack your squash equipment early to save last-minute problems. You should have: two identical rackets (that is, a spare); clean grips and spare grips (now is the time to change one if necessary, so that you don't find that you need a new grip, and don't have a spare one as you are going on court); secure shoes with clean soles; spare laces; grip aids and sweat bands if used; squash kit (cotton is best as it retains more sweat and gives it time to evaporate which is when heat loss occurs. This helps to keep the body temperature down a little to more efficient levels); a tracksuit for warming up and cooling down; a towel for rubbing down; a drink bottle.

MENTAL PREPARATION

Overall you want to be organised, to have minimised the chances of distractions and to have taken a positive attitude to the match while avoiding overconfidence and defeatism. You will have worked out a game plan in advance and set your goal of playing well rather than winning or losing.

During the physical warm-up you will endeavour to relax your muscles, to stay warm and relaxed and to start narrowing your focus of attention, running through the game plan and the knock-up check list.

Use visualisation, (*See* page 126), imagine yourself in specific situations playing well. When you step on court you should be physically and mentally ready to play and looking forward to it. You know what you are going to do in the knock-up, in the playing-in period of the match, how you want to play your game and you are focusing on these things.

WARM-UP

The warm-up prepares you physically and mentally for play. Arrive and change early for your matches so that you have plenty of time for a good warm-up. Five minutes will be better than nothing but you will be better prepared if you spend between ten and twenty minutes on this. Many top players would spend twenty to thirty minutes on their warm-up. Remember when you step on court you want to be completely warmed up and ready to play – not halfway there. You should feel warm and have started to sweat lightly (to feel the moisture on your skin), feel loose, flexible and 'on your toes'.

Try to avoid a time-lag between warming up and competition. If you cool down you should start some gentle warming exercises again before you go on court. Develop your own routine and make it a habit.

Your warm-up should raise your body temperature, heart and breathing rates, loosen your joints and stretch your muscles. A warm-up tracksuit can be very useful, especially in cold weather to help raise body temperature and then to keep you warm.

Your warm-up has three parts – warming, loosening and stretching.

Warming

Warm up easily and gently with running on the spot type exercises or whole body exercises for several minutes. Develop a little routine. Try astride jumps, punch-ups and skipping.

Loosening

Run through these 'top to toe' loosening exercises.

1 *Sky Reach* Arm straight overhead, reach as high as possible and hold, alternating sides. Ten repetitions.

2 *Head Turns* Turn your head to the left and hold, then to the right, back and forward, several times each way.

3 *Shoulder Shrugs* Bring the right shoulder up to your ear and hold; ten repetitions. Repeat on left.

4 *Arm Circling* Forward and backwards ten times each.

5 *Arm Flings* Pushing arms back towards each other behind the body, ten times.

6 *Trunk Twists* Arms straight in front, turn arms and trunk to the side as far as possible.

7 *Side Bends* Arms at side, bend sideways and reach down to touch below knee. Ten each side.

8 *Trunk Circling* Feet astride, bend down and touch right foot, swing across to left, swing up and over in line with shoulders and repeat. Ten each way.

9 *Hip Circling* Hands on hips, thrust pelvis forward, then to the side, back and side. Ten times each way.

10 *Ankle Circling* Ten full circles in and ten out with each foot.

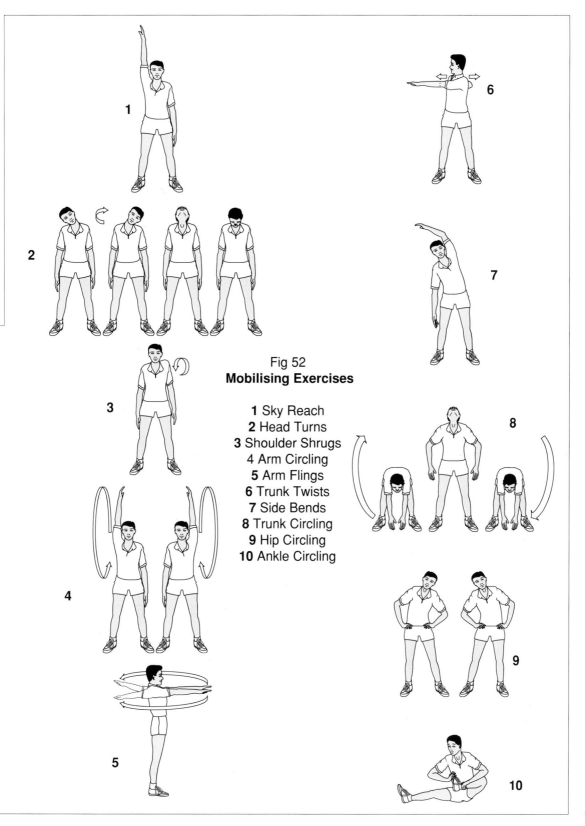

Fig 52
Mobilising Exercises

1 Sky Reach
2 Head Turns
3 Shoulder Shrugs
4 Arm Circling
5 Arm Flings
6 Trunk Twists
7 Side Bends
8 Trunk Circling
9 Hip Circling
10 Ankle Circling

Stretching

Stretch only when you are warm and start your stretching easily. Don't bounce.

Fig 53
Stretching

1 Lunge
2 Hamstring Stretch
3 Standing Quads Stretch
4 Groin Stretch
5 Calf Stretch/Achilles Stretch

1 *Lunge Stretch (Hip Flexor Stretch)*
This is a stretch for the front of the hip, groin and hamstring. Bend with the right leg forward, knee over the ankle, left leg straight behind with your weight on the ball of your foot. Use your hands for balance and slowly lower your shoulders in front of your right knee until you feel a good stretch in your groin, hip and hamstring. Hold for fifteen seconds, relax, repeat and then work on the other side.

2 *Hamstring Stretch*
(i) Sit with your legs straight in front, feet upright. Bend forward from the hips, keeping your back as straight as possible and your head up. Slide your hands down your legs to your toes and feel the tension in your hamstrings. Hold for twenty seconds. From this position you can reach down and pull your toes in towards you for a seated calf stretch.
(ii) Stand on one leg and place the back of your heel on a support about waist high and keep this leg straight. Slowly bend forward from the hips until you feel the tension in your hamstrings. Keep your head up as you bend forward. Hold for twenty seconds.

3 *Quads Standing Stretch*
Stand on your left leg, bend your right leg and using your left hand pull your right heel towards your buttock until you feel a light stretch in your quads. Hold for twenty seconds and repeat on the opposite side.

4 *Groin Stretch*
Sit tall, bend your knees and place the soles of your feet together. Hold on to your feet, let your knees fall easily to the floor and gently pull yourself forward. Rest your elbows on your legs as you bend forward but do not bend your head forward. Hold for twenty seconds.

5 *Calf Stretch*
Stand or lean on a wall with one leg forward, feet parallel and heels flat on the floor. Bend the forward knee until you feel a light tension behind the knee and on the calf of the back leg. Hold this for twenty seconds, relax slowly, then repeat for the other leg.

To create a stretch in the Achilles tendon lower your hips and bend your knees as far as possible without raising your heels.

KNOCK-UP

Most players usually use the knock-up poorly and in doing so miss a vital opportunity to be well prepared for their matches. Here you have the chance of five minutes' practice at your best hitting, the chance to groove and establish touch on your basic shots and the opportunity to start reading your opponent.

Use the knock-up well so that when the match starts you have already established tight, straight length and good width on the crosscourt which beats your opponent's volley and buries him right in the back corner. You are already volleying and looking for the volleying opportunities, varying the pace, have your lob working and feel secure on your drop. Now when you step into the match you just carry on.

Think about what you want out of your knock-up, plan a check list and then develop a little routine. The following is what I would suggest.

KNOCK-UP CHECK LIST

1 Line up the ball

Don't waste the knock-up with rushed and scrappy shots. Initially take your time; prepare your racket early, move your feet, get in the best position, pause, and play your best shots. Develop a rhythm so you are hitting sweetly.

2 Length

Play one or two shots to yourself (not every time – don't hog the ball) before crossing the ball to your opponent. Make sure you get the ball right into the back, to rebound off the back wall and cling. Establish this straight, tight length now and hold on to it in the match. Get your thinking working. Is your shot short? Yes? Lift the next one higher.

Plate 58 –
The knock-up is an opportunity to practise your best hitting, groove your main shots and focus your concentration before you play

3 Width

Don't just hit the ball across to your opponent, practise the shot you want to use in a game. Drive the ball past your opponent into the corner. Play it wide to beat the volley and target the side, floor and back. Practise a few crosscourts off the back wall. Vary the pace of these shots.

4 Volley

Concentrate on the first three points of the checklist first and then play a few volleys. You want to start your match ready to take any opportunities, not hanging around in the back of the court. Feed a few balls up for yourself and crosscourt for the nick behind the service box.

5 Lob

It can take a little time to get your touch working in a game, so start early. Practise the tactical idea of lobbing when under pressure. You have a whole range of paces available that you will want to use in a game to a greater or lesser extent. Start in the knock-up by getting used to the lob.

You will know from the experience of playing on different courts that conditions and temperatures can vary considerably, affecting the flight of the ball. Get a feel for this with a few lobs.

6 Drops

Practise your drops safely, using a short swing with cut and build up confidence on this so that you will have already played some before that first opportunity crops up in a game.

Practise dropping off an opponent's boast, perhaps playing a few little shots from the cutting exercise (see page 103).

READING AN OPPONENT

Practise reading your opponent's shots in the knock-up. Make a decision (but don't move) before he hits (See page 68).

STRENGTHS AND WEAKNESSES

Run through your own check list and get the six things above working in your game rather than becoming totally obsessed with testing out your opponent. Do, however, observe your opponent and make mental notes. For example, ask yourself questions like the following, and plan answers.

Q *Is he volleying well?*

A Yes, I will have to keep it straight and low. Crosscourts must be wide. He is better on the forehand-attacking volley, so if I have to lob I better hit to his backhand.

Q *What is he like out of the back?*

A He seems to boast a lot so perhaps I will be able to get in with my straight drop. He boasts more on the backhand so perhaps play deep crosscourts there but I will have to pass the volley.

Q *Which side does he seem strongest on?*

A He seems good on both sides but has cracked a few nice backhand kills so I will have to be careful not to play short there.

Q *What are his best shots?*

A He's good on the drive and volley but may be a bit loose down the backhand. I will rally down there for good length.

Q *What are his favourite shots?*

A He seems to like attacking volleys so any high shots need to be tight and if I have put up a loose one I can anticipate a short shot and start moving forward.

Q *How is he moving?*

A It is hard to say but he seems a little slow to the front and to turn for the hard low balls. Maybe I can catch him out with counterdrops when he attacks and perhaps some long drops when he tires. Any ball in the middle I will hit low and hard crosscourt.

INTO THE MATCH

In many ways you start your match just carrying on with your knock-up play. Remember a match is a best of five so you are not going to win it in the first few minutes. Use this as a playing-in period, establishing your length and tight basic game, and try to hold on to this throughout the match.

However, if the opportunity is there to dominate or pressurise your opponent early, take it.

CHAPTER 10

Match Play

Everything that has been said before in this book is designed, in the end, to improve your play in matches. This is where you are under pressure, have to adapt your shots and tactics to your opponent's game, work out how you are going to rally and what opportunities you will look for.

Playing on the day is not something that has to be left to chance. Just as you organise your other squash activities you can plan, prepare, practise and programme your matches. This section will give you some ideas on how to evaluate these so that you can improve and do it better next time.

Match play is where you have to front up. A large part of this book has emphasised the activities you can do to lift your level but in the end you have to do it in matches. There is no substitute for hard matches at your level.

Search out different types of players to play. Play different types of matches at different courts and venues. Play hard competitive matches. There is no substitute for this experience. Take your losses and victories away and learn from them.

Here are some ideas that may help you in your play and in learning from that experience.

START WITH DEFENCE

The first battle in squash is for the high ground – the T. From this central position you control the territory of the court. You are in the best position to cover all your opponent's moves. You are in the best position to apply pressure, move your opponent and attack when opportunities occur.

When you are out of position, you can still use these plays and often will if there is a good opportunity, but your chances of success are reduced – it is harder to deprive your opponent of time, move the ball away from him, play shots that will die before he can recover them and then to cover his options.

Start with defence. Get the ball past your opponent into the back corners and win the T. Get length and win the T. This is the first tactic of squash. Ask a coach why you didn't play well and this is the first thing he will look at. When you lose length you fail to put your opponent out of position and you fail to win the T.

Start each match, game and rally with defence. This is what you build your game on. Get the ball back, don't risk mistakes, don't give your opponent easy opportunities, tighten up loose areas before moving, attacking and pressurising your opponent.

Establish this length in the knock-up, emphasise it at the start and hang on to it throughout the match.

Possession of the T will change, but if you don't get that feeling of having the T and time, then this first basic part of your game is not working.

SET UP RALLIES

Don't just think of winning points in squash, think of winning rallies. Develop a rally plan and practise it. Practise different types of rally so that you can use these to counter different styles of play. A plan for your rallies will help your decision-making.

Here is a simple seven-stage plan for setting up your rallies that can be easily adapted. Try out parts of it in easy practice games and build these up so that you are familiar with them when you come to play your matches.

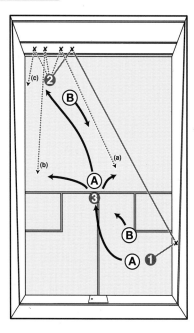

Fig 54
Following Up

1 Player **A** boasts moving **B**
from the backcourt over the
diagonal to the front.
2 Three of **B**'s options are:
(a) the crosscourt;
(b) the straight drive; and
(c) straight drop.
3 A follows up quickly on the
boast and is in position to
intercept **B**'s drives or seize on
the drop before **B** has
recovered position

1 Drive Straight

Tight, straight driving will pull your opponent out of the centre and give you a good chance of taking the T and getting your opponent behind you. Set up this basic pattern of straight driving of varying length and pace, persist with it a little, get it tight, and there is not much your opponent can do about it. If it becomes predictable and this is a problem, then you can change it by introducing more crosscourts and variations.

2 Look for Opportunities to Crosscourt

If you can pass your opponent with a crosscourt it is a better shot than the straight drive as it doesn't come out of the back as much and can often force a boast. When it is played hard and low a crosscourt can pass an opponent and die before or on the back wall, perhaps winning the rally or forcing a weak return.

The crosscourt, however, is a 'loose' shot, spending much of its time out from the side wall and risking interception.

Keep your rallies mainly straight and look for opportunities to crosscourt when your opponent is slightly out of position to one side, back off the T, in the process of recovering it, or hanging into the side looking for the straight drive.

Pick balls to crosscourt that come off the back sufficiently to allow you the correct angle.

3 Look for Opportunities to Volley

Set up your straight rallies, varied with crosscourts, and look for opportunities to volley. As you move out of the back corners, study your opponent and be prepared to volley. If your straight shot is not coming off the back much, making a crosscourt difficult, hang in to the side looking for weaker straight drives to volley. Look for weak crosscourts you can intercept with a volley drop or straight volley.

4 Look for Openings

Move your opponent around when a gap appears. Use it to hit the ball as far away from him as possible. Boast when your opponent is behind and drop when your opponent has been forced to boast from the back.

Apply pressure when your opponent is faltering, when you have an easy ball and when you have the centre ground.

Attack when you have an easy ball and your opponent is out of position.

5 Follow Up

Try to predict your opponent's moves, especially when he is under pressure at the front. Follow up quickly looking for the intercept. When under pressure your opponent's shots will probably become more predictable. If your opponent is in the front court, volley long; if in the back court, volley or move him short.

6 Return to Defence

One foray into attacking play is not necessarily a rally won. Often you will see a player, disappointed by a missed opportunity, throw a rally away in a series of rash shots or a player under pressure attempt a risky outright winner from an unlikely position. Don't waste points like this. Return to defence whenever you need to and set up a rally again. This is really the art of rallying; set up a rally, explore an opening, return to defence and set it up again. This pattern should be repeated over and over again.

7 Create Openings and Apply Pressure

Don't be too comfortable in setting up nice rallies and in sitting around waiting for opportunities – go out and force them. Play tight shots that will force weak replies and apply pressure to force errors and create openings for a winning shot.

PLAY YOUR GAME

Often you will see a player depressed in the changing room – it wasn't the defeat that was depressing, he just didn't play well. He hadn't got his game together. Perhaps he wasn't allowed to or perhaps he was vague about what he was trying to do and allowed his opponent to dictate the type of game they played. You will have seen this when you have watched squash – one player hits hard, so his opponent hits hard; a player slows the game, so his opponent slows the game; a player plays lots of shots, so his opponent plays lots of shots.

Don't follow your opponent or play your opponent's game. Impose your game on your opponent as much as you can. If you can do this, you have picked the battleground that is to your advantage.

Your opponent will be trying to impose his game on you tactically, physically and mentally. In doing so he will be trying to neutralise, counter and disrupt what you want to do.

Prepare to play your game. Practise it and

Plate 59 –
Chris Walker is quickly on to a volleying
opportunity presented by Simon Parke

rehearse it mentally. Use the knock-up and set up rallies to a pattern. But be prepared to adapt your play to counter your opponent's game. This is your game plan.

GAME PLAN

A game plan is where you adapt your game to an opponent's strengths and weaknesses.

Think of an opponent, real or imaginary. Where is he strong? What are his best shots and where does he play them from? Avoid these areas. For example, if your opponent is very good at the front of the court you have to be very discriminating about when you play short. If your opponent is deadly on the volley you have to be very careful about putting loose balls in the air. If your opponent is brilliant at intercepting crosscourts with winning volleys you must play mainly straight and pick your crosscourts very carefully.

Where does this opponent catch you out? What winners does he play and where does he play them from? Where does he give you trouble and force weak balls?

Plan your game to avoid playing to your opponent's areas of strength.

Does your opponent like a fast or slow game, long rallies or short. What sort of game does he like to play? Counter these game types.

What is your opponent's fitness like? How will he handle long rallies and a long hard game?

Where is your opponent weak?

Is there part of the game where your opponent is relatively weak – on one side or the other, back or front? Is there an area he doesn't move to or change direction to well? Which part of the court is he weaker in? Play to here. Where is he predictable? Set up these opportunities.

Where are you relatively stronger in your game? Manoeuvre play into this area.

If you are fitter and faster, then obviously you don't want to play short, slow-paced rallies.

Plan your games. Prepare for specific opponents. Set up the rallies you want, to the areas you want. Use the shots, paces and combinations that are to your advantage.

BEATING BETTER PLAYERS

You can beat players who are better than you. You can also lose to players who are not as good.

Think of all the skills, shots and abilities that make up a squash player. It may be that an opponent has an admirable list of playing qualities, many of which are better than yours, but there may be areas where you have a small advantage. Try to play the game in this area.

Don't play to an opponent's strong points. For example, don't: play long punishing rallies against a fitter player; emphasise short shots against a player who is fast to the front with good counterdrops; lob against an excellent volleyer; play hard crosscourts against a fast-pressure player.

Play to an opponent's weakness. You have a whole range of tactics to use – different paces, placements and shots you can play with, various lengths of rallies and matches and the different speeds and pressure they can be played at.

Consider your opponent's attributes and make judgements on fitness, temperament, tactics and shots.

In your game, play on your strengths and your opponent's weakness. This way it is possible to beat players who in many ways are better than you.

Squash allows you a wide range of shots and game types to try to defeat an opponent. Adapt your game and use these to defeat opponents, even better opponents. That's part of the appeal of the game.

COUNTERING GAME TYPES

Part of the art of a good squash player is in playing the best type of game to beat an opponent, the game that best counters his type of game.

For example, how would you play someone who runs further, faster and hits the ball harder than you? Obviously it is not to your advantage to confront your opponent with a long, hard-hitting game.

Plate 60 –
Jahangir Khan winds up in a endeavour to turn the pressure on Jansher Khan

Practise different game types so that you can adapt your play to counter your opponent's game and concentrate on his relative weaknesses.

How would you counter opponents who play these types of game. Attempt to answer the questions before reading the answers here.

1 Slow Game

Q *How should I play against a slow-ball player who plays high shots, lobs and drops?*

A Try to impose your game on your opponent. Don't get sucked into playing your opponent's game or become frustrated or impatient. Vary the pace of your shots and try to keep some pressure in the game. (If you don't hit some shots hard, the ball will cool and this will only be to your opponent's advantage.)

Volley as much as you can, concentrating on deep, wide and safe volleys. Get right up on the T and look for the drops. Look for the opportunity to counterdrop if your opponent drops from the back.

2 The Hard-Hitting Game

Q *How should I play a hard-hitting opponent?*

A Don't be tempted into trying to outhit your opponent. Vary the pace. Lift the ball high and deep whenever you are under pressure. Play positively. Move into and out of defence and apply pressure when the opportunity arises.

3 The Shot-Maker

Q *What should I do against a very good shot-maker?*

A Deprive the shot-maker of opportunities to play shots. Keep the ball wide and deep, be patient and be ready to counterattack. Take your opportunities as they come, but don't play your opponent's game and start going for a lot of shots.

Try to apply pressure to give your opponent less time on the ball.

4 The Volleyer

Q *How do I play an opponent who hogs the T and volleys everything?*

A Deprive the player of opportunities to volley easily. Keep it mainly straight and use extra width

on the crosscourts. Go very high or lower and harder on drives. Recover the T quickly, especially if you have conceded an opening.

An emergency measure is to consider more short shots. A decision on this would depend on your opponent's ability at the front and your ability to cover.

5 The Retriever

Q *How do I play someone who just seems to get every ball back?*

A It's easy to become tired, frustrated and impatient playing a retriever. You must play positively but you can't afford mistakes. Play defensively, vary the pace and continually look for opportunities to move into pressure, positional and attacking play. Follow up on opportunities so that these become bursts of activity. Attack in these bursts and pace yourself through the match.

CHANGING YOUR GAME

There is an old rule in squash: change a losing game, don't change a winning game.

There are a whole range of shots, paces and patterns of play which a player uses in a game. If playing a losing game, change the emphasis of these. Alter the tactical balance in your game – the balance between defence and attack, between positional play and pressure play, and between hard and soft shots. Shift the emphasis from where you are making mistakes, playing loose shots or

Plate 61 –
Australian Liz Irving slows the game against England's hard hitting Suzanne Horner

168

being beaten, to where you are relatively stronger.

To be able to use different strategies, play different types of game and vary your tactics so that you become familiar with them. Practise this in practice games.

WINNING SQUASH

Develop a mentality in your match play where you are thinking positively about playing your best. Focus your thinking and effort into the things that will help you do this. Don't be distracted. Discard all other thoughts.

Here are the ten secrets of winning squash.

1 Win the T

The player in front wins. The player who controls the T, controls the game. Win the T with length.

2 Win the Rallies

Squash is a rallying game. Set up rallies, take charge of them and pick the openings.

3 Recover from Poor Positions

When in poor situations winning players don't waste points with rash shots or give them away easily. They concentrate on length and width, on playing tight shots that will allow them to recover the T and when they are under pressure, they lob.

4 Know When to Attack

In squash as in all warfare when you are in a weak position you retreat, regroup and fight again. Attack here could be suicidal.

Attack involves risk and you should attack when you have the advantage. This means two things: firstly that you have an easy ball; and secondly that your opponent is out of position.

Plate 62 –
Susan Devoy waits until she has Cassie Jackman out of position and an easy ball before she attacks

Plate 63 –
A fine sense for the gap. Here the attacking player has used an ample margin of error above the tin to play a soft, winning drop shot. The straight dying length drive was an alternative. Obviously the crosscourt was the wrong shot

5 Sense the Gaps

Winners sense the gaps, are on to them quickly and make their opponents run. Sense your opponent's position and the gaps between this and the T.

6 Pick When to Pressurise your Opponent

The secret of winning squash is to play well at the right time. Pace yourself throughout a match so that you still have something for the vital moments. Apply pressure when your opponent tires, starts making mistakes or loses concentration.

7 Pick Where to Pressurise your Opponent

Study your opponent's game, monitor it, learn as you go along. Work out where his play is weakest, where mistakes are made, play is loose and where he is limited. Apply pressure here.

8 Keep your Opponent Guessing

Winning players keep their opponents guessing by varying paces and shots. They use variations from the same situation, so that as soon as an opponent is on to their shots or combinations they use another.

Use surprise shots, disguise, deception, half volleys and anticipatory intercepts. Save some surprises for your opponent.

9 Talk Positively to Yourself

One of the secrets of winning squash is willing yourself to win. In all the ups and down of a match, and despite the pressures, anxieties and distractions, winners keep concentrating and stay confident. Winners accept the challenge of competition positively, while the inner dialogue of losers becomes negative – losers seek excuses.

10 Prepare to Win

Winning players prepare to win. They are not the players who are late to the venue, who are running around at the last minute with equipment problems and who take a game to get warmed up.

They are organised, arrive early, get warmed up and are mentally prepared.

WHEN THINGS GO WRONG

In match play things can go wrong. Imagine that suddenly your opponent is in front, dominating, that your play is rushed, loose and that you are scrambling to recover your opponent's shots.

When things go wrong the first thing to check is length. From outside the court it is an obvious problem but inside when you rush, you often compound the problem. You rush because you have not time and you have not time because you are not creating it with good length.

Lose your length and your opponent has less distance to move, is on to the ball more quickly, perhaps before you have recovered your position. By making the ball go to the back of the court, and forcing your opponent to wait for it to come off the back wall, you are creating time. Even against a superior player there is a momentary respite. You have time: time to move to the T, time to anticipate and time to seize on any loose ball to work or attack.

If you lose your length there is one simple answer – hit higher.

Imagine now that you are playing an opponent who seems to be able to play shots at will, shots that beat you or shots which you have difficulty reaching. What can you do in a game where your shots ricochet around the court and an opponent easily reads and intercepts them where your crosscourts come through the middle and straight drives drift out from the side?

Any time your opponent is playing good shots you must ask yourself where he is playing them from. Don't give your opponent these opportunities. Try to play fewer looser crosscourt and boast shots and straighten up your game. Tighten up.

When you rush or are anxious you can mistime slightly and your shots won't be as accurate as the ones that are well lined up. This gives your opponent the opportunity of putting you under more pressure and hence compounds the problem.

The only way to break out of this vicious circle is to slow down and take more time on your shots. Prepare your racket as you move, make a definite stop before hitting and hit higher and softer to give yourself more time.

If you lose your length or your play becomes loose, concentrate on these things:

1 If you play a 'short' drive, correct this immediately by aiming the next shot significantly higher.

2 If you lose your length, set a new policy of aiming higher. Play into that part of the wall above the cut line.

3 If your game is loose, providing opportunities for your opponent, slow down. Concentrate on three things – preparing for your shot, making a definite stop on balance, playing more high straight and high wide shots to give yourself time.

4 If your crosscourts and boasts are drifting out into the middle of the court, stop playing them.

5 If your crosscourts are being volleyed, aim wider across the court and into the side wall.

6 If your straight drives from the front are coming out from the side wall, angle your body to the side more and let the ball come behind the right angle before impact.

7 If your straight drives from the back are deflecting off the side wall, stop running into the ball and position yourself further away and to the side of it.

MONITORING YOUR GAME

Squash is all action. There is little time in a match to sit back and work out what you are doing and how you could do it better – this must be done on the move.

Improving your tactical understanding by studying and observing tactics, practising tactics, developing good tactics in Your Game, preparing for matches well and developing game plans are all useful but on court everything is not going to be perfect and you just have to make it work.

Former World Champion Ross Norman puts it rather well.

> You're monitoring your game the whole time. You're monitoring how you're feeling, how he is feeling, how the game's going, whether you're winning or losing, everything about the game you're gauging all the time.
>
> If you hit a particular shot and your opponent puts a few down, keep that in the back of your mind so that when you get half an opportunity, you can create that situation again.

Of all the things you are trying to do in your game and of which you must be aware, your attention must focus on the key areas that are really important in that particular match situation. Where are you in trouble? Where is your opponent taking advantage? Can you tighten up here?

Where can you take advantage? Can you anticipate more? Can you apply more pressure?

Keep your thinking simple. Be aware of what happened in the last rally and make positive resolutions about this. Encourage yourself as you go along. Will yourself on. For example, say to yourself 'Come on, you could have volleyed that' and then go out and take the next volleying opportunity.

Don't let your concentration wander. Don't become distracted by the crowd, the referee, an opponent's gamesmanship or worry about your equipment. Focus your concentration on what is happening and what is important.

CHECK LISTS

Have little check lists that you can use at the end of rallies. Develop your own.

Here is an example. You could quickly follow this line of thinking and ask yourself these questions.

1 Length

Am I getting length? And in considering this, consider width and whether you are varying the pace. Am I getting the ball past my opponent? Am I forcing my opponent to take the ball off the back? When was the last time he had to take the ball off the back wall?

2 T

Am I on the T before he hits? Can I recover quicker? Am I in front?

3 Watching

Do I know what shot is coming up next? Did I see that shot coming? Am I watching?

4 Pressure

Have I got pressure on my opponent? Should I hit harder or look to volley more?

5 Attack

Am I taking my opportunities? Am I looking to attack?

Pause for a second or two before serving. Quickly consider the check list. Decide what to do. Don't be rushed into receiving. Concentrate on getting it past your opponent.

TAKING ADVICE

The giving and taking of advice between games is a precarious business and it is often difficult for the adviser to separate himself emotionally from the contest.

It is for the advisers to remind themselves frequently that they are not dealing with robots who will follow instructions exactly. The overwhelming impulse is to say too much and dilute the impact of what could have been a couple of succinct points.

Firstly an adviser should consider a player's mental state. In general he will want to encourage, be positive and build up confidence – not depress.

Advice should be simple, brief, concentrating on one or two key points and perhaps on where a player is obviously not coping well with his opponent's game. Advice should be provided within a player's capability.

The best way to go about this relationship is to practise it. Ideally the adviser and coach will have discussed a game plan which may include a contingency plan. After it is all over there should be a debriefing.

SERVING AND RECEIVING

In traditional scoring, points can only be won on service and only lost when receiving. Risk-taking then can be varied with a little more risk being taken when serving and less when receiving.

Receiving means that you have just lost a rally (except perhaps for the first point in the match). This is generally the time to think defensively, especially of length and winning the T, and most importantly of avoiding a lapse in concentration.

When receiving, play a more defensive game; when serving, a more attacking one.

PACE YOURSELF

Matches ebb and flow. It is the player who has strength and energy and who plays well in the end who wins. Squash rewards persistence.

If you go flat out from the start of a match you may indeed tire. Save a little energy in reserve for emergencies and so that you can put the pressure on when it is really going to count. Play hard to put pressure on your opponent and soft to relieve pressure on yourself. If you can feel yourself getting tired, predict it and slow down. If you have been working very hard and are on the losing end of the rallies, again slow down, save something so that you are still in good condition to fight out the final rallies.

Don't give up if you are behind. It is quite possible your opponent may not play well throughout the whole match.

Plate 64 –
In traditional scoring the server can take a little more risk, and attack; while the receiver who is in danger of losing points should minimise the risks and play more defensively

EVALUATE
Some players never improve because they always do the same things. It will be difficult to improve your match play if you don't try to learn from your match experience. This means being a little self-critical, rather than making excuses.

Learn from your mistakes. Evaluate what you have done. Analyse your matches (*See* Chapter 1), evaluate your game, (*See* Chapter 3), solve the problems (*See* Chapter 4) and work at improving your game (*See* Chapter 5).

Use match analysis, video, coaches' observations and experience, and ask senior players and opponents for their views on your game.

In a Nutshell

Twenty key points to excelling at squash

1 Set some goals for your game. What would you realistically like to achieve in the longer term?

2 Analyse your game and make a list of the things you need to improve on.

3 Improve your game by concentrating your effort on these things.

4 Work out a long-term programme, with specific phases, that builds up to when you want to play your best.

5 Develop monthly and weekly programmes that balance out fitness activities, solo practice, pairs practice, practice games and matches.

6 Develop your own solo and pairs practice routines.

7 Work on the problem areas in your game – minimise errors and loose shots, avoid playing a loose game, recognise tactical errors.

8 Work out clear targets for all your shots. Understand exactly where you want the ball to go.

9 Practise to improve and groove your shots. Line up the ball.

10 Be aware of your movement and work to improve it in pairs practice and practice games.

Endeavour to recover the T before your opponent hits.

11 Work on your fitness so that you can pressurise your opponents and still perform at the end of long, hard matches.

12 Improve your basics. Remember better players are better at the basics.

13 Learn the ten basic tactics. Discipline yourself to use these, practise game types and combinations. Learn the ten tactical errors and work to eliminate these from your game.

14 Prepare mentally and physically for your matches.

15 Use a game plan for your matches.

16 Use a knock-up check list.

17 Develop mental toughness and concentrate on playing your best.

18 Watch better squash.

19 There is no substitute for hard matches. Play some hard matches and some better players to help you step up to a higher level.

20 Evaluate your game. Learn from your experiences and mistakes. Don't make excuses. Take advice.

Into Action

Ten steps to help you get into action and improve your game

Complete the assessment and planning tasks set on these pages.

Help

Squash Rackets Association

(The national governing body for squash in England)

Westpoint
33–34 Warple Way
Acton
London W3 ORQ

Tel: 081 746 1616
Fax: 081 746 0580

World Squash Federation

(The international federation of the national governing bodies)

6 Havelock Road
Hastings
East Sussex
England TN34 1BP

Tel: 0424 429245
Fax: 0429 429250

The National Coaching Foundation

(Information service for coaches)

4 College Close
Beckett Park
Leeds LS6 3QH

Tel: 021 414 5843
Fax: 021 471 4691

Squash Player Magazine

67–71 Goswell Road
London EC1V 2EN

Tel: 071 250 1881
Fax: 071 410 9440

Squash Player Coaching Service

460 Bath Road
Longford
Middx UB7 0EB

Tel: 0753 682309
Fax: 0753 680799

The Rules of Squash

Approved by the World Squash Federation at its twenty-second Annual General Meeting, Vancouver, Canada, 13 October 1992. Effective from 1 May 1993.

(These rules will be updated by the WSF in 1997)

1 . THE GAME
The game of Squash is played between two players, each using a specified racket, with a specified ball, and in a court constructed to WSF specified dimensions.

Note
When the words "he", "him" and "his" are used in the rules they shall be taken to mean "she" and "her" as appropriate.

2. THE SCORE
A match shall consist of the best of three or five games at the option of the organisers of the competition. Each game is to nine points, in that the player who scores nine points wins the game, except that, on the score being called eight-all for the first time, the receiver shall choose before the next service is delivered to continue that game either to nine points (known as "Set one") or to ten points (known as "Set two") in which latter case the player who scores two more points wins the game. The receiver shall in either case clearly indicate his choice to the Marker, Referee and his opponent.

The Marker shall call either "Set one" or "Set two" as applicable before play continues.

The Marker shall call "Game ball" to indicate that the server requires one point to win the game in progress or "Match ball" to indicate that the server requires one point to win the match.

3. POINTS
Points can be scored only by the server. When the server wins a stroke he scores a point; when the receiver wins a stroke he becomes the server.

4. THE SERVICE
4.1 The right to serve first is decided by the spin of a racket. Thereafter, the server continues to serve until he loses a stroke, whereupon his opponent becomes the server, and this procedure continues throughout the match. At the commencement of the second and each subsequent game the winner of the previous game serves first.

4.2 At the beginning of each game and each hand the server has the choice of serving from either box and thereafter shall serve from alternate boxes while remaining the server. However, if a rally ends in a let he shall serve again from the same box.

Note To Officials
If it appears that the server intends to serve from the wrong box, or either player appears undecided as to which is the correct box, the Marker shall advise which is the correct box. If the Marker makes an error with this advice, or there is any dispute, the Referee shall rule on the correct box.

4.3 For a service to be good there shall be no foot fault and the ball, before being struck, shall be dropped or thrown and shall not hit the walls, floor, ceiling or any object(s) suspended from the walls or ceiling; it shall be served directly onto the front wall between the cut line and the out line so that on its return, unless volleyed, it reaches the floor within the quarter of the court opposite to the server's box. Should a player, having dropped or thrown the ball, make no attempt to strike it, the ball shall be dropped or thrown again for that service. A player with the use of only one arm may utilise his racket to propel the ball into the air before striking it.

4.4 A service is good when it does not result in the server serving his hand out. The server serves his hand out and loses the stroke if:

4.4.1 The ball, after being dropped or thrown for service, touches the wall(s), floor, ceiling or any object (s) suspended from the walls or ceiling before being served. — Called "Fault".

4.4.2 At the time of striking the ball the server fails to have part of one foot in contact with the floor within the service box without any part of that foot touching the service box line (part of that foot may project over this line provided that it does not touch the line). — Called "Foot fault".

4.4.3 The server makes an attempt but fails to strike the ball. — Called "Not up".

4.4.4 The ball is not struck correctly. — Called "Not up".

4.4.5 The ball is served out. — Called "Out".

4.4.6 The ball is served against any part of the court before the front wall. — Called "Fault".

4.4.7 The ball is served onto or below the cut line. — Called "Fault" if above the board and "Down" if on or below the board.

4.4.8 The first bounce of the ball, unless volleyed by the receiver, is on the floor on or outside the short or half court lines of the quarter court opposite to the server's box. — Called "Fault".

4.4.9 The ball, after being served and before it has bounced more than once on the floor and before it has been struck at by the receiver, touches the server or anything he wears or carries. — Called "Down".

4.5 The server must not serve until the Marker has completed calling the score.

Note To Officials
The Marker must not delay play by the calling of the score. However, if the server serves or attempts to serve prior to the calling of the score, the Referee shall stop play and require the server to wait until the calling of the score has been completed.

5. THE PLAY
After a good service has been delivered the players return the ball alternately until one fails to make a good return, the ball otherwise ceases to be in play in accordance with the rules or on a call by the Marker or Referee.

6. GOOD RETURN

6.1 A return is good if the ball, before it has bounced more than once upon the floor, is returned correctly by the striker onto the front wall above the board without first touching the floor or any part of the striker's body or clothing, or the opponent's racket, body or clothing, provided the ball is not hit out.

6.2 It shall not be considered a good return if the ball touches the board before or after it hits the front wall and before it bounces on the floor, or if the racket is not in the player's hand at the time the ball is struck.

7. LET

A let is an undecided rally. The rally in respect of which a let is allowed shall not count and the server shall serve again from the same box.

8. STROKES

A player wins a stroke:

8.1 Under Rule 4.4 when the player is the receiver.

8.2 If the opponent fails to make a good return of the ball when the opponent is the striker, unless a let is allowed or a stroke is awarded to the opponent.

8.3 If the ball touches his opponent or anything he wears or carries when his opponent is the non-striker, except as is otherwise provided for in Rules 9, 10 and 13.1.1. In all cases the Referee shall rule accordingly.

8.4 If a stroke is awarded to him by the Referee as provided for in the rules.

9. HITTING AN OPPONENT WITH THE BALL

If the ball, before reaching the front wall, hits the striker's opponent or his racket, or anything he wears or carries, the ball shall cease to be in play and:

9.1 Unless Rule 9.2 applies, the striker shall win the stroke if the return would have been good and the ball would have struck the front wall without first touching any other wall.

9.2 If the return would have been good but the striker has either followed the ball round and turned or allowed it to pass around him — in either case by striking the ball to the right of his body after the ball had passed to his left (or vice versa) then a let shall be allowed in all cases.

Note To Referees
If the striker, having turned or allowed the ball to pass around him, chooses not to continue the rally due to reasonable fear of striking his opponent and, in the opinion of the Referee, a reasonable possibility of this occurring did exist and the striker would have been able to make a good return, then a let shall be allowed.

9.3 If the ball either had struck or would have struck any other wall and the return would have been good, a let shall be allowed unless, in the opinion of the Referee, a winning return has been intercepted, in which case the striker shall win the stroke.

Note To Referees
The stroke award provisions of Rule 9 do not apply to turning, ball passing around the striker, or further attempts.

9.4 If the return would not have been good, the striker shall lose the stroke.

Note To Officials
When a player has been struck by the ball as described in Rule 9, the Marker shall call "Down". The Referee shall assess the trajectory of the ball and make all further decisions.

10. FURTHER ATTEMPTS TO HIT THE BALL

If the striker strikes at and misses the ball he may make further attempts to strike it. If, after being missed, the ball touches his opponent or his racket, or anything he wears or carries, then, if, in the opinion of the Referee:

10.1 The striker could otherwise have made a good return a let shall be allowed, or

10.2 The striker could not have made a good return he shall lose the stroke.

If any such further attempt is successful resulting in a good return being prevented from reaching the front wall by hitting the striker's opponent or anything he wears or carries, a let shall be allowed in all circumstances. If any such further attempt would not have resulted in a good return, the striker shall lose the stroke.

11. APPEALS

The loser of a rally may appeal against any decision of the Marker affecting that rally.

An appeal to the Referee under Rule 11 should be prefaced with the words "Appeal please". Play shall then cease until the Referee has given his decision.

If an appeal under Rule 11 is disallowed the Marker's decision shall stand. If the Referee is uncertain he shall allow a let except where provided for in the Note To Referees after Rule 11.2.1 and Notes To Referees C and D after Rule 11.2.2.

Appeals upheld or Referee intervention under Rule 20.4 are dealt with in each specific situation below.

Note To Referees
A pointing gesture is not an appeal.

11.1 Appeals on Service

11.1.1 If the Marker calls "Fault", "Foot fault", "Not up", "Down" or "Out" to the service the server may appeal. If the appeal is upheld a let shall be allowed.

11.1.2 If the Marker fails to call "Fault", "Foot fault", "Not up", "Down" or "Out" to the service the receiver may appeal, either immediately or at the end of the rally if he has played or attempted to play the ball. If, in the opinion of the Referee, the service was not good he shall stop play immediately and award the stroke to the receiver.

11.2 Appeals on Play other than Service

11.2.1 If the Marker calls "Not up", "Down" or "Out" following a player's return, the player may appeal. If the appeal is upheld the Referee shall allow a let except that if, in the opinion of the Referee:
— The Marker's call has interrupted that player's winning return, he shall award the stroke to the player.
— The Marker's call has interrupted or prevented a winning return by the opponent, he shall award the stroke to the opponent.

Note To Referees
In the latter case the Referee shall also award the stroke to the opponent if he is unsure whether the Marker's call was correct.

11.2.2 If the Marker fails to call "Not up", "Down" or "Out" following a player's return the opponent may appeal either immediately or at the end of the rally if he has played or attempted to play the ball. If, in the opinion of the Referee, the return was not good he shall stop play immediately and award the stroke to the opponent.

Notes To Referees
A. No appeal under Rule 11 may be made after the delivery of a service for anything that occurred before that service.

B. Where there is more than one appeal in a rally (including an appeal under Rule 12) the Referee shall consider each appeal.

C. If a return is called "Not up", "Down" or "Out" by the Marker and that same return subsequently goes down or out the Referee, on appeal, if he reverses the Marker's call or is unsure, shall then rule on the subsequent occurrence.

D. If a service is called "Fault", "Foot fault", "Not up", "Down" or "Out" by the Marker and that service subsequently goes down, not up or out, or is again a fault, the Referee, on appeal, if he reverses the Marker's call or is unsure, shall then rule on the subsequent occurrence.

12. INTERFERENCE

12.1 When it is his turn to play the ball a player is entitled to freedom from interference by his opponent.

12.2 To avoid interference the opponent must make every effort to provide the player with:

12.2.1 Unobstructed direct access to the ball.

12.2.2 A fair view of the ball.

12.2.3 Freedom to hit the ball.

12.2.4 Freedom to play the ball directly to the front wall.

12.3 Interference occurs if the opponent fails to fulfil any of the requirements of Rule 12.2, irrespective of whether he makes every effort to do so.

Note To Referees

(G1) A. In 12.2.1 the opponent must move to allow the player direct access to the ball as soon as the opponent has completed his own return, i.e. at the completion of a reasonable follow-through of his racket swing. The player must also make every effort to get to and where possible play the ball.

B. In 12.2.2 fair view of the ball applies only to its rebound from the front wall.

(G2) C. In 12.2.3 freedom to hit the ball requires that the opponent permit the player an arc of racket swing comprising reasonable backswing, strike at the ball and reasonable follow-through.
Interference caused by a player's excessive backswing can not result in the award of a stroke to that player.
A player's excessive follow-through may cause interference for the opponent when it becomes the latter's turn to play the ball.

12.4 A player encountering what he considers to be interference has the choice of continuing with play or of stopping and appealing to the Referee.

(G3) 12.4.1 The correct method of appeal, whether a let or a stroke is sought by the player, is with the words "Let please".

(G4) 12.4.2 An appeal may be made only by the player. The appeal must be made either immediately the interference occurs or, where the player clearly does not continue with play beyond the point of interference, without undue delay.

12.5 The Referee shall decide on the appeal and shall announce his decision with the words "No let", "Yes let" or "Stroke to . . . (name of appropriate player)". In assessing the interference situation the only relevant opinion is that of the Referee and his decision shall be final.

12.6 The Referee shall not allow a let and the player shall lose the rally if:

12.6.1 There has been no interference.

12.6.2 Interference has occurred but either the player would not have made a good return or he has not made adequate effort to get to and where possible play the ball.

12.6.3 The player has clearly accepted the interference and played on.

(G5) 12.6.4 The player has created his own interference in moving to the ball.

12.7 The Referee shall allow a let if there has been interference which the opponent has made every effort to avoid and the

player would have made a good return.

12.8 The Referee shall award a stroke to the player if:

12.8.1 There has been interference which the opponent has not made every effort to avoid and the player would have made a good return.

12.8.2 There has been interference which the opponent has made every effort to avoid and the player would have made a winning return.

12.8.3 The player has refrained from hitting the ball which, if hit, would clearly have struck his opponent going directly to the front wall; or to a side wall but in the latter case would have been a winning return (unless in either case turning, ball passing around player or further attempt applies).

12.9 The Referee is also empowered to allow a let under Rule 12.7 or to award a stroke under Rule 12.8 without an appeal having been made, if necessary stopping play to do so.

12.10 The provisions of Rule 17, Conduct On Court, may be applied in interference situations. The Referee shall, stopping play if it has not already stopped, apply an appropriate penalty if:

(G6) 12.10.1 The player has made unnecessary physical contact with his opponent or vice versa.

12.10.2 The player has endangered his opponent with an excessive racket swing.

13. LETS

In addition to lets allowed under other rules, lets may or shall be allowed in certain other cases.

13.1 A let may be allowed:

13.1.1 If owing to the position of the striker, the opponent is unable to avoid being touched by the ball before the return is made.

Note To Referees

This rule shall include the cases where the striker's position is in front of his opponent, making it difficult for the latter to see the ball, or where the striker allows the ball to pass close to him and the ball hits his opponent who is behind the striker. This is not, however, to be taken as conflicting in any way with the duties of the Referee under Rule 12.

13.1.2 If the ball in play touches any article lying on the floor.

Note To Referees

The Referee shall ensure that no articles are placed on the floor by the players.

(G7) 13.1.3 If the striker refrains from hitting the ball owing to a reasonable fear of injuring his opponent.

Note To Referees

This shall include the case of the striker wishing to play the ball onto the back wall.

13.1.4 If, in the opinion of the Referee, either player is distracted by an occurrence on or off the court.

13.1.5 If, in the opinion of the Referee, a change in court conditions has affected the result of the rally.

13.2 A let shall be allowed:

13.2.1 If the receiver is not ready and does not attempt to return the service.

13.2.2 If the ball breaks during play.

13.2.3 If the Referee is asked to decide an appeal and is unable to do so.

13.2.4 If an otherwise good return has been made but either the ball lodges in any part of the playing surface of the court preventing it from bouncing more than once upon the floor, or the ball goes out on its first bounce.

13.3 If the striker appeals for a let under Rules 13.1 (2 to 5), in order for a let to be allowed he must have been able to make a good return. For a non-striker appeal under Rules 13.1.2, 13.1.4 and 13.1.5 this is not a requirement.

13.4 No let shall be allowed under Rules 13.1.3 and 13.2.1 if the striker attempts to play the ball but may be allowed under Rules 13.1.2, 13.1.4, 13.1.5, 13.2.2, 13.2.3 and 13.2.4.

13.5 The appeals requirements of Rule 13 are:

13.5.1 An appeal by the player is necessary for a let to be allowed under Rules 13.1.3 (striker only), 13.1.4, 13.2.1 (striker only) and 13.2.3.

13.5.2 An appeal by the player or Referee intervention without appeal is applicable to Rules 13.1.2, 13.1.5, 13.2.2 and 13.2.4.

13.5.3 Where a player is struck by the ball as described in Rule 13.1.1 the Referee shall decide without appeal whether a let is to be allowed or the stroke awarded to the striker.

14. THE BALL

14.1 At any time, when the ball is not in actual play, another ball may be substituted by mutual consent of the players, or on appeal by either player at the discretion of the Referee.

Note To Referees
Either player or the Referee may examine the ball at any time it is not in actual play to check its condition.

14.2 If a ball breaks during play, it shall be replaced promptly by another ball.

Note To Referees
The Referee shall decide whether a ball is broken.

14.3 If a ball has broken during play but this has not been established, a let for the rally in which the ball broke shall be allowed if the server appeals prior to the next service or if the receiver appeals prior to attempting to return that service.

Note To Referees
(G8) If the receiver appeals prior to attempting to return service and, in the opinion of the Referee, the ball break occurred during that service, the Referee shall allow a let for that rally only, but if unsure he should allow a let for the previous rally.

14.4 The provisions of Rule 14.3 do not apply to the final rally of a game. An appeal in this case must be immediately after the rally.

14.5 If a player stops during a rally to appeal that the ball is broken only to find subsequently that the ball is not broken, then that player shall lose the stroke.

15. WARM UP

15.1 Immediately preceding the start of play the two players together shall be allowed on the court of play a period of five minutes for the purpose of warming up the ball to be used for the match.
    After two and a half minutes of the warm up, the Referee shall call "Half time" and ensure that the players change sides unless they mutually agree otherwise. The Referee shall also advise when the warm up period is complete with the call of "Time".
    An interval of up to ninety seconds shall be permitted between the end of the warm up and start of play.

15.2 Where a ball has been substituted under Rule 14 or when the match is being resumed after considerable delay, the Referee shall allow the ball to be warmed up to playing condition. Play shall then resume on the direction of the Referee, or upon mutual consent of the players, whichever is the earlier.

Note To Referees
The Referee must ensure that both players warm up the ball fairly (Rules 15.1 and 15.2). An unfair warm up shall be dealt with under the provisions of Rule 17.

15.3 The ball may be warmed up by either player between the end of the five-minute warm up and start of play, between games and when his opponent is changing equipment.

16. CONTINUITY OF PLAY '

After the first service is delivered play shall be continuous so far as is practical provided that:

16.1 At any time play may be suspended, owing to bad light or other circumstances beyond the control of the players, for such period as the Referee shall decide. The score shall stand.
    If another court is available when the court originally in use remains unsuitable, the match may be transferred to it if both players agree or as directed by the Referee.
    In the event of play being suspended for the day the score shall stand unless both players agree to start the match again.

16.2 An interval of ninety seconds shall be permitted between all games. Players may leave the court during such intervals but must be ready to resume play by the end of the stated time.
    By mutual consent of the players play may recommence prior to the expiry of the ninety-second time interval.

(G9) 16.3 If a player satisfies the Referee that a change of equipment, clothing or footwear is necessary, the player may leave the court. He is required to effect the change as quickly as possible and shall be allowed a period not exceeding ninety seconds for this purpose.

16.4 When fifteen seconds of a permitted ninety-second time interval remain the Referee shall call "Fifteen seconds" to advise the players to be ready to resume play. At the end of this interval the Referee shall call "Time".
    It is the responsibility of the players to be within earshot of the court to hear the calls of "Fifteen seconds" and "Time".

Notes To Referees
A.   Should one player fail to be ready to resume play when "Time" is called, the Referee shall apply the provisions of Rule 17.

B.   Should neither player be ready to resume play when "Time" is called the Referee shall apply the provisions of Rule 17 for both players.

(G10)16.5 In the event of an injury to a player the Referee shall decide if it was:

16.5.1 Self-inflicted

16.5.2 Accidentally contributed to or accidentally caused by his opponent.

16.5.3 Caused by his opponent's deliberate or dangerous play or action.

Notes To Referees
A.   In all injury situations, the Referee must determine that the injury is genuine.

B.   In Rule 16.5.1, the Referee may allow the injured player up to three minutes to recover from the injury. This time interval may be extended at the discretion of the Referee. If additional recovery time is needed beyond that permitted by the Referee, the Referee shall require the player to continue play; or concede the game, accept the time interval and then continue play; or concede the match.

C.   In Rule 16.5.2, the Referee must not interpret the words "accidentally contributed to" or "accidentally caused by" to include the situation where the injury to the player is as a result of that player occupying an unnecessarily close position to his opponent.

D. In Rule 16.5.2 the Referee shall allow reasonable time for the injured player to recover, having regard to the time schedule of the competition.

The injured player must by the end of this period of time resume play or concede the match. If play is resumed the score at the time of injury shall stand, except that if play is resumed on another day the match may start again if both players agree.

E. In Rule 16.5.3 the Referee may, at his discretion, apply an appropriate Rule 17 penalty, except that if the injured player requires time to recover the Referee shall award the match to the injured player.

F. In all cases a player shall not resume play while a wound which is bleeding remains uncovered and the flow of blood continues.

(G11)16.6 The Referee shall apply the provisions of Rule 17 to a player who, in his opinion, delays play unreasonably. Such delay may be caused by:

16.6.1 Unduly slow preparation to serve or to receive service.

16.6.2 Prolonged discussion with the Referee.

16.6.3 Delay in returning to the court, having left under the terms of Rules 15.1, 16.2 or 16.3.

17. CONDUCT ON COURT

If the Referee considers that the behaviour of a player on court could be intimidating or offensive to an opponent, official or spectator, or could in any way bring the game into disrepute, the player may be penalised.

(G12) Offences which should be dealt with under this rule include audible and visible obscenities, verbal and physical abuse, dissent to Marker or Referee, abuse of racket or ball and coaching, other than during the interval between games. Other offences include unnecessary physical contact and excessive racket swing (Rule 12.10), unfair warm up (Rule 15.2 Note To Referees), late back on court (Rule 16.4 Notes to Referees A and B), deliberate or dangerous play or action (Rule 16.5.3) and time wasting (Rule 6.6)

(G 13) For these and any other offences which, in the opinion of the Referee, justify the application of this rule, one of the following penalty provisions may be applied.

Warning by the Referee (called a Conduct Warning)
Stroke awarded to opponent (called a Conduct Stroke)
Game awarded to opponent (called a Conduct Game)
Match awarded to opponent (called a Conduct Match)

Notes To Referees

A. If the Referee stops play to give a warning a let shall be allowed.

B. If the Referee stops a rally to award a conduct stroke then that stroke award becomes the result of the rally. If the Referee awards a conduct stroke at the conclusion of a rally, the result of the rally stands and the conduct stroke award is additional but without change of service box.

A conduct stroke awarded at the end of a game shall be carried over to the next game.

C. If the Referee awards a game that game shall be the one in progress or the next game if one is not in progress, in which latter case the interval between games shall not apply. The offending player shall retain any points already scored in the game awarded.

18. CONTROL OF A MATCH

A match is normally controlled by a Referee, assisted by a Marker. One person may be appointed to carry out the functions of both

Referee and Marker. When a decision has been made by the Referee he shall announce it to the players and the Marker shall repeat it with the subsequent score.

Note To Officials

(G14) A. It is desirable to have separate Officials to carry out the roles of Marker and Referee.

B. Players are not permitted to request a change of Marker or Referee. The Tournament Referee has the sole right to replace a Marker or Referee before or after the commencement of a match.

19. DUTIES OF A MARKER

19.1 The Marker shall call the play, followed by the score, with the server's score called first. He shall call "Fault", "Foot fault", "Not up", "Down", "Out" and "Hand-out" as appropriate, and shall repeat the Referee's decisions.

(G15)19.2 If the Marker makes a call the rally shall cease.

Note To Markers

If the Marker is unsighted or uncertain he shall make no call.

19.3 If play ceases and the Marker is unsighted or uncertain he shall advise the players and shall call on the Referee to make the relevant decision; if the Referee is unable to do so a let shall be allowed.

Note To Markers

Markers must use recognised calls, including when the rally has ceased (Appendix 2.2).

20. DUTIES OF A REFEREE

20.1 The Referee shall allow or disallow appeals for lets, and award strokes; make decisions where called for by the rules, including all cases when a player is struck by the ball, and for injuries; and shall decide all appeals including those against the Marker's calls or lack of calls. The decision of the Referee shall be final.

20.2 The Referee shall exercise control:

20.2.1 Upon appeal by one of the players, including an appeal against any specification.

20.2 2 As provided for in Rules 4, 8, 9, 10, 11, 12, 13, 14, 15, 16, 17, 18 and 19.

20.3 The Referee shall not intervene in the Marker's calling of the score unless, in the opinion of the Referee, the score has been called incorrectly in which case he shall have the Marker call the correct score.

Note To Officials

Both the Marker and Referee are required to record the score.

20.4 The Referee shall not intervene in the Marker's calling of the play unless, in the opinion of the Referee, the Marker has made an error in stopping play or allowing play to continue, in which case the Referee shall immediately rule accordingly.

20.5 The Referee is responsible for ensuring that all rules relating to time are strictly enforced.

20.6 The Referee is responsible for ensuring that court conditions are appropriate for play.

20.7 The Referee may award a match to a player whose opponent fails to be present on court, ready to play, within ten minutes of the advertised time of play.

APPENDIX 1

OFFICIAL GUIDELINES ON RULES INTERPRETATIONS FOR PLAYERS AND REFEREES

Guideline numbers are referenced in the Rules.

LIST OF CONTENTS

INTRODUCTION

The over-riding principle governing the Rules of Squash and their interpretation is to allow a fair result to each match. This requires that the Referee implements the Rules fairly for both players from the time the match starts until its conclusion.

The following Official Guidelines on interpretations are those which have been approved by the Rules and Referees Committee of the WSF and should be read in conjunction with the Rules.

G1. MAKING EVERY EFFORT

The outgoing striker is required to make every effort to clear the ball after playing his return. His route should be on a path which allows the incoming striker direct access to the ball, provided the incoming striker has not moved in to play the ball so quickly that he blocks the outgoing striker's exit.

However, it is equally important for the incoming striker to make every effort to get to and where possible, play the ball. If the incoming striker does not make every effort to get to the ball, then that is a significant factor in the Referee's assessment of whether or not that player could have reached the ball and made a good return.

The degree of effort that is required by the incoming striker, in order to demonstrate that he was indeed making every effort, is for the Referee to decide. Players should note that this does not give them licence to physically abuse their opponents and unnecessary physical contact will be penalised under Rules 12/17.

A Referee, however, should not refuse lets in situations where the player was clearly making every effort (albeit short of physical contact with his opponent) to get to and play the ball and had demonstrated to the Referee that he would have reached the ball.

In giving his decision the Referee must weigh up the amount of effort being made by both players. In cases where the Referee assesses that sufficient effort has not been made by either player, he should take that into account when making his decision.

G2. TIMING OF APPEALS

The timing of an appeal on interference is important.

In the case of an appeal concerning fair view and freedom to hit the ball directly to the front wall (commonly known as 'crossing the flight'), the Referee must consider the situation at the time the player could have hit the ball.

In the case of interference on backswing the appeal must be immediate, and before the player makes any attempt to play the ball. Any attempt to hit the ball after backswing interference has occurred indicates that the striker has accepted the interference and thus forfeits his right of appeal.

If in the act of playing the ball, which includes the downswing

and hit, there is interference, an appeal may be allowed. If this appeal is made at the completion of the racket swing the Referee may allow a let or award a stroke if in his opinion the interference has affected the outcome of that return.

G3. METHOD OF APPEAL

The correct method of appeal in interference situations is with the words "Let please".

Other forms of appeal are sometimes used by players including a raised hand or racket, especially where communication between players and Referee is poor.

A Referee accepting any form of appeal other than the standard "Let please" must be satisfied that an appeal is actually being made (not a rally conceded), if necessary clarifying this with the player.

G4. APPEALS

If a player makes a prompt appeal because of interference and his opponent's service or return subsequently goes down or out, the Referee should not consider the appeal but should rule on the service or return and award the stroke to the player.

G5. CREATED INTERFERENCE

At all times a player must be allowed direct access to play the ball and his opponent, having completed his own return, must always endeavour to provide this direct access.

However, sometimes the situation arises where the opponent has caused no interference (ie. he has clearly provided the required direct access) but the player has taken an indirect route to the ball which takes him through, or very close to, the opponent's position. He then appeals for a let because he has been 'obstructed' in his access to the ball.

But there is no genuine reason for this indirect route. In effect he has "created his own interference" where none otherwise existed and if he appeals for a let he should not be allowed one. Whether he could have made a good return is not even a consideration; in order to remain in the rally the player must get to and play the ball.

This is not to be confused with two situations where a player in attempting to extricate himself from a position of disadvantage is denied direct access to the ball. The first is where a player is "WRONG FOOTED", and anticipates his opponent hitting the ball one way, starts moving that way, but having guessed wrongly changes direction to find his opponent in the way. In this situation he should be allowed a let on appeal if he has recovered so as to show conclusively that he could have made a good return. In fact had the incoming striker been prevented from playing a winning return he may be awarded a stroke.

Secondly, if a player plays a poor return and puts his opponent in a position of advantage he should only be given a let if, in taking the direct line to the ball for his next return, he has shown conclusively that, but for the interference, he would have been able to get to the ball.

G6. UNNECESSARY PHYSICAL CONTACT

Unnecessary physical contact is both detrimental to the game and potentially dangerous. In blatant cases the Referee should stop the rally and award the appropriate penalty accordingly. The Referee should also be aware of a player who "pushes off" his opponent. Where this has no significant effect on the opponent, then the rally should be allowed to continue and a warning given at the end of the rally.

G7. APPEALS FOR FEAR OF INJURY

When an appeal for a let has been made and there has been no interference the Referee's decision is usually "No let". However, occasionally, although interference as defined in Rule 12.2 does not exist, there may be reasonable fear of injury in which case a let should be allowed under Rule 13.1.3.

G8. BROKEN BALL

When the receiver makes an appeal prior to attempting to return the service, the Referee has discretionary power to decide whether to replay the previous rally or to allow a let in respect of the rally in which the ball was found to be broken.

G9. CHANGE OF EQUIPMENT

In order to avoid the situation of one player gaining an unfair rest interval through a change of equipment, the Referee should note that before allowing a player to leave the court to change equipment, the Referee must be satisfied that there has indeed been a material deterioration of the equipment.

The preference for another racket, or a different pair of shoes where no physical deterioration is evident, is not sufficient reason for allowing a change of equipment. The Referee should also note that although up to 90 seconds are allowed for a change of equipment players are required to carry out the change as quickly as possible. If a player loses a contact lens or his glasses break, then following the appropriate time interval for change of equipment, he must continue play or an appropriate Rule 17 penalty will be applied.

If a player is unable to resume play because he has no alternative equipment then the Referee should award the match to the opponent.

G10.   ILLNESS/INJURY ON COURT
If, during a match, a player feels ill such that he needs to leave the court, he should advise the Referee who may allow him up to three minutes to recover. If extra time beyond that permitted is needed or if the Referee does not permit him recovery time, the player must concede the game, take the 90-second interval, then be ready to resume play. A player may concede only one game. If, after taking the 90-second interval, he is unable to continue play, he shall then concede the match.

If, however, a player is sick on court, so that the court conditions are such that play is prevented from continuing, then the Referee should award the match to his opponent irrespective of whether the sick player is able to continue or not (Rule 17 Conduct On Court).

Similarly, if a player suffers from a nose bleed and as a result the court conditions are impaired to the extent that they are detrimental to the match in progress, then his opponent should be awarded the match. (NB: This refers to a "natural" nose bleed rather than one caused by collision where the relevant injury rule would apply).

In all the above cases the Referee's decision with regard to court conditions is final.

Players should note that where an injury is sustained which is entirely self-inflicted, including injury caused by a player being struck by his opponent's racket when the player has occupied an unnecessarily close position to the opponent, a time interval of up to three minutes (which can be extended solely at the discretion of the Referee) may be permitted for the player to recover. After that time the Referee will require the player to continue; or concede the game, accept the interval and then continue play; or concede the match.

Players should also note that irrespective of the cause of any injury they are not permitted to resume play while a wound which is bleeding is not securely covered or where blood flow continues from an uncovered wound.

G11 .   TIME WASTING
Time wasting represents an attempt by one player to gain an unfair advantage over his opponent. Prolonged discussion with the Referee and slow preparation to serve or receive service are particularly mentioned (Rule 16.6). Where this occurs the Referee should apply an appropriate Rule 17 penalty at the earliest opportunity

It should be noted that while excessive ball bouncing prior to service does constitute time wasting, the server should not be considered to have served his hand out.

During game intervals the Referee is required to call "15 seconds" to indicate that the players have 15 seconds to return to court and be ready to resume play. It is the responsibility of players to be within earshot to hear the call. Players should note that the call of "15 seconds" is advice to return to court. A player who is not ready to resume play on the call of "Time" is deliberately or otherwise gaining an unfair advantage and should be penalised under Rule 17.

G12.   COACHING DURING MATCHES
Coaching of players may occur only during the interval between games. Coaching should not be taken to mean brief comments of encouragement between rallies which clearly have no effect on the continuity of play. The Referee is expected to exercise discretion in deciding between such comments and coaching a player

The use of external communication aids is prohibited.

The Referee may stop coaching in any form during play by applying Rule 17. Conduct on Court, to the player being coached.

G13.   PROGRESSION OF PENALTIES
The penalties available to the Referee under Rule 17 are:
> A warning
> A stroke
> A game
> The match

The guidelines for applying the penalties are as follows:

The first penalty imposed by the Referee for a particular offence may be at any level to suit the seriousness of the offence, ie. a warning, stroke, game or match. However, any second or subsequent penalty for the same type of offence may not be of a lesser severity than the previous penalty for that offence. Thus the Referee may award several warnings or several strokes for the same type of offence if he felt that the offence did not warrant a stronger punishment.

When issuing penalties the Referee should use the following terminology:

Conduct warning . . . . . . (player's name) for . . . . . (offence).
Conduct stroke. . . . . (player's name) for . . . . . (offence), stroke to
(opponent's name)
Conduct game. . . . . (player's name) for . . . . . (offence), game to
(opponent's name)
Conduct match . . . . . (player's name) for . . . . . (offence), match to
(opponent's name).

G14.   SINGLE OFFICIAL
It may not always be possible to have two officials for a match. A single official would act as the Marker initially, but when there was an appeal he would then take on the role of the Referee and give his decision, on appeal, as the Referee.

Whilst this situation is not recommended, it does happen, and the single official should know that he acts as the Marker and then on appeal, as Referee. It is not correct to say that because there is only one official there is no Referee.

G15.   MARKER'S CALLS
The Marker must call to stop a rally if, in his opinion, a player has failed to deliver a good service or to make a good return.

However, if because of a service or return which was obviously not good, both players cease play without the Marker making a call, then the appropriate call of "Not up", "Down" or "Out" may be omitted.

GENERAL GUIDELINES

G16.   SHAPING TO PLAY THE BALL
When a player shapes to play the ball on one side and then brings the racket across his body to take the ball on the other side (ie. from right to left or vice versa) then this is NOT considered to be either turning or making a second attempt, and the provisions of Rule 12 apply if interference occurs. This position frequently occurs after the ball has hit the side/front wall nick and then rebounds into the middle of the court.

G17.   MARKER'S GUIDELINES
In general the correct order of calls is:
> 1. Anything affecting the score.
> 2. The score (with the server's score always called first).
> 3. Comments on the score:

Examples are:
> "Not up, hand-out 4-3".
> "Down, 8-all, set one, game ball".
> "Out, 8-all, set two".
> "Yes let, 3-4".
> "No let, hand-out, 5-7".
> "Stroke to White, 8-2, match ball".
> "Foot fault, hand-out, love all".
> "Fault" (appeal by server, Referee unsure). "Let, 8-3, game ball"

Match introduction:
> "White serving, Black receiving, best of 5 games, love-all".

Start of subsequent game:
> "Black leads one game to love, love-all".

G18.   ADDRESSING THE PLAYERS
The use of first names should be avoided to eliminate any risk of familiarity with either player which could be interpreted as favouritism by the opponent.

G19.   EXPLANATION BY REFEREES

Following an appeal by a player, the Referee will normally give his decision and play resumes.

However, on some occasions it may be appropriate to explain the decision in order to clarify the situation for the players. Where the Referee feels this is appropriate, then he should give his decision followed by a concise and objective statement of explanation.

APPENDIX 2.1

DEFINITIONS (SINGLES)

APPEAL
A player's request to the Referee to consider an on or off court situation.
"Appeal" is used throughout the rules in two contexts:–
1) Where the player requests the Referee to consider varying a Marker's decision.
2) Where the player requests the Referee to allow a let.
The correct form of appeal by a player is "Appeal please" or "Let please".

ATTEMPT
The Referee shall decide what is an attempt to play the ball. An attempt is made, when in the opinion of the Referee, the striker has moved his racket towards the ball from the backswing position.

BOARD
The lowest horizontal marking on the front wall, with the tin beneath it covering the full width of the court.

BOX (SERVICE)
A square area in each quarter court bounded by part of the short line, part of the side wall and by two other lines, and from within which the server serves.

COMPETITION
A championship tournament, league or other competitive match.

CORRECTLY
The ball being hit by the racket, (held in the hand) not more than once nor with prolonged contact on the racket.

CUT LINE
A line upon the front wall, 50 millimetres in width, the top edge of which is 1.83 metres above the floor and extending the full width of the court.

DOWN
The expression used to indicate that an otherwise good service or return has struck the board or tin or has failed to reach the front wall; or that a player has been struck by the ball before it has bounced more than once upon the floor. ("Down" is also used as a Marker's call).

GAME
Part of a match, commencing with a service and concluding when one player has scored or been awarded nine or ten points (in accordance with the rules).

GAME BALL
The state of the score when the server requires one point to win the game in progress. ("Game ball" is also used as a Marker's call).

HALF-COURT LINE
A line set upon the floor parallel to the side walls, dividing the back of the court into two equal parts, meeting the short line at its midpoint to form the "T".

HALF TIME
The midpoint of the warm up ("Half time" is also used as a Referee's call).

HAND
The period from the time a player becomes server until he becomes receiver.

HAND-OUT
Condition when a change of server occurs. ("Hand-out" is also used as a Marker's call to indicate that a change of hand has occurred).

MATCH
The complete contest between two players, commencing with the warm up and concluding when both players have left the court at the end of the final rally (covers broken ball rule).

MATCH BALL
The state of the score when the server requires one point to win the match. ("Match ball" is also used as a Marker's call).

NOT UP
The expression used to indicate that the ball has not been struck in accordance with the rules. "Not up" applies when 1) the ball is not struck correctly by the server or striker, 2) the ball bounces more than once upon the floor before being struck by the striker, 3) the ball touches the striker or anything he wears or carries other than his racket, 4) the server makes an attempt but fails to strike the ball. ("Not up" is also used as a Marker's call).

OFFICIALS
The Marker and the Referee.

OUT
The expression used to indicate that 1) the ball has struck the out line, or a wall above the out line, or the ceiling, or any fitting attached to the ceiling and/or wall above the out line or 2) the ball has passed through any fitting attached to the ceiling and/or wall above the out line or 3) in addition to 1) and 2) on courts which are not fully enclosed the ball has passed over the out line and out of the court without touching any wall or, if no out line is provided, passed over any wall and out of the court. ("Out" is also used as a Marker's call).

OUT LINE
A continuous line comprising the front wall line, both side wall lines and the back wall line and marking the top boundaries of the court.

Note: When a court is constructed without provision of such a line, ie. the walls comprise only the area used for play, or without part of such a line (eg. a glass back wall) and the ball in play strikes part of the horizontal top surface of such a wall and deflects back into court, the ball is out. The decision should be made in the normal manner by the Marker, subject to appeal to the Referee.

POINT
A unit of the scoring system. One point is added to a player's score when he is the server and wins a stroke.

QUARTER (COURT)
One half of the back part of the court which has been divided into two equal parts by the half-court line.

RALLY
A service only or service and any number of returns of the ball, ending when the ball ceases to be in play.

REASONABLE
The initial action used by a player in moving his racket away from his body as BACKSWING preparation prior to racket movement towards the ball for contact. A backswing is reasonable if it is not excessive. An excessive backswing is one in which the player's racket arm is extended towards a straight arm position and/or the racket is extended with the shaft approximately horizontal. The Referee's decision on what constitutes a reasonable as distinct from excessive backswing is final.

REASONABLE
The action used by a player in continuing the movement of his racket after it has FOLLOW-THROUGH contacted the ball. A follow-through is reasonable if it is not excessive. An excessive follow-through is one in which the player's racket arm is extended towards a straight arm position with the racket also extended with the shaft horizontal — particularly when the extended position is maintained for other than a momentary period of time. An excessive follow-through is also one in which the arm extended towards a straight position takes a wider arc than the continued line of flight of the ball, even though the racket is on the correct vertical position. The Referee's decision on what constitutes a reasonable as distinct from excessive follow-through is final.

SERVICE
The method by which the ball is put into play by the server to commence a rally.

SHORT LINE
A line, 50 millimetres in width, set out upon the floor parallel to and 5.44 metres from the front wall and extending the full width of the court.

SPECIFIED
The description given to balls, rackets and courts that meet existing WSF specifications.

STRIKER
The player whose turn it is to hit the ball after it has rebounded from the front wall, or who is in the process of hitting the ball, or who — up to the point of his return reaching the front wall — has just hit the ball.

STROKE
The gain achieved by the player who wins a rally, either in the course of play or on award by the Referee, and which results in either the scoring of a point or change of hand.

TIN
Situated between the board and the floor covering the full width of the court and constructed in such a manner as to make a distinctive noise when struck by the ball.

TOURNAMENT DIRECTOR
The person responsible for the conduct of players and officials throughout the tournament.

TOURNAMENT REFEREE
The person given overall responsibility for all marking and refereeing matters throughout the tournament, including the appointment and replacement of officials to matches.

GENERAL NOTE
The use of the word "shall" in the rules indicates compulsion and the lack of any alternative. The word "must" indicates a required course of action with considerations to be taken into account if the action is not carried out. The word "may" indicates the option of carrying out or not carrying out the action.

APPENDIX 2.2

MARKER'S CALLS (SINGLES)

The recognised Marker's calls are defined below.
Calls made by the Marker as referred to in:

Rule 19 DUTIES OF A MARKER

Fault   To indicate that the service is a fault.
              See Rules 4.4.1, 4.4.6, 4.4.7, 4.4.8.

Foot Fault To indicate that the service is a foot fault. See Rule 4.4.2.

Not Up   To indicate that the ball has not been struck in accordance with the rules. See Definitions, "NOT UP".

Down   To indicate that an otherwise good service or return has struck the board or tin or has failed to reach the front wall, or that a player has been struck by the ball before it has bounced more than once upon the floor See Definitions "DOWN".

Out   To indicate that an otherwise good service or return has gone out. See Definitions "OUT" and "OUT LINE".

Hand-Out   To indicate that the server has become the receiver, ie. a change of server has occurred. See Definitions "HAND-OUT" and "HAND".

Call made by the Marker as referred to in:

Rule 2 THE SCORE

4-3   An example of the score. The server's score is always called first, thus in this example the server leads by four points to three. If points are equal the wording used is "all" (eg. "love-all").

Set One   To indicate that the game in progress is to be played to nine points after the score has reached 8-all (called once only in any game).

Set Two   To indicate that the game in progress is to be played to ten points after the score has reached 8-all (called only once in any game).

Game Ball To indicate that the server requires one point to win the game in progress. See Definitions "GAME BALL".

Match Ball To indicate that the server requires one point to win the match. See Definitions "MATCH BALL".

Calls made by the Marker as referred to in:

Rule 18 CONTROL OF A MATCH (Repeating Referee Decisions).

Yes Let   Call made by the Marker after the Referee has ruled that a
Let   rally is to be replayed.
Stroke To Call made by the Marker after the Referee has awarded
(Name of stroke to that player.
Player)
No Let   Call made by the Marker after the Referee has disallowed an appeal for a let.

APPENDIX 2.3

REFEREE'S CALLS

Stop	To stop play.
Time	To indicate that a period of time prescribed in the rules has elapsed.
Half Time	To advise players of the mid-point of the warm up period.
Yes Let	When allowing a let, following a player's appeal for a let.
No Let	When disallowing a player's appeal for a let.
Stroke To	To advise that the player named is to be awarded a stroke. (PLAYER'S NAME)
Fifteen Seconds	To advise the player(s) that fifteen seconds of a permitted ninety-second time interval remain.
Let	(May be accompanied by an explanation). To advise that a rally is to be replayed in circumstances where the wording "YES LET" is not applicable.
Conduct Warning	To advise a player that he has committed an offence under Rule 17 Conduct on Court, and is being given a warning.
Conduct Stroke	To advise a player that he has committed an offence under Rule 17 Conduct on Court, and that a stroke is to be awarded to his opponent.
Conduct Game	To advise a player that he has committed an offence under Rule 17 Conduct on Court, and that a game is to be awarded to his opponent.
Conduct Match	To advise a player that he has committed an offence under Rule 17 Conduct onCourt, and that the match has been awarded to his opponent.

APPENDIX 3

SEATING OF OFFICIALS

The correct position for refereeing and marking a Squash match is one located at the centre of the back wall, as close to that wall as is physically possible, above the out line on the back wall, and preferably with seating.

APPENDIX 4

POINT-A-RALLY SCORING

The following variations to the Rules of the International Singles Game of Squash apply if point-a-rally scoring (PARS) is used:

2.   THE SCORE
A match shall consist of the best of three or five games and each game shall be played to nine or fifteen points at the option of the organisers of the competition.
        Where each game is to fifteen points, the player who scores fifteen points wins the game, except that on the score being called fourteen-all the receiver shall choose, before the next service is delivered, to continue that game either to fifteen points (known as "Set one") or to seventeen points (known as "Set three") in which latter case the player who scores three more points wins the game.
        The receiver shall in either case clearly indicate his choice to the Marker, Referee and his opponent.
        Where each game is to nine points, the player who scores nine points wins the game, except that on the score being called eight-all the receiver shall choose, before the next service is delivered, to continue that game either to nine points (known as "Set one") or to eleven points (known, as "Set three") in which latter case the player who scores three more points wins the game. The receiver shall in either case clearly indicate his choice to the Marker, Referee and his opponent.
        The Marker shall call either "Set one" or "Set three" as applicable before play continues.
        The Marker shall call "Game ball" to indicate that either player requires one point to win the game in progress, "Match ball" to indicate that either player requires one point to win the match, and "Match ball, game ball" if one player requires one point to win the match and his opponent requires one point to win the game in progress.

3.   POINTS
Points can be scored by either player. When the server wins a stroke he scores a point and retains the service; when the receiver wins a stroke he scores a point and becomes the server.

Note: Modifications to definitions of "Game ball", "Match ball", "Point", and "Stroke" and the appropriate Marker's Calls apply in accordance with the requirements of Rules 2 and 3 of this appendix.

APPENDIX 5

EXPERIMENTAL RULES

The World Squash federation may from time to time request or authorise its members to carry our certain rules experiments.
        Tournament organisers using experimental rules shall specify at the time of entry the manner in which any rules, definitions or appendices differ from those of the WSF.

APPENDIX 6

DIMENSIONS OF A SINGLES COURT

Dimensions
        Length: 9750mm between plaster faces.
        Breadth: 6400mm between plaster faces.

        Height to lower edge of cut line on front wall: 1780mm
        Height to lower edge of front wall line: 4570mm
        Height to lower edge of back wall line: 2130mm

Distance to nearest edge of short line from back wall: 4260mm
Height to upper edge of board from floor: 480mm
Thickness of board (flat or rounded at top): 15mm top to 45mm bottom (splayed)

Side wall line: the diagonal line joining the front wall line and the back wall line.

The service boxes shall be entirely enclosed on three sides within the court by lines, the short line forming the side nearest to the front wall, the side wall bounding the fourth side.

The internal dimensions of the service boxes shall be 1600mm.

All dimensions in the court shall be measured, from junction of the floor and front wall — 1 metre above the finished floor level.

All lines shall be 50mm in width. All lines shall be coloured red.

In respect of the outer boundary lines on the walls, it is suggested that the plaster should be so shaped as to produce a concave channel along such lines.

APPENDIX 7

SPECIFICATIONS OF A WSF YELLOW DOT
CHAMPIONSHIP SQUASH BALL
Revised WSF specification – effective 13 October 1990

The following specification is the standard for a WSF Yellow dot Championship Squash Ball.

Diameter (mm)	40.0 +or– 0.5
Weight (gm)	24.0 +or– 0.5
Stiffnes (N/mm) @ 23 degrees C.	3.2 +or– 0.4
Rebound resilience @ 23 degrees C.	16-17 inches
@ 45 degrees C.	26-28 inches

Annual General Meeting resolution, 26 September 1993:

"The WSF recognises that a yellow dot Squash Ball which meets either of the following will be accepted for Championship play:

a) A rebound resilience as tested by the British standards Institution:

@ 23 degrees C	15-18 inches
@ 45 degrees C	26-31 inches

OR:

b) A rebound resiliencs as tested by the Rubber Research Institute of Malaysia:

@ 23 degrees C	16-17 inches
@ 45 degrees C	26-28 inches

PROVIDING THAT:
The ball also meets peviously agreed diameter, weight, stiffness and seam strength requirements as laid down by the WSF and as tested by either authority."

APPENDIX 8

DIMENSIONS OF A SQUASH RACKET

Revised WSF specification — effective 12 November 1991

Dimensions   Maximum length: 686 mm.
                Maximum width, measured at right angles to the shaft: 215 mm.
                Maximum length of strings: 390 mm.
                Maximum strung area: 500 sq. cms.
                Minimum width of any frame or any structural member (measured in plane of strings): 7 mm.
                Maximum depth of any frame or other structural member (measured at right angles to plane of strings): 26 mm.

Minimum radius of outside curvature of frame at any point: 50 mm.
Minimum radius of curvature of any edge of frame or other structural member: 2 mm.

Weight
Construction

Maximum weight: 255 gm.

a) The head of the racket is defined as that part of the racket containing or surrounding the strung area.
b) Strings and string ends must be recessed within the racket head or, in cases where such recessing is impractical because of racket material, or design, must be protected by a securely attached bumper strip.
c) The bumper strip must be made of a flexible material which cannot crease into sharp edges following abrasive contact with the floor or walls.
·d) The bumper strip shall be of a white, colourless or unpigmented material. Where for cosmetic reasons a manufacturer chooses to use a coloured bumper strip, then he shall demonstrate to the satisfaction of the WSF that this does not leave a coloured deposit on the walls or floor of the court after contact.
e) The frame of the racket shall be of a colour and/or material which will not mark the walls or floor following an impact in normal play.
f) Strings shall be gut, nylon or a substitute material, provided metal is not used.
g) Only two layers of strings shall be allowed and these alternately interlaced or bonded where they cross, and the string pattern shall be generally uniform and form a single plane over the racket head.
h) Any grommets, string spacers or other devices attached to any part of the racket shall be used solely to limit or prevent wear and tear or vibration, and be reasonable in size and placement for such purpose. They shall not be attached to any part of the strings within the hitting area.
·i) There shall be no unstrung areas within the racket construction such that will allow the passage of a sphere greater than 50 mm in diameter.
·j) The total racket construction including the head shall be symmetrical about the centre of the racket in a line drawn vertically through the head and shaft and when viewed face on.
k) After the date of implementation of this specification — 12 November 1991 — all changes to the racket specification will be subject to a notice period of two years before coming into force.
Note: *Under clause k) rules marked thus · will come into force on 1 January 1994.*

The World Squash Federation shall rule on the question of whether any racket or prototype complies with the above specifications, or is otherwise approved or not approved for play and will issue guidelines to assist in the interpretation of the above.

APPENDIX 9

COLOUR OF PLAYERS' CLOTHING

Organisers may specify regulations concerning players' clothing which must be complied with in their particular tournament or tournaments.

APPENDIX 10
(Amended at the 1993 AGM)

EYEGUARDS

Although the risk of injury in Squash is very low it is recommended that, when the avoidance of eye injury is of particular importance to a player, protective eyeguards manufactured to an appropriate National Standard are worn properly over the eyes at all times during play. It is the reponsibility of the player to ensure that the quality of the product is satisfactory for the purpose.

Note: As at september 1993 National Standards for Racket Sport Eye Protection are published by the Canadian Standards Association, the United States ASTM and Standards Australia.

SQUASH COURT DIMENSIONS

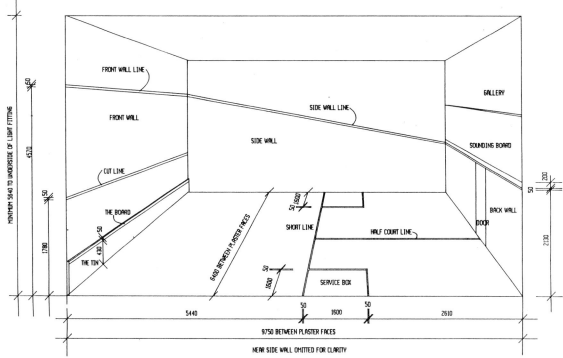

Index

Plates are indicated by page numbers in **bold**.
Figures are indicated by page numbers in *italics*.